JAPAN'S EMERGENCE AS A GLOBAL POWER

**Other Titles in the Greenwood Press Guides
to Historic Events of the Twentieth Century**
Randall M. Miller, Series Editor

JAPAN'S EMERGENCE AS A GLOBAL POWER

James I. Matray

Greenwood Press Guides to
Historic Events of the Twentieth Century
Randall M. Miller, Series Editor

Greenwood Press
Westport, Connecticut • London

Library of Congress Cataloging-in-Publication Data

Matray, James Irving, 1948–
    Japan's emergence as a global power / James I. Matray.
        p.   cm.—(Greenwood Press guides to historic events of the twentieth century,
    ISSN 1092–177X)
    Includes bibliographical references and index.
    ISBN 0–313–29972–2 (alk. paper)
    1. Japan—History—1945–   2. Japan—Economic policy—1945–
    I. Title.   II. Series.
    DS889.M345767   2001
    952—dc21   00–039356

British Library Cataloguing in Publication Data is available.

Library of Congress Catalog Card Number: 00–039356
ISBN: 0–313–29972–2
ISSN: 1092–177X

First published in 2001

Greenwood Press, 88 Post Road West, Westport, CT 06881
An imprint of Greenwood Publishing Group, Inc.
www.greenwood.com

Printed in the United States of America

∞™

The paper used in this book complies with the
Permanent Paper Standard issued by the National
Information Standards Organization (Z39.48–1984).

10 9 8 7 6 5 4 3 2 1

Copyright Acknowledgments

The author and publisher gratefully acknowledge permission for use of the following material:

Map of modern Japan reprinted from *The Rise of Modern Japan: Political, Economic, and Social Change since 1850*, by W. G. Beasley, with the permission of Orion Publishing Group Ltd.

Northern Territories map reprinted from *The Soviet Union and Postwar Japan: Escalating Challenge and Response*, by Rodger Swearingen, with the permission of the publisher, Hoover Institution Press. Copyright © 1978 by the Board of Trustees of the Leland Stanford Junior University.

Ryukyu Islands map reprinted with permission of the University of Hawai'i Press, Honolulu, Hawai'i.

East Asia map reprinted from *Japan among the Powers, 1890–1990*, by Sidney Giffard, with the permission of Yale University Press.

Document 7 excerpted from Asahi Shimbunsha, ed., *Shiryo Maji Hyakunen* [A Documentary History for the Meiji Centennial] (Tokyo: Asahi Shimbunsha, 1966), pp. 561–62. Reprinted with permission of M. E. Sharpe, Inc., Publisher, Armonk, NY 10504.

Document 13 reprinted with permission of Simon & Schuster from *The Japan That Can Say No: Why Japan Will Be First among Equals*, by Shintaro Ishihara. Translated by Frank Baldwin. English translation Copyright © 1991 by Shintaro Ishihara.

Document 15 excerpted from "Japan Is Twenty Years Behind," by Kiichi Miyazawa, *New Perspectives Quarterly* 15 (Winter 1998). Reprinted with permission of *New Perspectives Quarterly*.

Contents

A photographic essay follows page 82.

Series Foreword

As the twenty-first century opens, it is time to take stock of the political, so-cial, economic, intellectual, and cultural forces and factors that made the twentieth century the most dramatic period of change in history. To that end, the Greenwood Press Guides to Historic Events of the Twentieth Century presents interpretive histories of the most significant events of the century. Each book in the series combines narrative history and analysis with primary documents and biographical sketches, with an eye to providing both a reference guide to the principal persons, ideas, and experiences de-fining each historic event, and a reliable, readable overview of that event. Each book provides analyses and discussions, grounded in both primary and secondary sources, of the causes and consequences, in thought and ac-tion, that give meaning to the historic event under review. By assuming a historical perspective, drawing on the latest and best writing on each sub-ject, and offering fresh insights, each book promises to explain how and why a particular event defined the twentieth century. No consensus about the meaning of the twentieth century emerges from the series, but, collec-tively, the books identify the most salient concerns of the century. In so do-ing, the series reminds us of the many ways those historic events continue to affect our lives.

Each book follows a similar format designed to encourage readers to consult it as both a reference and a history in its own right. Each volume opens with a chronology of the historic event, followed by a narrative over-view, which also serves to introduce and examine briefly the main themes and issues related to that event. The next set of chapters is composed of topical essays, each analyzing closely an issue or problem of interpretation introduced in the opening chapter. A concluding chapter suggesting the long-term implications and meanings of the historic event brings the strands of the preceding chapters together while placing the event in the larger historical context. Each book also includes a section of short biographies of the principal persons related to the event, followed by a section introducing and reprinting key historical documents illustrative of and pertinent to the event. A glossary of selected terms adds to the utility of each book. An annotated bibliography—of significant books, films, and CD-ROMs—and an index conclude each volume.

The editors made no attempt to impose any theoretical model or historical perspective on the individual authors. Rather, in developing the series, an advisory board of noted historians and informed high school history teachers and public and school librarians identified the topics needful of exploration and the scholars eminently qualified to examine those events with intelligence and sensitivity. The common commitment throughout the series is to provide accurate, informative, and readable books, free of jargon and up to date in evidence and analysis.

Each book stands as a complete historical analysis and reference guide to a particular historic event. Each book also has many uses, from understanding contemporary perspectives on critical historical issues, to providing biographical treatments of key figures related to each event, to offering excerpts and complete texts of essential documents about the event, to suggesting and describing books and media materials for further study and presentation of the event, and more. The combination of historical narrative and individual topical chapters addressing significant issues and problems encourages students and teachers to approach each historic event from multiple perspectives and with a critical eye. The arrangement and content of each book thus invite students and teachers, through classroom discussions and position papers, to debate the character and significance of great historic events and to discover for themselves how and why history matters.

The series emphasizes the main currents that have shaped the modern world. Much of that focus necessarily looks at the West, especially Europe and the United States. The political, commercial, and cultural expansion of the West wrought largely, though not wholly, the most fundamental changes of the century. Taken together, however, books in the series reveal the interactions between Western and non-Western peoples and society, and also the tensions between modern and traditional cultures. They also point to the ways in which non-Western peoples have adapted Western ideas and technology and, in turn, influenced Western life and thought. Several books examine such increasingly powerful global forces as the rise of

Islamic fundamentalism, the emergence of modern Japan, the Communist revolution in China, and the collapse of communism in eastern Europe and the former Soviet Union. American interests and experiences receive special attention in the series, not only in deference to the primary readership of the books but also in recognition that the United States emerged as the dominant political economic, social, and cultural force during the twentieth century. By looking at the century through the lens of American events and experiences, it is possible to see why the age has come to be known as "The American Century."

Assessing the history of the twentieth century is a formidable prospect. It has been a period of remarkable transformation. The world broadened and narrowed at the same time. Frontiers shifted from the interiors of Africa and Latin America to the moon and beyond; communication spread from mass circulation newspapers and magazines to radio, television, and now the Internet; skyscrapers reached upward and suburbs stretched outward; energy switched from steam, to electric, to atomic power. Many changes did not lead to a complete abandonment of established patterns and practices so much as a synthesis of old and new, as, for example, the increased use of (even reliance on) the telephone in the age of the computer. The automobile and the truck, the airplane, and telecommunications closed distances, and people in unprecedented numbers migrated from rural to urban, industrial, and ever more ethnically diverse areas. Tractors and chemical fertilizers made it possible for fewer people to grow more, but the environmental and demographic costs of an exploding global population threatened to outstrip natural resources and human innovation. Disparities in wealth increased, with developed nations prospering and underdeveloped nations starving. Amid the crumbling of former European colonial empires, Western technology, goods, and culture increasingly enveloped the globe, seeping into, and undermining, non-Western cultures—a process that contributed to a surge of religious fundamentalism and ethno-nationalism in the Middle East, Asia, and Africa. As people became more alike, they also became more aware of their differences. Ethnic and religious rivalries grew in intensity everywhere as the century closed.

The political changes during the twentieth century have been no less profound than the social, economic, and cultural ones. Many of the books in the series focus on political events, broadly defined, but no books are confined to politics alone. Political ideas and events have social effects, just as they spring from a complex interplay of non-political forces in culture, society, and economy. Thus, for example, the modern civil rights and woman's rights movements were at once social and political events in cause and consequence. Likewise, the Cold War created the geopolitical framework for dealing with competing ideologies and nations abroad and served as the touchstone for political and cultural identities at home. The books treating political events do so within their social, cultural, and economic contexts.

Several books in the series examine particular wars in depth. Wars are defining moments for people and eras. During the twentieth century war became more widespread and terrible than ever before, encouraging new efforts to end war through strategies and organizations of international cooperation and disarmament while also fueling new ideologies and instruments of mass persuasion that fostered distrust and festered old national rivalries. Two world wars during the century redrew the political map, slaughtered or uprooted two generations of people, and introduced and hastened the development of new technologies and weapons of mass destruction. The First World War spelled the end of the old European order and spurred communist revolution in Russia and fascism in Italy, Germany, and elsewhere. The Second World War killed fascism and inspired the final push for freedom from European colonial rule in Asia and Africa. It also led to the Cold War that suffocated much of the world for almost half a century. Large wars begat small ones, and brutal totalitarian regimes cropped up across the globe. After (and in some ways because of) the fall of communism in eastern Europe and the former Soviet Union, wars of competing cultures, national interests, and political systems persisted in the struggle to make a new world order. Continuing, too, has been the belief that military technology can achieve political ends, whether in the superior American firepower that failed to "win" in Vietnam or in the American "smart bombs" and other military wizardry that "won" in the Persian Gulf.

Another theme evident in the series is that throughout the century nationalism has continued to drive events. Whether in the Balkans in 1914 triggering World War I or in the Balkans in the 1990s threatening the post–Cold War peace—or in many other places—nationalist ambitions and forces would not die. The persistence of nationalism is yet another reminder of the many ways that the past becomes prologue.

We thus offer the series as a modern guide to and interpretation of the historic events of the twentieth century and as an invitation to consider how and why those events have defined not only the past and present but also charted the political, social, intellectual, cultural, and economic routes into this century.

Randall M. Miller
Saint Joseph's University, Philadelphia

Preface

Entering a new millennium has caused people around the world to reflect on the past. Journalists and newscasters devoted considerable time during 1999, for example, to compiling lists of the most significant people and events of the twentieth century. *Time* magazine named Albert Einstein as the last century's most important person. The *Entertainment and Sports Programming Network* (*ESPN*) picked basketball player Michael Jordan of the Chicago Bulls as the greatest athlete of the twentieth century. There even was a ranked list of the fifty most influential songs of the last century. Historians would have difficulty agreeing on a ranking of the century's one hundred most important events or individuals. But there might be more consensus on a list of the nations that have had the greatest influence on international affairs during the twentieth century. The United States would be an easy choice. Also, the Soviet Union obviously was a key player, but its revolutionary birth and humiliating death gave this nation an artificial quality. Japan might deserve the top spot, given its arrival as a world power not once, but twice in the past century.

This book provides a concise summary and analysis of Japan's emergence for a second time in the twentieth century as a global power. The book's focus is on international affairs, covering domestic developments in Japan that have had an important impact on foreign policy. Japan first emerged as a world power in 1905, after decisively defeating tsarist Russia in the Russo-Japanese War and securing international recognition of its imperial holdings in East Asia.

But the Japanese already had displayed a kind of national inferiority complex that provides an important, although admittedly partial, explanation for policies leading to unwinnable wars first against China and then against the United States. Japan's recovery from the devastation of defeat in World War II and military occupation under a conquering foreign power was certainly one of the most remarkable achievements in recent history. But what emerged in Japan after 1945 was an unconventional global power, one that concentrated on economics rather than politics while preferring a reactive, rather than a proactive approach to meeting challenges abroad. Although this book cannot predict the future, it might provide clues about whether Japan will become an authentic global power in the new millennium.

Chapter 1 presents an overview of developments in Japan from 1945 to 1999. Subsequent chapters discuss in more detail events and patterns emerging during the years since World War II. Chapter 2 describes the reasons for Japan's rise as a postwar economic power. Japan's relationship with the United States receives attention in Chapter 3, and Chapter 4 focuses on interaction with the Communist nations of the Soviet Union and China. Chapter 5 covers developments in Korea and Southeast Asia, and the final chapter summarizes events in the last decade of the twentieth century. In preparing this book, I have depended on the writings of experts on recent Japanese history. Of indispensable importance was the information and analysis in Mikiso Hane's *Modern Japan: A Historical Survey*, Gary D. Allinson's *Japan's Postwar History*, Paul J. Bailey's *Postwar Japan: 1945 to the Present*, and John K. Fairbank, Edwin O. Reischauer, and Albert M. Craig's *East Asia: Tradition and Transformation*.

I am extremely grateful to Randall M. Miller, the series editor, for his unfailing support and encouragement in the course of this project. Also, Barbara Rader of Greenwood Press displayed incredible patience, as well as a talent for gentle prodding, and she deserves credit for her superb editing of the manuscript for length. I extend thanks to my department head and college dean for the sabbatical leave and course reduction that freed time for me to prepare this book. I am indebted to Nayan Chanda for prompt permission to use material from the *Far Eastern Economic Review*. Hyung-gu Lynn and Aaron Forsberg offered valuable advice on selecting documents and subjects for biographies. Kamimura Naoki of Hiroshima City University supplied key documents, and Henmi Teidi translated them. I thank my colleague Kenneth J. Hammond for reviewing the final manuscript for accuracy and providing guidance in adding clarifications. Juanita Stern, as always, provided outstanding secretarial assistance. Of special value were the love and support from my wife, Karin, and our children, Ben and Amanda. Ben was indispensible in performing photocopying services on demand and at the last minute. Finally, I dedicate this book to Robert J. Koss and William Fleming, two dedicated and inspiring middle school teachers at Central School in Evergreen Park, Illinois who first sparked my interest in history.

Abbreviations

ADB	Asian Development Bank
APEC	Asia-Pacific Economic Cooperation forum
AMF	Asian Monetary Fund
ANZUS	Australia, New Zealand, United States Security Pact of 1951
ASEAN	Association of Southeast Asian Nations (Brunei, Indonesia, Malaysia, Philippines, Singapore, Thailand, and Vietnam)
ASPAC	Asian and Pacific Council
CHINCOM	China Committee for East-West Trade Policy
COCOM	Coordinating Committee for East-West Trade Policy
DPRK	Democratic People's Republic of Korea
DSP	Democratic Socialist Party
EAEC	East Asia Economic Cooperation forum
EPA	Economic Planning Agency
ESB	Economic Stabilization Board
GATT	General Agreement on Tariffs and Trade
GDP	gross domestic product
GNP	gross national product
G-7	Group of Seven (Canada, France, Germany, Italy, Japan, United Kingdom, and the United States)

IMF	International Monetary Fund
JCP	Japan Communist Party
JSEC	Japan-Soviet Economic Committee
JSP	Japan Socialist Party
LDP	Liberal Democratic Party
MITI	Ministry of International Trade and Industry
NAFTA	North American Free Trade Agreement
NATO	North Atlantic Treaty Organization
NPR	National Police Reserve
ODA	Official Development Assistance
OECD	Organization for Economic Cooperation and Development
PKO	Peacekeeping Operations bill
PLO	Palestine Liberation Organization
PRC	People's Republic of China
ROC	Republic of China
ROK	Republic of Korea
SCAP	Supreme Commander of the Allied Powers
SDF	Self-Defense Forces
SDP	Socialist Democratic Party
SEATO	Southeast Asia Treaty Organization of 1954
UN	United Nations
UNCHR	United Nations Commission on Human Rights
UNHCR	United Nations High Commissioner for Refugees

Chronology of Events

1945

July   Allies issue Potsdam Declaration demanding Japan's immediate surrender in World War II

August   United States drops atomic bomb on Hiroshima

Soviet Union declares war on Japan and attacks Japanese forces in Manchuria and Korea

United States drops atomic bomb on Nagasaki

Emperor Hirohito announces Japanese surrender on the radio to Japanese people

Prince Higashikuni becomes prime minister

General Douglas MacArthur arrives in Japan

September Japanese formal surrender ends World War II

U.S. occupation begins

MacArthur receives "Initial Post-Surrender Policy"

October   Shidehara Kijuro replaces Prince Higashikuni as prime minister

Supreme Commander of the Allied Powers (SCAP) issues Civil Liberties Directive

Japan Communist Party (JCP) is legalized

November	MacArthur approves plan for break-up of *zaibatsu* ("financial clique")
December	Creation of Allied Council and Far Eastern Commission
	State Shinto Directive separates religion from state
	Diet passes Trade Union Law guaranteeing workers the right to organize and strike

1946

January	Emperor Hirohito renounces his divinity
	First political purge directive is issued
	Abolition of Army and Navy ministries
April	First postwar Diet elections are held, with women for the first time voting and standing as candidates for election
May	Yoshida Shigeru, head of conservative Liberal Party, becomes prime minister
	Tokyo War Crimes Trials open proceedings
October	Diet passes Land Reform Bill
November	Promulgation of new constitution to become effective in May 1947

1947

January	MacArthur prohibits planned General Strike
April	First Diet elections under new constitution are held
	Japan Socialist Party (JSP) holds most seats in Diet
	Socialist leader Katayama Tetsu forms coalition and becomes prime minister
May	New constitution is implemented
	Postwar Diet holds first session under new constitution
	Diet passes Labor Standards Law, establishing Ministry of Labor
	Local Autonomy Law is enacted
	Diet passes Fundamental Law of Education
	Adoption of plan calling for the dissolution of all excessive concentrations of economic power

| December | Diet passes Law for the Elimination of Excessive Concentration of Economic Power, giving power to a commission under SCAP to dissolve any company that it judged too large or monopolistic |

1948

January	Termination of *zaibatsu* dissolution program
March	Ashida Hitoshi, leader of conservative Democratic Party, becomes prime minister following Katayama's resignation
July	Right of public workers to strike is revoked
October	Truman administration approves NSC-13, establishing as the "prime objective" of U.S. policy in Japan achieving economic growth and political stability over a quick peace settlement and social reform. This marked adoption of the "reverse course" in U.S. occupation policies
	Yoshida Shigeru becomes prime minister after Ashida resigns amid charges of bribery and corruption
November	War Crimes Trials end with seven defendants, including Tojo Hideki, condemned to death
December	National Public Service Law denies civil servants the right to strike and engage in collective bargaining

1949

January	Lower house elections give Yoshida's Liberal Party a plurality of seats
	Dodge Plan of financial retrenchment is implemented, leading to massive unemployment
	Ministry of International Trade and Industry (MITI) replaces Ministry of Commerce and Industry
May	Reparations program is terminated
October	SCAP formally ends censorship
December	Yen is stabilized at 360 to the (U.S.) dollar

1950

| January | Beginning of year-long purge of Communists and leftists results in the dismissal of thousands from public sector jobs |
| | Sohyo labor federation is formed |

April	United States appoints John Foster Dulles to negotiate Japanese Peace Treaty
June	U.S. government urges government of Japan to initiate rearmament
	Outbreak of the Korean War
July	National Police Reserve is created
August	Korean War begins to stimulate economic revival in Japan
	Diet passes Foreign Investment Law

1951

April	General Matthew B. Ridgway becomes SCAP after relief of MacArthur
June	Purge restrictions on 69,000 persons are lifted
September	San Francisco Conference
	Signing of Japanese Peace Treaty, to become effective in April 1952
	Signing of U.S.-Japan Security Treaty
	Yoshida refers to U.S. retention of Okinawa as a source of "pain and anxiety" for the Japanese people
October	Japan Socialist Party splits over U.S.-Japan Security Treaty ratification

1952

February	U.S.-Japan Administrative Agreement is signed
April	Japan regains sovereignty as U.S. occupation ends
	Peace treaty is signed with Nationalist government under Chiang Kai-shek on Taiwan recognized as the Republic of China, ignoring Mao Zedong's government in Beijing
	Peace treaty is signed with India
May	May Day Incident occurs with anti-American riots
July	Subversive Activities Prevention Law is passed
September	Soviet Union vetoes Japan's membership application to United Nations
October	National Police Reserve is reorganized to become the National Security Force

1953

July   Cease-fire agreement ends fighting in the Korean War

1954

March   U.S.-Japan Mutual Defense Assistance Agreement is signed

June   Police Law recentralizes Police Administration

Self-Defense Forces (SDF) is established under civilian control, replacing National Security Force

United States conducts atomic tests on Bikini island resulting in a Japanese ship, the *Lucky Dragon*, being showered with nuclear fallout

September   Japan Defense Agency established to supervise SDF

November   Peace treaty and reparations agreement are signed with Burma

December   Hatoyama Ichiro, former purged politician and leader of the Democratic Party, becomes prime minister

1955

August   First Ban the Atom Bomb World Conference is held in Hiroshima

September   Japan is admitted to the General Agreement on Tariffs and Trade (GATT)

October   Two factions of JSP reunite

Economic Planning Agency is established

November   Two top conservative parties merge to form the Liberal Democratic Party (LDP)

December   Population reaches 89 million

1956

April   Hatoyama Ichiro is elected first president of the LDP

May   Fisheries agreement is concluded with the Soviet Union

Peace treaty and reparations agreement are signed with the Philippines

June   School Boards Law abolishes local elective school boards after massive demonstrations and fights in the upper house of the Diet

October   Diplomatic relations are restored with the Soviet Union

November	Hatoyama resigns as prime minister
December	Japan is admitted as a member of the United Nations
	Ishibashi Tanzan becomes prime minister

1957

February	Kishi Nobusuke becomes prime minister
May	First election since the creation of the LDP results in the party receiving 57.8 percent of votes cast
June	U.S. president Dwight D. Eisenhower promises the return of Okinawa during summit with Kishi
	Kishi-Eisenhower agreement on reducing U.S. troops and military facilities in Japan is signed
August	Nationwide teacher demonstrations protest the government's rating system and the reintroduction of moral education into the school curriculum
December	Treaty of Commerce is signed with the Soviet Union

1958

January	Peace treaty and reparations agreement are signed with Indonesia
May	Nagasaki flag incident offends the People's Republic of China (PRC), and Beijing terminates trade with Japan
September	Negotiations begin to renew U.S.-Japan Security Treaty
October	Kishi shelves Police Duties Amendment bill in response to violent opposition in the Diet

1959

March	Formation of the People's Council for Preventing Revision of the Security Treaty signals growing opposition to revised U.S.-Japan Security Treaty
	Asanuma Inejiro delivers anti-American statement in Beijing
April	Crown Prince Akihito marries a commoner
August	Agreement is signed with North Korea for repatriation of Koreans

1960

January	Kishi leaves for Washington, D.C., to sign the new U.S.-Japan Mutual Security and Cooperation Treaty

	JSP supporters of the renewal of the U.S.-Japan Security Treaty split from the party and found the Democratic Socialist Party (DSP)
February	Revised U.S.-Japan Security Treaty is submitted to the Diet for ratification
May	Kishi's extension of the Diet session to ensure ratification of the U.S.-Japan Security Treaty leads to a JSP boycott and massive demonstrations against renewal of the agreement
June	Diet ratifies renewal of revised U.S.-Japan Security Treaty and U.S.-Japan Administrative Agreement
	President Eisenhower cancels visit to Japan in response to continuing public protests against the treaty that climax in the death of a female student
July	Ikeda Hayato becomes prime minister
	PRC resumes trade with Japan
September	Ikeda announces the Income Doubling Plan
October	Assassination of JSP secretary-general Asanuma Inejiro
	Peace treaty and reparations agreement are signed with South Vietnam
November	Bitter year-long Miike Mines strike is settled

1961

June	Ikeda summit with U.S. president John F. Kennedy
	Agreement is signed for Japanese repayment of GARIOA (Government Aid and Relief in Occupied Areas) debts covering the cost of the U.S. occupation
November	First meeting of Joint U.S.-Japanese Committee on Trade and Economic Affairs that Ikeda and Kennedy created during June summit

1962

January	First meeting of U.S.-Japan Cultural Conference that Ikeda and Kennedy organized during June summit
February	Okinawa's legislature appeals to the United Nations for action to end U.S. colonial occupation of the Ryukyus
	Ikeda tours Europe

November	Liao-Takasaki five-year trade agreement is the fifth one to be signed with the PRC since 1952
December	Machinery exports exceed textiles exports

1963

December	Republic of China on Taiwan suspends trade with Japan to protest trade agreements with the PRC

1964

January	Merger creates Mitsubishi Heavy Industries
April	Japan is admitted to the Organization for Economic Cooperation and Development (OECD)
	Japan enters the International Monetary Fund
October	Bullet train from Tokyo to Osaka begins operation
	Summer Olympic Games are held in Tokyo
November	Sato Eisaku becomes prime minister
	Yoshida brokers deal to resume trade with the Republic of China on Taiwan
	First visit of U.S. nuclear-powered submarine to Japan
	Komeito (Clean Government) Party is formed, advocating the views of the Soka Gakkai religious sect

1965

January	Sato summit with President Lyndon B. Johnson
June	Treaty normalizes relations with South Korea, with ratification in December
July	LDP loses majority in Tokyo Assembly elections
August	Sato is first postwar prime minister to visit Okinawa
	Formation of Citizens' Federation for Peace in Vietnam (Beheiren) signals beginning of anti–Vietnam War protest movement in Japan
December	Population reaches 98 million

1966

July	Site is chosen in Chiba Prefecture for new Narita International Airport to serve Tokyo

	Peace treaty and reparations agreement are signed with Singapore
	Tokyo Conference on aid to Southeast Asia
August	Japan joins Asian Development Bank at its inception
November	Sato summit with Johnson

1967

May	Komeito Party wins first Diet seats, as the LDP for the first time loses a majority of popular votes cast
November	Sato summit with Johnson
	Sato tours Southeast Asia
December	Sato enunciates Three Non-Nuclear Principles
	First anti-pollution lawsuit is brought against a company in Niigata, with other lawsuits following soon thereafter
	Anti–Vietnam War demonstrations and strikes increase in number and intensity

1968

January	U.S.S. *Enterprise*, a nuclear-powered aircraft carrier, visits U.S. naval base at Sasebo
April	Agreement with the United States for the return of Bonin, Iwo Jima, and Marcus Islands to Japan's administrative control, to become effective in June
May	U.S.S. *Swordfish* allegedly releases nuclear waste in Sasebo Harbor
June	U.S. plane crash brings demands to move airbase
	Student demonstrations take place at many universities
August	Law allows police access to universities to restore order
October	Kawabata Yasunari wins Nobel Prize in literature
	New Japan Steel Company is formed following the merger of Yawata and Fuji Steel companies
December	U.S.S. *Plunger* visits Sasebo, resulting in revival of the anti-nuclear debate
	First surplus in trade with the United States

1969

January	Riot police evict students occupying Tokyo University buildings

May	Completion of Tokyo-Kobe Expressway
July	U.S. president Richard Nixon enunciates "Nixon Doctrine" on Guam, precluding future commitment of U.S. ground troops in Asia
August	Diet passes University Reform Law
November	Nixon-Sato communiqué promises the return of Okinawa in 1972 during summit meeting
December	Citizens movements spread over environmental issues
	Japan becomes the top television manufacturer in the world

1970

February	Japan signs Nuclear Non-Proliferation Treaty, but the Diet fails to ratify it
	Japan launches first satellite
March	Hijacking of Japan Airlines flight to North Korea
	World Exposition is held in Osaka
May	Sato pledges 1 percent of gross national product (GNP) in foreign aid
June	U.S.-Japan Mutual Security and Cooperation Treaty is renewed indefinitely despite huge public demonstrations
October	Sato is reelected to unprecedented fourth term as prime minister
	Sato summit with Nixon
	Sato becomes first Japanese prime minister to address United Nations
November	Right-wing novelist Mishima Yukio commits suicide after abortive appeal to end the Self-Defense Forces
December	Three policemen die in demonstration against Narita International Airport

1971

February	Start of compulsory expropriation of land for Narita International Airport
April	Last Okinawa Day demonstration
July	Environmental Protection Agency is established

	First Nixon Shock announces U.S. intention to normalize relations with the PRC
August	Second Nixon Shock announces dollar devaluation and 10 percent surcharge on U.S. imports
	Nixon meets Emperor Hirohito in Anchorage, Alaska
October	Japan formally accepts new "voluntary" textile quotas
December	Agreement revalues yen at 308 to the dollar
1972	
January	Nixon-Sato communiqué outlines new foundations for U.S.-Japanese relations
February	Winter Olympic Games in Sapporo
May	United States returns Okinawa to Japanese control
	Left-wing terrorist group, the Japanese Red Army, forms links with the Palestinian Popular Front for the Liberation of Palestine and carries out an attack at Lod Airport in Tel Aviv, Israel, in which 26 people die
July	Tanaka Kakuei becomes prime minister
September	Tanaka summit with Nixon in Honolulu
	Relations are normalized with the PRC in the Tanaka–Zhou Enlai communiqué
	Formation of the Japan Foundation
November	Japan closes embassy on Taiwan
December	Diet passes National Environmental Preservation Law
	Yen appreciates to 272 to the dollar
1973	
July	Tanaka summit with Nixon
August	South Korean CIA agents arrest Kim Dae-jung in Tokyo and take him back to South Korea for execution
September	Normalization of relations with North Vietnam
	Oil price crisis forces Tanaka to scale down and then abandon ambitious regional development plan
December	Diet approves Three Non-Nuclear Principles

Tanaka tours Europe

1974

January	Tanaka's tour of Southeast Asia is met with hostile demonstratrions in Thailand, Indonesia, and the Philippines
April	Taiwan suspends flights with Japan in response to signing of PRC-Japan air agreement
August	Japanese youth shoots and kills wife of South Korean president Pak Chung-hui
September	Nuclear leak occurs on experimental nuclear-powered *Mutsu*
November	Gerald R. Ford becomes first sitting U.S. president to visit Japan for summit in Tokyo
	Charges of corruption force Tanaka to resign
December	Miki Takeo becomes prime minister
	Sato wins Nobel Peace Prize

1975

January	Miki lobbies for reforms to end LDP factionalism and illegal campaign contributions
March	Diet passes Political Funds Control Law
July	International Ocean Exposition opens on Okinawa
August	Issuance of Miki-Ford communiqué reaffirms defense alliance and bilateral commitment to security in Asia after the end of the Vietnam War
September	Resumption of flights between Taiwan and Japan
October	Emperor Hirohito and his wife visit the United States
November	First summit of six major industrial democracies, or G-6 (Britain, France, Italy, Japan, the United States, and West Germany), takes place in France
December	Population reaches 112 million

1976

February	U.S. Senate holds hearings on the Lockheed Scandal, which implicates the Tanaka government in taking bribes
	First criminal indictments occur in the Minamata pollution case

May	Diet ratifies the Nuclear Non-Proliferation Treaty
June	Six members of the LDP split and create the New Liberal Club (NLC)
July	Tanaka is arrested and indicted in the Lockheed Scandal
	First meeting of Japan-U.S. Subcommittee for Defense Cooperation
	Final payment of reparations to the Philippines
September	Soviet pilot with MiG 25 defects to Japan
November	Diet endorses a defense spending ceiling of 1 percent of the GNP
December	Fukuda Takeo replaces Miki as prime minister

1977

March	Fukuda summit with U.S. president Jimmy Carter
April	Critical mass is attained by first fast breeder reactor
May	Violent demonstration at Narita International Airport causes one fatality
August	Fukuda tours Southeast Asia, promising increased aid and announcing Fukuda Doctrine
November	Appointment of Ushiba Nobuhiko to a cabinet post to supervise resolving trade problems with the United States
December	Life expectancy rate reaches highest in the world

1978

January	One hundred Chinese fishing boats descend on Senkaku Islands
April	Fukuda summit with Carter
May	Narita International Airport opens amid continuing opposition from local farmers
August	MITI sets voluntary limits on auto exports
	The Sino-Japanese Long-Term Trade Agreement and the Japan-PRC Treaty of Peace and Friendship are signed
December	Yen rises to 175 to the dollar
	Ohira Masayoshi becomes prime minister

1979

January   First uniform national university entrance examinations take place

Ohira makes trip to Beijing

April   Enshrinement of 14 class "A" war criminals at the Yasukuni Shrine, where Japanese military war dead are venerated

Chisso executives are found criminally responsible in the Minamata pollution case

June   Issuance of Carter-Ohira proclamation during Carter's visit to Japan

Textile trade dispute with the United States is settled

30 percent increase in oil prices occurs

July   Fifth summit of industrialized democracies is held in Tokyo, Canada having joined to create the G-7

October   Assassination of South Korean president Pak Chung-hui

November   Komeito Party announces support for renewal of the U.S.-Japan Mutual Security Treaty

1980

January   Ohira tours Pacific nations

March   Japan participates in "RIMPAC 80" military exercises with United States, Canada, Australia, and New Zealand

May   Ohira summit with Carter in Washington, D.C.

Lower house passes surprise no-confidence vote

JSP announces end to opposition to U.S.-Japan Mutual Security and Cooperation Treaty and Japanese Self-Defense Forces

June   Ohira dies suddenly of a heart attack

The LDP wins a surprise victory in Diet elections

July   Suzuki Zenko becomes prime minister

1981

January   February 7 is designated "Northern Territories Day"

Commission on Administrative Reform is established and calls for reduced public expenditures and privatization

	Suzuki tours Southeast Asia
May	Suzuki summit with U.S. president Ronald Reagan
	Voluntary auto export agreement is signed with the United States

1982

January	School textbook revision controversy starts
	Diet passes Health Law for the Elderly
	Report of the Commission on Administrative Reform recommends privatization of three public corporations
August	Japanese-Korean agreement settles textbook crisis
	Japan gains membership in the U.N. Commission on Human Rights
November	Nakasone Yasuhiro becomes prime minister

1983

January	Third Market Opening Package with the United States is signed
	During summit with Reagan, Nakasone promises to enhance Japan's defense capabilities
	LDP bargain with eight-member NLC retains Diet majority
	Diet passes Structural Reform Law for Specified Industries, resulting in privatization of Nippon Telephone and Telegraph in 1985
October	Tanaka is convicted in Lockheed Scandal
	Disneyland opens in Japan
November	Reagan summit in Tokyo with Nakasone

1984

March	Nissan announces plans to build a factory in England
	Citrus and meat import deal is signed with the United States
	Nakasone visits the PRC

1985

| January | Nakasone summit with Reagan |
| | Anti-Japanese demonstrations in China |

	Toyota announces plans to build factories in the United States and Canada
	Diet passes Equal Employment Opportunity Act
	Steel export agreement is signed with the United States
September	"Plaza Agreement" with the United States allows the value of the dollar to slide, the yen to appreciate, and exports of heavy industry to drop
	Diet revises National Pension Law
	Telecommunications and tobacco monopolies are privatized
December	Population reaches 121 million

1986

April	Nakasone summit with Reagan
	Doi Takako is elected leader of the JSP, becoming the first woman to head a major political party
	The LDP wins large majorities in both Diet houses
	Nakasone wins one-year extension as prime minister
	Semi-conductor trade agreement is signed with the United States

1987

January	Nakasone summit with Reagan
	Nakasone withdraws controversial tax reform plan
	Japan National Railways is broken up into seven separate companies and privatized
	Defense expenditures surpass 1 percent of GNP
	Nakasone tours Southeast Asia
June	Toshiba Scandal occurs, resulting in a ban on importation of its products into the United States for five years
September	Nakasone summit with Reagan
October	Decline of 14.9 percent in stock market prices
	Takeshita Noboru replaces Nakasone as prime minister

1988

July	Recruit-Cosmos Scandal occurs

August	Takeshita makes trip to the PRC
December	Record trade surplus with the United States

1989

January	Emperor Hirohito dies
	Rengo union federation is formed, unifying most unions for the first time
February	Diet passes revised tax reform proposal
	Takeshita summit with U.S. president George Bush takes place when Bush travels to Tokyo for Hirohito's funeral
	Chinese prime minister Li Peng visits Tokyo
April	Diet enacts a 3 percent consumption, or general sales, tax
June	Recruit-Cosmos Scandal forces Takeshita to resign
July	The LDP loses its majority in upper house election
	Kaifu Toshiki becomes prime minister
September	Kaifu summit with Bush
	Formation of the Asia-Pacific Economic Cooperation (APEC) forum
November	Heisei era begins when Emperor Akihito is enthroned
December	Japan becomes largest foreign aid donor in the world
	Reductions in overseas investments continue

1990

January	Kaifu tours Europe
February	The LDP wins a narrow majority in lower house elections
March	Kaifu in Washington, D.C., calls for "global partnership" to deal with terrorism, drugs, and environmental damage
	South Korean prime minister No Tae-u visits Tokyo
May	Kaifu tours Southeast Asia
August	Economic sanctions are imposed on Iraq in response to its invasion of Kuwait
	Kaifu commits $1 billion for actions against Iraq
September	Diet authorizes $4 billion for military buildup in Saudi Arabia and the Persian Gulf

Diet delegation visits North Korea

North Korean–Japanese talks on recognition begin

1991

January   Kaifu pledges $9 billion more to finance conduct of the Gulf War

                Kaifu visits South Korea and apologizes for Japan's massacre of Korean protesters in 1919

April   Soviet president Mikhail Gorbachev visits Japan

                Japanese minesweepers are sent to the Persian Gulf

                Economic recession begins after huge decline in stock market prices

May   First use of the term *kenbei* ("dislike of the United States")

July   Kaifu summit with Bush

September   Emperor Akihito tours Indonesia, Malaysia, and Thailand

October   Miyazawa Kiishi becomes prime minister

1992

January   Miyazawa visits South Korea

February   Bush visits Tokyo with top U.S. auto executives

June   Diet approves Peacekeeping Operations bill, authorizing the deployment of Self-Defense Forces (SDF) units abroad for noncombatant purposes

                1,800 SDF forces are sent to Cambodia for peacekeeping operations

                Official Development Assistance (ODA) Charter adds four human rights provisions for receipt of economic aid

July   Miyazawa summit with Bush

                Emperor Akihito visits the PRC

                Suspension of normalization talks with the Democratic People's Republic of Korea after North Korean agents capture Japanese citizens and take them to North Korea

August   Nikkei stock prices reach 1,400-point decline over the prior nine months, as economic recession deepens

                Japan New Party is formed under Hosokawa Morihiro

1993

January	Miyazawa in Thailand pledges participation of Japan in long-term regional security discussions
	SDF forces participate in peacekeeping operations under UN auspices in Mozambique
March	Refusal to sign Bangkok Declaration on Human Rights
July	LDP dissidents form Shinseito and Sakigake parties
	The LDP loses a majority in House election
	Seven-party coalition replaces LDP government under Hosokawa as prime minister
November	Diet passes Environmental Basic Law
	Hosokawa agrees to open domestic market to foreign rice imports at GATT talks

1994

January	Diet passes major election reform bill ending multiple representation in districts, to become effective in 1995
	SDF forces participate in peacekeeping operations under UN auspices in Rwanda
April	Hata Tsutomu becomes prime minister
June	Murayama Tomiichi becomes second Socialist prime minister, leading a JSP-LDP coalition government
	New Life, DSP, CGP, JNP, and Shinseito parties dissolve and then join to form the Shinshinto Party
December	Oe Kenzaburo wins Nobel Prize in literature
	Voluntary auto export restraints are ended

1995

January	Kobe earthquake kills over 5,000 in western Japan
March	Poison gas attack in Tokyo subway kills 12 people in the name of the Aum Shinrikyo religious sect
June	Diet passes diluted war apology resolution on eve of 50th anniversary of Japan's surrender in World War II
	The PRC launches missiles across the Taiwan Strait, causing Japan to suspend economic assistance

September	U.S. soldiers on Okinawa rape a Japanese girl, intensifying popular demands for the United States to close all its bases on the island
November	Russian president Boris Yeltsin and Murayama issue a communiqué pledging action to end the Kurile dispute and sign a peace treaty by the end of the century
	Diet raises consumption tax to 5 percent, to become effective in 1997
December	Government report announces banks with a total of $375 billion in nonperforming loans
	Yen rises to 79 to the dollar

1996

January	Hashimoto Ryutaro becomes prime minister
April	U.S. president Bill Clinton visits Tokyo, promising to negotiate arrangements for closing or relocating some U.S. bases from Okinawa

1997

September	Announcement of Japan-U.S. Agreement on Defense Cooperation Guidelines
November	Hokkaido Takushoku Bank and Yamaichi Securities declare bankruptcy, setting off financial crisis
December	Kyoto Conference on global warming

1998

January	Government announces banks have a total of $658 billion in nonperforming loans
April	Hashimoto announces 10 percent reduction in foreign economic aid
August	Obuchi Keizo becomes prime minister
	North Korea launches a missile into Japan's airspace, causing Tokyo to suspend funding for two light water reactors, food assistance deal, and normalization talks
October	Diet passes Obuchi's six bills to resolve the banking crisis
	Obuchi pledges $30 billion in new foreign loans and other arrangements
November	Jiang Zemin of the PRC visits Japan

1999

March	A Japanese destroyer fires on two suspected North Korean spy ships
May	Diet approves new Defense Cooperation Guidelines
July	Diet authorizes "research councils" to reconsider provisions in the Constitution, such as Article 9
September	Three banks merge to form the largest in the world
	Accident at nuclear plant kills two workers and exposes 47 others to nuclear contamination
December	Economic sanctions on North Korea are ended, and normalization negotiations resume

2000

February	Lower house of the Diet passes bill to reduce by 50 its number of proportional representatives
March	Japan pledges 100,000 tons of food aid to North Korea
	North Korea drops demand for $10 billion in reparations from Japan and agrees to investigate charges that its agents kidnapped Japanese citizens
April	Prime Minister Obuchi suffers an incapacitating stroke, leaving him in a coma
	Volcano erupts on east coast of Japan, forcing mass evacuation
	Mori Yoshiro becomes prime minister
May	Obuchi dies
June	Mori forms coalition government after LDP fails to win a majority in lower house Diet elections
July	G-8 summit on Okinawa, Russia having joined the group
August	Economy stagnant, as land prices continue to fall and bond market remains weak

JAPAN'S EMERGENCE AS A GLOBAL POWER EXPLAINED

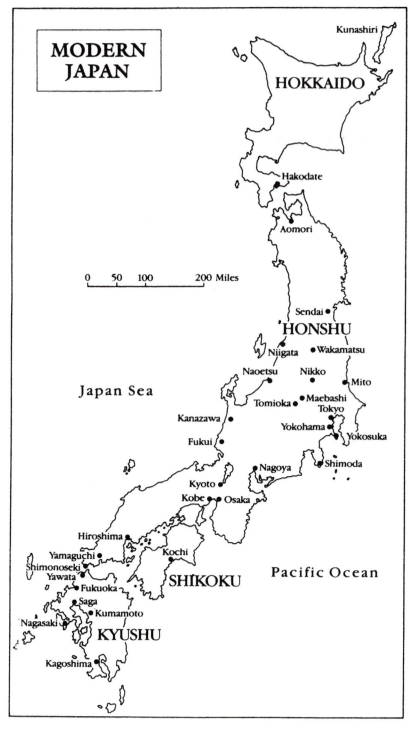

Modern Japan

I

Reprise of the Rising Sun

After World War II Japan forced the world to revise the definition of what constitutes a world power. Traditionally, commanding military might and political influence determined whether a nation could achieve and retain status as a decisive international player. But after its defeat in World War II, Japan adopted a new constitution prohibiting the maintenance of a military establishment capable of waging anything but defensive war. After 1945, Japan shifted its attention to expanding its economic power and projecting it abroad. No nation has transformed itself into a global economic power as rapidly as postwar Japan. But major changes in world affairs in the 1970s raised pressure on Japan to extend the realm of its international activism beyond trade and investment. In the last decade of the twentieth century, as a new international order emerged after the collapse of the Soviet Union and the end of the Cold War, demands for Japan to perform as a traditional world power grew stronger.

No nation has yet matched postwar Japan's capacity to exert decisive influence on world affairs without the option of applying military sanctions. During World War II, Japan fought to establish East Asia as its political and economic preserve to the exclusion not only of the West but also of the Soviet Union and its Communist adherents. Although the United States and its allies acted decisively to prevent Japan from achieving dominance in the Pacific arena, Japan's brief rule over much of Asia destroyed the old colonial order Western imperialism had created. Defeat in World War II ended Japanese efforts to construct a self-sufficient and mutually beneficial economic and cultural community in East Asia under its allegedly enlightened direction and benevolent leadership through traditional military means. Ironically, Japan's surrender left it under U.S. control and vulnerable to Communist penetration. After the U.S. occupation ended in 1952, Japan moved peacefully to realize its dream of the 1930s to create a "Co-Prosperity Sphere" in Asia with itself at the center as an economic rather than a military superpower.

This chapter presents a historical overview of Japan's relations with the world community from the end of World War II through the remainder of the twentieth century. The Japanese people and their culture deserve most of the credit for the emergence of Japan as a global power after the war. The United States, however, played a critical role as well, reconstructing Japan politically, socially, and economically. U.S. occupation brought about nothing less than a second opening of Japan. Its impact was as decisive as had been Commodore Matthew C. Perry's arrival in 1853 that initiated Japan's rapid modernization and Westernization. But rather than embarking on a course of military expansion, the Japanese after 1945 became passionate pacifists. Resistance to U.S. dictates was futile, of course, but the Japanese reacted to American guidance with positive if not enthusiastic cooperation. Japan then focused its attention on rapid economic development, becoming one of the most productive and prosperous nations in the history of humankind.

ENDURING THE UNENDURABLE

Japanese citizens heard the voice of Emperor Hirohito for the first time on August 15, 1945, when he announced Japan's surrender in World War II, imploring his people to "endure the unendurable." Defeat had left Japan in ruins. In a prewar population of 71 million, over 2 million Japanese had died, of whom 668,000 were civilians. Air and naval bombardment in combination with fires had devastated 66 major cities, destroying or damaging factories and wiping out 2.3 million civilian houses. Conscription, deaths, and evacuation cut the urban population in half. Industrial production was at 30 percent of prewar levels, and agricultural output was meager because of inadequate labor, capital, and fertilizer. There were shortages of everything, and inflation raged at 10 percent per month. People were ill-clothed and hungry, having to trade prized family possessions just to buy enough rice to survive. But it was a combination of psychological trauma and spiritual emptiness that made rapid recovery seem impossible. The Japanese suffered from a palpable lack of direction in August 1945, as a citizenry that had recently prepared for a final battle in defense of the home islands now faced a future seemingly without purpose. Traditional discipline evaporated, as survival frequently required defiance of authority. Worst of all, Japan had to confront the frightening prospect of foreign occupation. Remarkably, the Japanese people accepted surrender and humiliation with courage and dignity.

Japan expected a harsh and vindictive occupation, but the American rule was benevolent and constructive. Accustomed to disciplined and loyal obedience to superior authority, the Japanese people at first merely tolerated an uneasy cooperation with the occupiers. U.S. president Harry S. Truman appointed General Douglas MacArthur to command the U.S. occupation. As Supreme Commander of the Allied Powers (SCAP), he and his staff enacted a series of reforms that helped create an open society in Japan based on capitalism and representative government. To achieve the central goal of eliminating the foundations of Japanese authoritarianism and militarism, SCAP closed munitions factories, packing them for shipment as reparations to the victims of previous Japanese aggression. SCAP also disbanded ultranationalist groups, released political prisoners, and disestablished the state religion of Shintoism. War crimes trials resulted in the execution or imprisonment of twenty-five wartime leaders, and the prohibition of 220,000 others from participation in politics. SCAP drafted the 1947 constitution that made the emperor, who had renounced his divinity in 1946, "the symbol of the state" and vested all power in a Diet (legislature) with election of representatives based on universal suffrage. Peerage for 913 families ended. Under Article 9, Japan renounced war forever.

Understanding the complexities of administering a nation with an alien culture and language, the United States did not impose direct military rule on Japan, as it did in Germany. MacArthur supervised a huge bureaucracy in Tokyo, but SCAP governed through the Japanese themselves. Staff sections paralleled ministries in the emperor's government, with military government teams to monitor implementation of occupation policy. In the first postwar elections in April 1946, a total of 363 political parties fielded candidates. The Liberal Party won the most seats, but because SCAP had purged its leader, Hatoyama Ichiro, for his links with the wartime governments, Yoshida Shigeru, for the first of two times during the U.S. occupation, became prime minister, setting the example as a cooperative partner. Elections for representatives to the Diet followed under the new constitution in 1947, but Japan's legislature had very little power to make independent decisions. In essence, peace brought the replacement of one military government with another of foreign origin. Predictably, U.S. officials made mistakes, such as trying without permanent success to decentralize local government and the police force. SCAP's reforms made major strides toward democratization and demilitarization, but its economic policies were far less successful.

During the U.S. occupation, the prime minister and Diet were handmaidens of SCAP, implementing the American reform program with little resistance. Guiding U.S. officials was the fundamental premise that the concentration of wealth in Japan had nurtured authoritarianism and imperialist expansion. Thus, it seemed, destroying old economic elites and distributing the ownership of production would promote competition and equality, contributing to the emergence of democracy and political stability. SCAP immediately froze the assets of the great family-dominated industrial combines, or *zaibatsu* ("financial cliques"), such as Mitsubishi, Mitsui, Sumitomo, and Yasuda. The first wave of "trust-busting" dissolved 83 holding companies and reorganized 5,000 others. Anti-monopoly laws sought to replace large banks and *zaibatsu* with smaller companies, in which the public now could buy stock. What individual wealth the war failed to destroy, SCAP eliminated with proposals to the Diet resulting in the imposition of a 90 percent tax on capital, as well as steep income and inheritance taxes.

Patterned after Franklin D. Roosevelt's New Deal, the Diet passed labor laws that guaranteed the right to organize unions, stage strikes, and bargain collectively. This resulted in the creation of a powerful union movement to protect worker rights. By 1949 the number of unions reached 35,000, with a membership of 6.5 million in a total work force of 15 million. The Domei union emerged as the main organizer of blue-collar workers, using collective bargaining to raise wages and expand benefits. Communists and Socialists, having been released from prison, quickly assumed leadership of the labor movement, organizing a string of strikes to achieve political aims.

Even more sweeping was SCAP's program of land redistribution, which created a class of small farmers. In 1945, 70 percent of farmers either were tenants or rented acreage affecting 46 percent of land in Japan. Under new laws, absentee owners and those holding over 10 acres were forced to sell their property to the government at a fraction of its worth. The government then sold the land to former tenants at low prices and with generous credit. At first, farmers could own a maximum of 2.5 acres and had to live on the land.

During 1947 the adverse impact of SCAP's economic reforms became apparent, as the atmosphere of physical and psychological devastation had not disappeared. Emphasis on revenge, reparations, and reform meant that nothing had been done to rebuild the markets, resources, and demand that were essential for recovery. Most Japanese still lived at the bare subsistence level with heavy reliance on the black market to provide daily necessities. Spiraling inflation negated the benefits of wage increases, and inadequate transportation limited marketing and distribution, which are indispensable for reviving industry or agriculture. Economic productivity in 1947 was still only slightly more than half of what it had been in 1936. Japan had only 1.8 million tons of mostly wooden shipping in 1945, a decline from the wartime high of 10 million tons. With no merchant marine and an unstable currency, it was impossible to regain access to foreign sources of raw materials for industrialization and external markets to end a serious adverse balance of trade.

Compounding an already desperate situation was a 10 percent increase in population to 80 million, as soldiers and other overseas Japanese returned to the home islands. Surviving on meager rations, Japan still had to import 1.7 million tons of food during 1948. Only American economic assistance, amounting to $429 million in 1949, averted catastrophe. It was the international implications of Japan's inability to move toward economic recovery that added urgency to the concerns of the American leaders. By late 1947 the rising power of the Communist Party in China, combined with the Soviet Union's control in northern Korea, created growing concern in the United States that a weak Japan would be a vulnerable and inviting target for Soviet expansion. Even more disturbing was leftist penetration of Japanese politics, creating intense fear that Communist subversion would result in a peaceful seizure of political power. Adding to U.S. alarm was steadily rising voter support for the Socialists from the Sohyo union, which represented highly politicized and internationally oriented government and white-collar employees. Sohyo demanded sympathy, or at least "positive neutrality," for the Communist bloc in the Cold War. Signaling a coming shift in U.S. policy, MacArthur prohibited a General Strike set for February 1947.

After less than two years of occupation, the United States abandoned any further reforms in favor of promoting rapid economic recovery, pursuing a "reverse course" aimed at transforming Japan into a bulwark against Soviet expansion in Asia. Vigorous measures followed to repress any leftist political activities, notably leading to the purge of Communist leaders from Japanese trade unions. Arguably more significant was an end to "*zaibatsu* busting" in the interests of promoting industrial recovery. The immense combines of the past resurfaced quickly—often with the same names, although no longer under direct family administration. Reestablishing links with recovering banks and trading companies, these postwar *zaibatsu*, known as *keiretsu*, led Japan's postwar economic revival. By 1946 these firms had formed the Federation of Economic Organizations, or Keidanren, which became the guiding force for big business. Representing about 700 industrial, financial, and commercial firms, the Keidanren was a powerful lobbyist thereafter for government policies favorable to corporate interests.

Elections under the new constitution in 1947 had made Socialist leader Katayama Tetsu prime minister until March 1948, when Ashida Hitoshi of the Democratic Party, his coalition partner, replaced him. Later that year, this new government fell after Ashida, following MacArthur's orders, banned a strike and then persuaded the Diet to pass laws outlawing work stoppages and unions for government workers. With its "reverse course" under way in October 1948, SCAP welcomed the return of Yoshida as prime minister; he soon demonstrated remarkable skill in manipulating American officials as he implemented his conservative agenda. But the Japanese people supported Yoshida's shift to the right because it delivered economic recovery. During January 1949 elections gave Yoshida's Liberal Party its first majority in the Diet, with the Democratic Party finishing second. The Japan Socialist Party (JSP) and the Japan Communist Party (JCP) won far fewer seats, reflecting the rising conservative mood among the Japanese people.

Yoshida was enthusiastic in implementing the "reverse course" because it advanced the interests of his allies, the conservative elite, and eliminated chances of a Communist political triumph. He believed, however, that the occupation had to end if Japan was to emerge as a genuine partner of the United States in the Cold War. MacArthur supported this position, although American military leaders feared the impact of losing U.S. military bases in Japan. During 1949 it became clear that the Japanese were beginning to tire of U.S. dictation, as economic recovery began and then accelerated after the outbreak of the Korean War in June 1950. Criticism became more open and vocal not only of unwise occupation policies but of arrogant Americans still enjoying privileges and luxuries in Japan. Thus, part of the "reverse course" became U.S. negotiations with Yoshida's government for a treaty to restore Japan's sovereignty. Ignoring the Soviet Union, which refused to cooperate, the United States and 48 other nations met in September 1951 at the San Francisco Conference to sign the Japanese Peace Treaty. Regaining its independence, Japan renounced all former colonial claims and agreed to pay reparations for its imperialist aggression during the war. But it had to accept dependence as well, signing a security pact with the United States that ensured military protection in return for the use of airbases.

RESTORATION AND RENEWAL

Japan formally regained its sovereignty on April 28, 1952. It could look to the future with optimism because economic recovery was under way and fundamental occupation policies had brought about desirable change. Prime Minister Yoshida took the lead in persuading the Diet promptly to reverse a few U.S. reforms, resulting in the passage of legislation to recentralize the police force, reclaim control over local government, replace elected with appointed school boards, and expand the Ministry of Education's power to standardize instruction. During the Korean War, strong pressure from the United States had caused Yoshida to convince the Diet to authorize the creation of a National Police Reserve to compensate for reduced military protection following wartime redeployment of American troops. In October 1952, this entity became the National Security Force and then in June 1954 the air, land, and sea Self-Defense Forces (SDF). But Yoshida and his conservative allies failed to pass revisions they desired in the constitution aimed at restoring the emperor's status and allowing full remilitarization. Vocal Socialist opposition to these changes, along with warnings that the security treaty with the United States would draw Japan into a new war, elicited considerable popular support.

Economic recovery after 1948 made it difficult for the JCP and the JSP to build significant popular support during the "Yoshida era." Along with revived industrial productivity beginning in coal, chemicals, shipping, and steel, Japan achieved agricultural self-sufficiency during 1950. In 1949, the United States had sent Joseph Dodge as advisor to the government, which implemented his plan of financial retrenchment to end inflation and create economic stability. Playing a major role in reviving the economy was U.S. spending during the occupation, which accelerated with orders for vehicles, supplies, and equipment to meet the needs of waging war in Korea. Overall, U.S. wartime procurement in Japan exceeded $4 billion, including spending on services and recreation. Economic growth was the natural result of the revival of a war-torn economy, at least once American efforts at business decentralization ended. Then Japan just had to reexploit existing favorable conditions that had fueled economic productivity before World War II.

Japan's success in regaining its economic strength would not have been as swift and complete without support from the United States. During 1952 and 1953 American financial assistance amounted to $800 million, holding steady thereafter at roughly $500 million annually until 1957. Just as important, the United States provided military protection, allowing Japan to maintain defense spending at below 1 percent of its gross national product (GNP) for decades, whereas U.S. allies in Europe would spend more than five times that amount. This enabled the Japanese to invest more money in peacetime industries. Admittedly, it served the security interests of the United States in the Cold War to promote Japan's return to economic health, thereby creating a strong diplomatic and economic ally that offered a desirable alternative to communism as a model for economic development in Asia. Japan would experience a brief recession following the end of the Korean War late in July 1953, but by 1954 its per capita production had regained prewar levels.

"Japanese industry," British diplomat and historian Hugh Cortazzi states succinctly, "was rebuilt behind protectionist walls and under government supervision."[1] Japan's economic recovery was complete by 1955, but exports and imports were still below prewar levels. A new export boom began that year, growing in size during the remainder of the decade as Japan systematically restored relations with its prior colonial possessions, especially in Southeast Asia. Once again, close relations with the United States spurred this economic expansion. The United States generously shared technology, giving Japan access to American patents and the latest innovations in equipment. It was less costly to buy licenses in the 1950s than to finance independent research and development. And U.S. occupation reforms in education also facilitated postwar economic growth. Curriculum revision replaced rote memorization and nationalist indoctrination with emphasis on encouraging imaginative and critical thought. Removal of barriers to promotion opened opportunities for advancement for those with intelligence and ability. As a result, Japan had the engineers and scientists needed to exploit access to new technology.

Economic recovery and renewed growth had a major impact on Japanese politics. Despite restoration of Japanese sovereignty, leftist agitation against the United States persisted. Any step to enhance the U.S. military presence in Japan set off angry protests. For example, on May 1, 1952, Socialists and Communists led demonstrations sparking widespread rioting, battles with police, and significant property damage. Although most Japanese were unhappy that Yoshida had approved allowing the United States to maintain its military bases in Japan, fearing the consequences of taking sides in the Cold War, the May Day turmoil fizzled. These acts of violence ran counter to the popular desire for stability after years of deprivation, discrediting the extreme left and causing voters to widen the conservative majority in the Diet in October 1952. But the government's signing of a revised adminstrative agreement in 1954 with the United States and refusal to resume trade with the People's Republic of China (PRC) boosted leftist popularity. Yoshida's arrogant and authoritarian behavior also discredited his leadership, bringing about his forced resignation.

Late in 1954, Hatoyama Ichiro, having recently reentered politics at the end of the U.S. occupation, replaced Yoshida as prime minister. Hayotama worked to reestablish Japan's position in the world community, restoring diplomatic relations with its closest neighbors. Continuing a pattern begun in 1954 with Burma, he reached a reparations settlement with the Philippines in 1956 while paving the way for accords with Indonesia and South

Vietnam later in the decade. In each case, Japan provided industrial goods as partial payment, implementing a so-called seed policy that opened markets for future exports with incentives for growth. Hatoyama adopted a "two China" policy that maintained official recognition of Chiang Kai-shek's government (which had fled to Taiwan after its defeat in the Chinese Civil War in 1949), while cultivating commercial contacts with Beijing. Private Japanese trade associations negotiated four economic deals with the PRC from 1952 to 1958, although only three of these arrangements were thoroughly implemented. During the same years, Japan's economic productivity increased by 7.2 percent annually.

Hatoyama also sought the renewal of ties with the Soviet Union, resulting in normalization of diplomatic relations, as well as a fisheries agreement in 1956. In December 1956, Japan's reward was admission to the United Nations. In 1957, despite continuing friction over disposition of the Kurile Islands, Tokyo and Moscow signed a commercial agreement. Hatoyama also negotiated Japan's participation in the General Agreement on Tariffs and Trade (GATT), obtaining temporary acceptance of protectionist policies on the condition that Tokyo would move promptly toward completely opening its markets to member nations. Meanwhile, in response to the reuniting of the JSP after a brief schism, Hatoyama presided over arguably the most important event in post-occupation Japanese politics—the political merger of the conservatives in 1955 to form the Liberal Democratic Party (LDP), which would hold power until 1993. But his renewed effort to alter the constitution and abolish Article 9 (which barred remilitarization) forced him to resign as prime minister late in 1956. A decade after the war, Yoshida and Hatoyama had restored Japan's economic stability and reintegrated the nation into the world community.

Dependence on the United States remained the most contentious issue in Japanese politics throughout the 1950s, hampering Tokyo's ability to pursue a vigorous strategy of global economic expansion. This became clear after Kishi Nobusuke became prime minister in February 1957. The JSP maintained pressure for a restoration of diplomatic relations with the PRC, arguing that Japan was following orders from the United States. Business and industrial leaders wanted to open the broad and inviting new market in China for an increasingly large amount of manufactured goods that Japan was producing, but they were less vocal in backing political normalization with Beijing. Kishi tried to accommodate the economic interest groups without alienating the United States, negotiating agreements to expand still limited opportunities for travel and trade. He refused to sever important economic and political relations with the Republic of China (ROC) on Taiwan, however, fearing that this would jeopardize relations with the United

States and thereby damage Japanese economic and security interests. Attempting to defuse attacks on the U.S.-Japanese relationship as semi-colonial, Kishi opened negotiations with U.S. legislators in Washington in September 1958 to revise the U.S.-Japan Security Treaty. He wanted changes resulting in a more equitable partnership.

Kishi's handling of the revision of the U.S.-Japan Security Treaty ignited the most serious domestic crisis in the postwar history of Japan. He persuaded Washington to accept a new agreement eliminating the U.S. right to intervene to suppress internal riots or disturbances in Japan. In addition, the agreement provided Japan with a consultative role in the implementation of U.S. policy in Asia, but it also authorized the retention of U.S. military bases in Japan. Protesters, angry over the continued U.S. military presence, staged massive street demonstrations against ratifying the revised treaty. Defying criticism, Kishi's associates forced ratification through a chaotic late-night session of the Diet while opponents were boycotting. Denunciations of the prime minister for undemocratic and illegal behavior were loud and intense. Displeasure with Kishi was widespread, especially after President Dwight D. Eisenhower cancelled a scheduled visit to Japan because domestic unrest had created security concerns. Once Kishi resigned, the turmoil quickly subsided. The treaty revision dispute was a key turning point in postwar Japanese history, as humiliation and paralysis of the government persuaded many that the time had come to focus on the future rather than the past. Leftist agitation against dependence on the United States and rightist pressure to change "MacArthur's Constitution" vanished as major items on the national agenda, clearing a path for Japan's emergence as a global power.

AN ECONOMIC GIANT

During the ten years following 1960, Japan emerged as the third largest industrial nation in the world. Historian Ardath Burks writes that economic "growth was the religion in the decade of the 1960s and conservative politicians the high priests of ritual GNP."[2] After adjustment for inflation, Japan's economy enjoyed an annual growth rate of 9.7 percent from 1960 to 1965 and 13.1 percent for the last five years of the decade. Japan's economic success was astonishing, as its GNP reached $202 billion in 1970 after a fourfold rise in the production of manufactured goods. Its economic output was more than that of the PRC, South Korea, South Vietnam, and India combined. During the 1950s Japan achieved full partnership with the United States and economic dominance in Asia. This set the stage for Tokyo to shift its emphasis, with the benefit of American military protection, toward expanding trade abroad. Its objective was nothing less than the creation of a commercial empire, which it had failed to achieve through military means during the first half of the twentieth century.

Average Japanese citizens deserve most of the credit for transforming what had been a shattered nation in 1945 into a global economic giant by 1970. The postwar rate of savings in Japan was very high, providing a huge pool of capital for investment in economic development. People willingly postponed short-term consumption in favor of promoting recovery, at first placing around 13 percent of their disposable income in postal savings and commercial banks. That figure jumped to 25 percent by 1974, reflecting a tacit national consensus placing a priority on achieving sustained economic growth. Because the government did not tax interest, it was not surprising that savings reached 40 percent of the GNP early in the postwar period. The Industrial Bank of Japan and the Japan Development Bank provided low-interest loans in anticipation of long-term returns rather than short-term dividends. Reversing the pattern in the United States, debt for Japan's companies typically was 80 percent, with the rest being equity. Postwar Japanese also displayed respect for a new group of professional industrial and financial managers. Gaining experience on the job during and after the U.S. occupation, these hardworking, competitive, innovative, and patriotic corporate leaders viewed economic growth as a way to refight and win the war, thereby atoning for defeat in World War II.

A symbiotic relationship between the government and the Keidanren was another important explanation for Japan's fantastic economic growth. Close ties between politicians and corporate leaders derived from money, school, marriage, business, and personal links. Reflecting the extreme elitism of postwar leadership in Japan, graduating from Tokyo University was almost a condition for gaining a top government position. Well into the 1970s the ruling LDP made no decisions without consulting the Keidanren, especially regarding the position of prime minister. It is not surprising that relaxation of laws against industrial and financial consolidation continued after the occupation ended. During the prewar era, four *zaibatsu* controlled nearly one-quarter of all capital in industry and finance. By 1970 eight *keiretsu* maintained the same level of economic dominance. Postwar corporations in Japan were organized around a small number of banks that comprised a financial community, known as *zaikai*, replacing prewar holding companies that U.S. occupation reformers had destroyed. By the early 1960s thirteen city banks controlled 60 percent of assets. Six large marketing companies, or *sogo shosha,* were another key component of these economic combines, controlling over half of all Japan's world trade. The *keiretsu*, historian Gary Allinson explains, built their economic power on "shared identity with a lead bank, common brand names, crossholding of shares, marketing coordination, intergroup sales and purchases, and informal personal relationships."[3]

Government management of economic development was an important factor in Japan's emergence as a global power. SCAP had promoted central planning during the U.S. occupation to accelerate economic recovery. Generous commercial agreements opened U.S. markets, and Washington persuaded its allies to follow suit. Once Japan regained its sovereignty, the Ministry of Finance, the Economic Planning Agency, and most important, the Ministry of International Trade and Industry (MITI) provided central guidance for the economy. Business ventures that the government targeted for development would receive subsidies, low-interest loans, credit allowances, and tax incentives. The Japanese government not only tolerated but encouraged mergers and the creation of cartels to boost competitive advantage in international trade. Careful studies of productivity patterns and world markets guaranteed that those businesses unlikely to prosper received no governmental support and had little chance for survival. Foreign economists identified MITI as the linchpin in a monolithic "Japan, Inc." MITI ensured that favored firms had access to the latest technological innovations on the best terms. Bureaucrats representing the cabinet provided direction to the Diet on imposing tariffs and limiting outside investment to close out foreign competition.

Achieving status as a global economic power would have been impossible had Japan not solved the problem of feeding its swelling postwar population, which grew from 71 million in 1937 to 98 million in 1965. Self-sufficiency in food production came after investment in technology and farm machinery, because Japan had limited arable land and no longer had access to any colonial possessions. Mirroring its approach to promoting industrial productivity, the government provided price supports for rice to increase output. Diversification was encouraged, as farmers began to produce wheat, soybeans, meat, and dairy products. Improved agricultural efficiency not only increased the food supply but also freed labor for work in the industrial sector. Japan benefited from a labor force that historically had been literate, skilled, loyal, and hardworking. Japan's employers developed a unique relationship with employees, providing regular pay raises and generous fringe benefits. Wages jumped by 10 percent annually from 1950 to 1968, whereas the consumer price index rose only 5.7 percent. Paternalism prevailed in Japanese firms. Lifetime employment for skilled workers in the *keiretsu*, where a majority worked, led to intense loyalty among employees that resulted in increased efficiency and productivity. Strikes occurred but were rarely violent and invariably brief.

Japan's sustained growth in the 1950s derived mainly from an expanded consumer market at home. Thereafter, with the fortuitous development of postwar multilateral trade, international commerce became steadily more important as a stimulant for economic growth. Initially Japan exported textiles, half of its prewar total, and inexpensive consumer goods, mainly toys, pottery, and cutlery, for sale in mainstream department stores, especially in the United States. American consumers developed a disdain for inferior products that were "Made in Japan" from cheap materials and with shoddy workmanship. Beginning in the 1960s, however, Japan began to market high-quality goods at modest prices around the world. Indeed, Japan demonstrated a remarkable ability to apply new technology quickly and then make innovative changes to meet consumer demand. Continuing to market textiles, metal products, machinery, and chemicals, the nation also became a leading exporter of cameras, radios, and motorcycles. The value of Japan's exports grew from $820 million in 1950 to $16.7 billion in 1969, producing a trade surplus in that year of $4 billion. By then Japan had started marketing automobiles, televisions, and calculators, as textiles constituted only 14.2 percent of total exports in 1969. By 1970, 30.8 percent of Japan's global trade was with the United States, 25.4 percent with non-Communist Asian nations, 15 percent with Europe, and 5.4 percent with the Soviet Union and the PRC.

Political stability in Japan after 1960 was another vital ingredient in promoting economic development. The LDP established and maintained a close relationship with business and industry. A solid majority of Japanese voters elected LDP candidates to office because government policy under that party's direction was deemed responsible for the nation's expanding prosperity. Ikeda Hayato, who became prime minister in 1960, initiated a pattern of LDP government leadership that identified and maintained as the overriding priority the establishing of Japan's status as a global economic power. A protégé of Yoshida, Ikeda had been minister of finance and then the head of MITI in a career typical of bureaucrats who followed him as prime minister. Conscious of how Kishi's heavy-handed leadership had created disruption at home and embarrassment abroad, Ikeda pursued a "low posture" (tei shisei) in both domestic affairs and foreign policy. Ikeda's Income Doubling Plan marked a watershed in government direction of Japan's postwar economic growth. It reflected an awareness that domestic consumption had not kept pace with the spectacular rise in economic production. The plan called for a dramatic jump in GNP and per capita income over ten years through tax cuts, low interest rates, and government spending. These measures, as well as relaxed regulation, stimulated a vast increase in productivity and full employment.

Luck was another factor explaining Japan's economic growth during the 1960s. Limited hydroelectric power and expensive coal might have caused an energy shortage, dampening industrialization. But Japan benefited along with other developed countries from access to cheap oil, imported in large tankers, from the Mideast. By 1960 oil equaled coal as Japan's main energy source. That year, major strikes in the coal mining industry prompted the government to adopt policies increasing dependence on imported oil, with serious negative consequences in the 1970s. But incredible economic growth distracted Japan's attention from its vulnerabilities. For example, its industrial expansion relied heavily on access not only to oil but to other raw materials, much as prewar Japan had done. The value of imports increased from $974 million in 1950 to $18 billion in 1970, with 75 percent of the total comprised of assorted ores, oil, coking coal, wool, cotton, steel scraps, rubber, lumber, and other raw materials. Japan built its prosperity not only on global trade but on protectionist legislation at home. Signaling the onset of trade friction with the United States, in 1961 American workers refused to use Japanese cloth because of discriminatory trade practices. Resumption of economic ties with Southeast Asia stimulated economic development in underdeveloped nations there, which later became Japan's competitors.

Ikeda was prime minister for four years, a period of domestic stability and international goodwill for Japan that climaxed with the holding of the 1964 Summer Olympic Games in Tokyo. The Japanese displayed a new sense of self-confidence derived from the recognition that Japan was again an important actor in global affairs. Sato Eisaku, who replaced Ikeda in November 1964, served as prime minister for seven years. His long tenure demonstrated the popularity of policies promoting economic growth and prosperity, as Sato built on the successes of his predecessor. Concluding prolonged negotiations, in 1965 he signed a treaty with South Korea that initiated an immense surge in trade with Japan's former colony. Under Sato, Japan shifted its emphasis to exploiting cheap foreign labor, as the government helped trade companies negotiate joint ventures and subsidies for operations in South Korea and Taiwan. In addition, he greatly increased Japanese grants and investments in Southeast Asia after helping create the Asian Development Bank in 1966. Developing nations throughout East Asia sent their young people to Japan for education and technical training. Further elevating its global profile, Japan hosted the World Exposition in Osaka during 1970.

As the decade ended, changes in international affairs were beginning to create pressure on Japan to alter its world role. For example, Sato strongly supported U.S. military intervention in Vietnam, but after 1969 deescalation and gradual withdrawal caused questions to be raised about the American commitment to preserve stability in the region or protect Japan. The PRC's explosion of a nuclear device in 1964, combined with the harsh rhetoric emanating from Beijing during the Cultural Revolution, produced grave security concerns for Japanese government leaders and the public. Critics of the LDP doubted if Japan could advance and protect its international economic and commercial interests while remaining a dependent junior partner of the United States. Sato responded with a more active foreign policy. In 1968 he regained control from the United States over the Bonin Islands, and the next year he secured a pledge from President Richard Nixon for the return in the near future of the island of Okinawa to Japan. While retaining the 1 percent GNP limit on defense spending, Sato enunciated the Three Non-Nuclear Principles, declaring that Japan would not build, keep, or use nuclear weapons. Japan was entering a new, less placid era of independence and assertiveness in world affairs.

STRUGGLING WITH INSTABILITY

Bureaucrats, bankers, and businessmen dominated a postwar Japanese government that was highly centralized and efficient. Until 1972, the LDP provided a reliable vehicle for their exercise of authority while maintaining strict party discipline and delivering on its promise to achieve economic expansion and a better quality of life. Per capita income rose from $284 in 1958 to $8,414 in 1983, but an obsession with development regardless of cost had negative consequences that caused growing public concern during the 1960s. Life in the Tokyo-Osaka industrial corridor typified modern Japan, where, amid traffic jams, noise, and pollution, people commuted for hours to service jobs and then returned to small, crowded, expensive apartments. Reacting to the failure of government to address the deterioration of social services and infrastructure, the Komeito (Clean Government) Party entered politics in 1964, acting as the political arm of the new Soka Gakkai (Value Adding Study Society), a lay group espousing Nichiren Buddhism and stressing exclusiveness, intolerance, and particularism. Rising support for this new party among alienated voters in the cities increased the LDP's dependence not only on corporate political contributions but also on electoral support from farmers to retain political power. Ironically, Japan's emergence as a true global power threatened the LDP's dominance because it seemed to require the abandoning of rice subsidies and protectionist trade policies.

Three developments brought an end to Japan's postwar political and economic stability. *First*, during the summer of 1971 President Nixon implemented dramatic changes in U.S. foreign policy that shocked the Sato government. After providing Tokyo with just a few hours' advance notice, the Nixon administration announced its plan to normalize relations with Beijing. Despite a strong desire to restore ties with the PRC, Tokyo had withheld recognition since its establishment in 1949. The second "Nixon Shock" was the announcement that the United States, responding to declining exports, would allow the dollar's value to float on world currency markets, making U.S. goods more competitive in world trade at the expense of Japan. Sato immediately traveled to the United States for consultations, complaining to Nixon that Japan had not received the treatment a "partner" deserved. The Nixon administration managed to ease tensions somewhat by setting a specific date for U.S. withdrawal from Okinawa as no later than May 1972. Nevertheless, Sato never recovered politically from this loss of face.

Second, an oil crisis began after the Yom Kippur War in Israel during October 1973. The oil-producing states of the Mideast imposed an embargo against those nations supporting Israel. The United States applied pressure on Japan, as well as its West European allies, not to submit to Arab dictates. But Tokyo distanced itself from Israel to facilitate access to oil, providing evidence that Japan was no longer a compliant tool of U.S. foreign policy. But Tokyo's self-serving behavior seemed inconsistent with its claim to status as a global power. Maintaining friendship with the Arab states did not stop Japan's energy costs from skyrocketing, as oil prices increased from $11 per barrel in 1973 to $24 in 1979 and then $35 by the early 1980s. Japan's leaders remained unwilling to take any action that might jeopardize access to oil, refusing, for example, to criticize Iran when Iranian students held 52 Americans hostage after seizing the U.S. Embassy in late 1979. Tokyo's silence won no favors from Iran, as Teheran halted oil exports after Japan objected to price increases early in 1980.

Criticism of the U.S.-Japanese relationship following the Nixon Shocks already had forced Sato to resign in July 1972 before the energy crisis began. This led to the *third* development shattering Japan's postwar stability when Tanaka Kakuei was elected prime minister. Tanaka, unlike his predecessors, had no university education and was not a former bureaucrat. A brash, self-made businessman who became wealthy in the construction industry, he built political power on his ability to deliver public works projects to his district and those of his adherents. But his triumph as president of the LDP caused factional feuds within the party to intensify. Worse, his habit of raising campaign contributions by promising political favors introduced the "black mist" of corruption as the most divisive issue in postwar Japanese politics. Tanaka, facing charges of corruption, resigned in November 1974 and was later convicted in the Lockheed Scandal for taking bribes while prime minister to approve an airplane procurement deal with that U.S. company. Thereafter public policy drifted, as a series of prime ministers struggled against factional opposition while searching for ways to resume economic growth. Corruption and economic stagnation brought a decline in the LDP's popularity. Only the sudden death of Prime Minister Ohira Masayoshi saved the party from devastating losses in lower house elections several years later in June 1980.

The Arab oil embargo had a dual impact on the Japanese economy. First, the government devised methods to increase energy conservation. Better technology led to lowered energy use (by 25 percent) in the production of cars, steel, and chemicals. Along with other measures, Japan reduced its dependence on oil from 80 percent to 61 percent. Publicity campaigns suggested to the public that the era of unlimited prosperity was over, requiring sacrifices to increase savings and reduce consumption. These government efforts contributed to the lowering of inflation while the annual rate of savings remained high at 15 percent of per capita income. Capital for investment therefore increased after 1974, but fears of overproduction translated into declining investment rates for the next fifteen years. During 1975, modest prosperity gradually resumed after two years of recession and trade deficits. Workers soon demanded and received pay raises, setting off the start of a long and serious depression during 1978 and 1979. It was clear that conservation alone would not restore Japan's economic health.

Second, Japanese leaders adopted a new industrial strategy that shifted emphasis from smokestack to high technology industries. By 1974 special government incentives went to advances in the production of electronics and construction equipment at the expense of plastics and synthetics. Joining textiles and coal, soaring energy costs caused shipping, chemical fertilizers, steel, aluminum, paper, and petrochemicals to be added to the list of failed industries. Given the emphasis on reduced domestic consumption, pressure to expand overseas trade accelerated. During the 1970s Japan exported many electronic devices, such as videocassette recorders, video cameras, and fax machines. But automobile production remained central to Japan's economic health, as the number of cars produced increased annually from 4.5 million in 1975 to 28.5 million in 1980, resulting in Japan ranking first in the world. The volume of exports of automobiles jumped from 117,809 in 1965 to 6.11 million in 1980. And to escape tariff barriers, car makers constructed plants in target countries, especially the United States. By the late 1980s, 14 of Japan's 25 biggest corporations still were producers of automobiles and electronics.

By 1980 Japan had restored its economic stability. Expanding industrial productivity brought annual increases in the GNP from 1975 to 1983. This combined with nearly full employment to boost the standard of living, as per capita income increased to $8,414 in 1983, compared with $12,485 in the United States. Several factors explain Japan's economic recovery after the energy crisis. Government direction of industrial development continued as in the past, resulting in the planned collapse of uncompetitive ventures. In 1981 there were 17,600 bankruptcies. This forced retrenchment allowed surviving *keiretsu* to become stronger through assimilation and adjustment to shifting market conditions. Large corporations changed policies, such as subcontracting to countless smaller firms that in slow economic times faced a precarious survival. By the early 1980s, 70 percent of Japanese companies were smaller firms that had 100 or fewer workers, constituting 60 percent of the labor force. Only 13 percent of workers were in companies of 1,000 employees or more. And *keiretsu* diversified, as Mitsui and Mitsubishi began building hydroelectric plants, chemical factories, and harbors worldwide.

Japan's managerial class still was more efficient in adapting and applying technology. But a major difference was a significant increase of investments in research and development, which rose during the 1970s to 6 percent of sales. Also, there was a new emphasis on improving quality, reflected in the intense competition to win the Deming Prize (named after a U.S. efficiency expert who had been an advisor during the U.S. occupation). Japan's companies focused on keeping production costs low, resulting in corporate executives, for example, taking lower salaries and not issuing large stock dividends. In 1982 Toyota's chief executive officer (CEO) earned $1.3 million, whereas his U.S. counterpart at Ford earned $7.3 million. Many bureaucrats and government leaders retired to top posts in business, industry, and finance, in part explaining a stronger sense of public duty. There was a tremendous increase in Japanese international investment as well, beginning early in the 1980s. The total rose from $7 billion in 1980 to $74 billion in 1984, as Japan passed the United States as the leading investor in the world.

An undervalued yen made prices lower for Japanese goods, enabling Tokyo to use a vast expansion of exports as a means to end the recessions of the 1970s. The value of Japanese imports declined from $141.6 to $130.6 billion from 1980 to 1985, whereas exports rose from $130 to $176 billion. Of course, the United States remained Japan's biggest market, consuming fully 35.3 percent of total exports. Inflation in the United States contributed to Japan's trade surplus, which exploded from $7 billion in 1980 to $39.5 billion in 1985. Washington protested that even though it allowed a flood of cars, steel, and electronic equipment to enter its market from Japan, tariffs and red tape kept Japan's doors shut to U.S. exports. In response, Japan accepted voluntary quotas on the export of cars, as it had earlier with textiles.

As it penetrated new markets in areas such as Latin America, Japan also built a trade surplus with the European Economic Community—to $9.3 billion in 1984. Despite a boom in Japanese tourism, some European nations, with complaints paralleling those of the United States, retaliated against Japan with trade restrictions.

Another tactic Japan used to attain economic recovery was an intensified penetration of Southeast Asia. When Tanaka visited Thailand and Indonesia in 1974, he received an angry greeting, reflecting dissatisfaction with Japan's failure to promote regional development. Tokyo responded with a vigorous policy to improve relations with its neighbors in Asia, especially the members of the Association of Southeast Asian Nations (ASEAN), which had been created in 1967. Pressure for more credit and economic aid caused the government to press Japanese companies to expand investment in Southeast Asia to improve communication and infrastructure. By 1980 more than half of all Japanese foreign investment went to the Philippines, Thailand, and Malaysia. Southeast Asia received 60 percent of all Japanese economic aid. In 1977 Prime Minister Fukuda Takeo pledged $1 billion to finance five projects in ASEAN nations. ASEAN members also received from Japan advice and assistance on how to market their manufactured goods in the United States. By 1981 the volume of Japan's trade with Southeast Asia reached $15.2 billion in exports and $21 billion in imports. An added bonus was trade with Indonesia that filled 63 percent of its oil needs.

U.S. détente with Moscow and Beijing under President Nixon provided one more opportunity for Japan to rebound from the adverse impact of the oil crisis. Tanaka visited the PRC in 1972, developing with the Chinese a formula to complete the normalization of relations and creating a framework for an increase in trade. In 1978 the signing of the Japan-PRC Treaty of Peace and Friendship helped promote travel and cultural exchanges between the two countries. Relations with the ROC became strained, but Japan maintained contacts and economic ties with Taiwan. Prime Minister Ohira Masayoshi's 1980 Comprehensive National Security Strategy signaled the abandonment of Ikeda's "low posture" in world affairs, envisioning Japan's emergence as an economic engine for development in Asia. Newly elected prime minister Nakasone Yasuhiro spoke of restoring relations with North Korea but visited South Korea in 1983 instead, arranging a $4 billion aid package. Japan also moved toward finalizing an agreement with Moscow to exploit resources in Siberia, especially oil, despite a continuing dispute regarding the Soviet Union's refusal to comply with Japan's demand for the return of islands in the Kuriles that the Soviets had occupied at the end of World War II.

Nakasone's election as prime minister in 1982 marked the completion of Japan's recovery from the shocks of the 1970s as well as a revival of unity within the LDP. His reliance on Tanaka to secure election prompted snide references to him as "Tanakasone," but he soon displayed his independence in energetically pursuing an expanded international role for Japan. For years Nakasone had been an advocate of reducing Japan's dependence on the United States through changing the constitution to permit remilitarization. Moderating his militant nationalism, he worked to strengthen relations with the United States, developing close ties with President Ronald Reagan through a series of personal meetings. Annual economic growth stabilized at about 4 percent under Nakasone, contributing to a revival of the LDP's popularity, as in 1986 the party gained an increased portion of votes (to nearly 50 percent) in lower house elections. But the government confronted the challenges of rising costs for anti-pollution and extensive welfare measures, as well as an aging population. During his term as prime minister, Nakasone presided over a new debate about Japan's future world role, making ill-defined references to the need for "internationalization." Despite this talk, as historian Michael Barnhart noted a decade later, "there has been little change in the fundamental order with Japan or the basics of Japan's foreign relations."[4]

ADRIFT IN A NEW WORLD ORDER

Japan's postwar emergence as a world power brought rising international scrutiny. Other industrialized nations became increasingly critical of Japan, as they had less success in restoring economic strength following the Arab oil embargo. In particular, Washington charged that Japan was the recipient of a "free ride" because American military protection was saving it from spending on defense. To placate the Americans, Japan agreed to underwrite $3 billion in annual defense expenditures totaling $7 billion. More contentious was trade friction, as the United States criticized Japan for dumping cheap goods on the American market while not providing access for foreign commodities to Japan. Japanese prime ministers made promises to end protectionism and cut exports, but nothing changed, prompting the Reagan administration to impose tariff restrictions on Japanese electronics in 1987. Reflecting the rising level of acrimony in Europe, one British observer referred to Japanese workers as "workaholics living in rabbit hutches."[5] Other critics ridiculed "education mamas" in Japan who devoted their lives to preparing their sons to pass a seemingly endless series of examinations that stressed rote memorization and recitation to gain entrance to top universities. In particular, outsiders faulted Japan for having a narrow outlook and an inward focus precluding change.

Escalating foreign criticism after 1980 brought a defiant response from the Japanese, who had developed pride in the success of their drive to be the top economic power in a hierarchical world order. Responding in kind to American "Japan bashing," the Japanese began a vigorous "America bashing." Sony president Morita Akio was arrogant and condescending in assessing the reasons for U.S. economic woes, attributing U.S. problems to corporate incompetence, lazy workers, and social decay. A growing sense of smugness surrounded this anti-Americanism. There also emerged a revival of militant nationalism. During 1982 a hit movie portrayed Japan as the victim, not the attacker, at Pearl Harbor. The minister of education infuriated Chinese, Koreans, and Southeast Asians when he authorized textbook revisions that stressed the benefits of prewar Japanese colonialism, referred to Japanese aggression during World War II as "advances," and ignored Japan's wartime atrocities. Despite his resignation and a public apology from Prime Minister Nakasone, few of Japan's imperialist victims accepted these acts as sincere. Japan generated further resentment when it campaigned for a permanent seat on the United Nations Security Council despite making no military contribution to the preservation of world stability.

Fueling Japanese confidence and optimism in the 1980s was an economy that was still prosperous and productive. An economic boom had started in late 1986 in response to low interest rates. Companies expanded operations to produce a flood of automobiles and electronic devices for export. Japan's trade surpluses grew, and the GNP jumped by 6 percent. Because population growth stabilized at 122 million late in the decade, most Japanese enjoyed the benefits of this economic expansion. Consumption was conspicuous, as more people than ever could afford to drive expensive cars, travel, and wear fancy clothes. A younger generation had no memory of postwar poverty and hardship. By the late 1980s Japanese youths watched American shows on television, ate at McDonald's, and listened to the music of Michael Jackson and Madonna. Even as American culture intruded into Japanese life, upbeat discussion of national character sparked a revival of admiration for Japanese tradition. When a pollster asked people in 1983 if they thought Japan was superior to nations in the West, 53 percent said yes as compared to only 20 percent in 1953.

Japan's economy still ranked third in the world in 1985, with its GNP reaching $1,329 billion (behind the United States at $3,987 billion and the Soviet Union at $2,064 billion). But the U.S. trade deficit had jumped from $300 million in 1975 to $40 billion by 1985, whereas its budget deficits rose steadily to well over $200 billion annually. Japan bought a majority of U.S.

government bonds, financing a mounting share of American indebtedness—in some years by as much as 40 percent. By 1988 Japan was the world's largest creditor nation. That year, on the list of the world's largest banks the Dai Ichi Kangyo Bank ranked seventh and the next nine all were Japanese. Japan's corporations bought electric companies, office buildings, and land throughout the world, with purchases in the United States stretching from Rockefeller Center in New York City to Pebble Beach Golf Course in California. Sony, following the lead of Matsushita, bought Columbia Pictures to control the software for music and films that hardware made in Japan conveyed in videocassette recorders and compact disk players. These acquisitions were symbols of Japan's new corporate wealth and power.

Rising world resentment of Japan translated into pressure on Tokyo to alter its world role, especially after 1989 with the end of the Cold War and then the fall of the Soviet Union two years later. Japan had moved in the direction of a more active world role after the oil crisis. For example, in 1975 it joined the Group of Seven (G-7) industrialized nations whose representatives met regularly to discuss global economic issues. In 1979 Japan condemned the Soviet invasion of Afghanistan and offered economic assistance to Pakistan and Turkey. Prime Minister Ohira's 1980 Comprehensive Security Strategy established as an objective the implementing of positive policy initiatives to build international stability and peace. Nakasone was outspoken in supporting the U.S. military buildup against the Soviet Union, announcing that Japan would defend sea lanes around the home islands. Under his leadership, Japan's total defense spending rose to rank third in the world at $45 billion annually, compared with $289 billion in the United States and $119 billion in the Soviet Union. But Iraq's invasion of Kuwait in August 1990 was a global public relations disaster for Japan. While condemning the Iraqi leader Saddam Hussein, the Japanese government was slow to provide either financial or material help in waging the Gulf War. In response to world criticism, Japan ultimately sent a medical staff and contributed $4 billion, later adding $9 billion more and deploying five minesweepers.

A rapid succession of prime ministers after Nakasone stepped down as prime minister late in 1987 prevented Japan from directly confronting and resolving these new international challenges. LDP factional infighting was the formula for government paralysis. Kaifu Toshiki, who had replaced Takeshita Noboru as prime minister in 1989, was incapable of acting quickly and decisively. He resigned in 1991 in the aftermath of brutal international criticism of Japan for its "checkbook diplomacy" during the Gulf War. Already, people were unhappy with Kaifu's signing in 1990 of the Structural Impediments Initiative, submitting to U.S. pressure to open Ja-

Japan makes its contribution to the Gulf War, telling Uncle Sam "Please, accept this." *Far Eastern Economic Review*, August 30, 1990.

pan's markets gradually to foreign imports. Particularly embarrassing was his inability to gain passage of the United Nations Peacekeeping Cooperation Law, allowing for deployment of troops abroad to deter war. Kaifu withdrew the measure in response to widespread fears that expanding the prime minister's power over use of the SDF would draw Japan into a foreign war. During 1992 the Diet passed the UN Peacekeeping Operations bill, making it possible to deploy SDF troops for peacekeeping duty in Cambodia later that year.

But the economy went into recession in 1991, halting growth in 1992 and registering only small increases over the next three years. This, combined with political turmoil, produced a mood of profound pessimism in Japan. Unwise investments at home in real estate and land plus plummeting stock market prices meant that borrowers could not repay huge bank loans. The government then raised interest rates and reduced spending, which made recovery more difficult. There were several reasons for Japan's downward economic slide. First, U.S. banks reduced investment and the Gulf War damaged consumer confidence in the United States, slowing the sale of Japan's exports. A recession in Europe after German reunification caused demand for Japanese goods there to vanish as well. Second, protectionism revived worldwide, resulting in voluntary and legal restraints on Japanese access to markets. Third, the yen's value rose from 139 to the dollar in 1989 to 79 briefly in 1995, making Japanese products more costly. Finally, Japan's increased output faced stiff competition from cheaper, high quality exports from Latin America, Southeast Asia, and Eastern Europe. Falling sales affected all industries and investment plummeted, forcing the sale of the prized Rockefeller Plaza and other prestigious properties.

A rising sense of isolation, vulnerability, and uncertainty returned to Japan during the late 1980s, after Nakasone had halted temporarily this pessimistic trend earlier in the decade. Plans were developed but never fully implemented to reduce the size of the bureaucracy, to make Japan's government smaller and more effective. Nor did the Diet revise the tax code, although it did privatize the government-operated Nippon Telephone and Telegraph and Japan National Railways. Government retrenchment reoriented reduced investment toward making Japan the leader in a new information society wherein advanced electronics and communication would make control databases accessible from computers in all homes. Japan's restructuring, or *kisei kanwa*, extended to business and industry, with an overriding objective to drive down costs and prices. Lowering labor costs and raising efficiency in production at home were key parts of the strategy, as well as exploiting cheap foreign labor, either through buying components or building plants abroad. But this led to reductions in domestic per capita income and a falling standard of living. During 1993, major companies fired workers in forced labor reductions. As family income declined, so did sales and savings. As the jobless rate passed an unprecedented 3 percent, Japan was experiencing the same anxieties as other industrialized nations.

By 1993 there were profound doubts in Japan about whether the nation had the ability to advance and protect its economic and security interests in a hostile and highly competitive world. Most people wanted to maintain a minimalist defense and passive foreign policy, but this no longer appeared possible. One positive sign was a continued expansion of trade in Southeast Asia, where total value reached $140 billion, almost equaling that of the United States. Japan also was providing larger amounts in assistance and investment for regional development. Nevertheless, uncertainties about the future in combination with a new bribery scandal prompted voters in 1993 to end the LDP's control of the government after factions broke away from the party. Only more instability followed, as Hosakawa Morihiro's resignation led to brief tenures for his successors as prime minister. For Japan's young voters, few of whom formed party ties, image was the prime concern. In 1995 a comedian in Tokyo and an entertainer in Osaka won races for governor, as voter turnout was the lowest in Japan's history for lower house races. Trade friction also continued with the United States, as the Clinton administration complained that of the 45 major trade agreements the two nations signed between 1980 and 1996, only 13 were producing the intended results.

Uncertainty, insecurity, and inequality had become the realities of life for Japan in the interdependent post–Cold War world of the 1990s. Discomfort about the future for many Japanese was greater than it had been during the 1930s when the nation was in the grip of militarism and authoritarianism. Despite an unprecedented postwar economic record of the GNP doubling every seven years, most observers thought the nation's future economic growth required expanding the domestic market to create an "economy of scale." Complicating Japan's challenge on the eve of the new century was the East Asia financial crisis that began in 1997. Asian nations over the prior decade borrowed large amounts of capital at low interest rates to finance extensive projects of an often dubious nature. But a strengthening U.S. economy subsequently boosted the value of the dollar, reducing Asian exports and profits and making repayment of debt increasingly difficult. In Japan, major financial institutions, notably Yamaichi Securities, collapsed under the weight of the $600 billion debt. In August 1998, failure to reverse the pattern of economic decline brought about the resignation of Prime Minister Hashimoto Ryutaro, who had revived and rejuvenated the LDP after 1995. His replacement, Obuchi Keizo, whose personality one observer likened to cold pizza, briefly found ways to reverse a pattern of economic decline and define a more active world role. But by late 1999 economic recession and domestic political discord had returned. In April 2000, Obuchi suffered an incapacitating stroke, leaving Japan adrift under a new prime minister again facing an uncertain future.

NOTES

1. Hugh Cortazzi, *The Japanese Achievement* (New York: St. Martin's Press, 1990), 250.

2. Ardath Burks, *Japan: Profile of a Post Industrial Power* (Boulder, CO: Westview Press, 1981), 143.

3. Gary D. Allinson, *Japan's Postwar History* (Ithaca, NY: Cornell University Press, 1997), 103.

4. Michael Barnhart, *Japan and the World since 1868* (New York: St. Martin's Press, 1995), 141.

5. Cortazzi, *The Japanese Achievement*, 279; Burks, *Japan*, 178.

however, was economic policy during the U.S. occupation. At first, SCAP attempted to impose a competitive free enterprise system, replacing Japanese historic traditions of government control, regulation, guidance, and intervention in the private economic sector. Starting in 1947, SCAP, acting to combat the perceived threat of Soviet political penetration through the Communist and Socialist parties, modified or "reversed" earlier reforms with enthusiastic support from Japanese conservatives who were fearful not only of popular democracy but also of unrestrained and unregulated economic competition. Firm actions limited labor militancy, ended the deconcentration of economic power, and removed leftist politicians from public office at all levels. Critics charged that this "reverse course" revived aspects of Japanese authoritarianism to serve Cold War aims. But it also had a positive impact on Japan's economic future, prompting the nation's leaders to embrace multilateralism, or participation by more than two states or parties, in financial and commercial matters to regain a place of prominence in world affairs.

Nor were U.S. motives in implementing the "reverse course" malevolent. Leaders in Washington sought to achieve Japan's economic recovery to end the growing cost of the U.S. occupation. More important, Communist military successes in the Chinese Civil War, climaxing in the creation of the People's Republic of China (PRC) in October 1949, transformed Japan into the linchpin of an American economic strategy to combat Communist expansion in Asia. Japan would be the center of a "Great Crescent" in the Pacific, joining together the nations of East Asia in a capitalist partnership fostering regional peace and prosperity. Washington's first step toward achieving this goal was to send to Japan Detroit banker Joseph M. Dodge with a comprehensive stabilization program, soon known as the Dodge Plan. Its aim was to promote financial discipline by imposing wage and price controls, balancing the budget, preventing inflationary loans, restraining government intervention in the private sector with subsidies, and ensuring allocation of raw materials for export production, all of which would result in the curbing of inflation, the expanding of domestic consumption, and the restoring of private control over foreign trade. U.S. advisors also provided training in management skills and quality control, and Japanese students attended business schools in the United States.

SCAP established the pattern of government bureaucrats formulating laws for the Diet's approval, causing one writer to deride the Japanese legislature as "the love child (ai-no-ko) of racially mixed parentage."[2] The Diet enacted legislation providing a brief set of guidelines for public policies but leaving to ministry bureaucrats the broad powers of interpretation and implementation. The same bureaucrats generally entered politics after rising through a government ministry, gaining election to about half the seats in the Diet. Another 25 percent were party politicians who served regional interests, with businessmen holding slightly fewer seats. Finally, the remaining legislators were assorted academics, media members, doctors, and lawyers. The majority, under the LDP's control until 1993, elected a prime minister, who then named party factional leaders—usually bureaucrats and technocrats—to serve in the cabinet. The Ministry of Finance, the Economic Planning Agency, and the Ministry of International Trade and Industry (MITI) dictated economic policy. Continuing the practice of the Economic Stabilization Board (ESB), which SCAP formed in August 1946, the government held consultations with management representatives. It eventually set up committees, or *shingikai*, with representatives from major interest groups to advise ministers, resolve differences, and build consensus for reports that often provided the basis for legislation approved in the Diet; the committees also acted thereafter to ensure compliance.

Japan's rise as a global economic power thus had roots in the practices and policies of the U.S. occupation. Having lost its vast empire, Japan had to focus inward, but militarism no longer drained its resources. Economic bureaucrats, having escaped competition for power from the military and the *genro* ("elder statesmen" who had restored the Meiji emperor in 1868 and unofficially dominated Japan's government until World War I), gained control over a planned industrial policy and exploited their education, ability, ambition, and determination to achieve economic growth. At MITI, they applied power directly to streamline industries and promote economic independence. Under the Foreign Exchange and Trade Control Law of 1949, MITI had authority over foreign exchange, export, and import licensing. In 1950 a very restrictive Foreign Investment Law coincided with MITI's fears of big companies in the West exploiting Japan. MITI absorbed the ESB, supervising technology imports and joint ventures. By 1963 it had negotiated over 2,500 contracts to acquire patents and technical aid, mostly in the United States. MITI also maintained rigid controls over food and fuel, and its power to grant import licenses enabled it to channel raw materials and machinery to the most promising industries. MITI made its first major adjustment in March 1952 when, in response to declining U.S. spending for the Korean War, it curtailed spinning production in the textile industry. In that year it also advised the largest companies in rubber and steel to lower production, and it even assigned quotas to each firm. MITI used its authority repeatedly thereafter to transform Japan into a global economic power.

ECONOMIC APPRENTICE

Implementation of the Dodge Plan brought economic stability in 1949, but Japan made limited progress toward full recovery until the Korean War began in June 1950. After the Truman administration halted Japanese reparations payments in May 1948, Congress for the first time approved $180 million specifically to revive Japan's economy. Direct U.S. aid reached a total of $1.8 billion in 1952. To further spur recovery, the United States set the exchange rate to Japan's advantage at 360 yen to the dollar, thereby expanding U.S. purchases of Japanese goods and creating a trade imbalance. But war in Korea provided the spark that ignited Japan's postwar economic boom, as the United States spent $4 billion in special procurements over three years on supplies, equipment, services, and recreation. During 1952, U.S. government purchases in Japan reached $800 million, constituting 38 percent of Japan's total foreign earnings. Following the end of the Korean War in July 1953, U.S. military spending continued to pump money into the Japanese economy. From 1951 to 1956, military purchases in Japan paid for over one-quarter of Japanese imports. U.S. spending in Japan totaled $5.5 billion from 1951 to 1960, but a chronic trade deficit persisted.

Japan suffered a brief recession after Korea in 1953 and 1954, but then experienced the "Jimmu boom"—named after the founder of Japan because it was the first post-occupation economic surge—until late 1957, resulting in the GNP rising from $15.3 billion in 1952 to ultimately $51.9 billion in 1962. In 1960, international economists began to refer to Japan as an economic "miracle" that had high productivity, harmonious labor relations, and a high rate of savings. During the prior decade, its GNP growth averaged about 12 percent annually, with domestic consumption absorbing 90 percent of this productivity. Industries that registered the greatest growth were textiles, steel, chemicals, vehicles, and coal mining, generating large profits that owners reinvested to expand facilities. More jobs boosted consumption and savings, providing incentive and capital for investment. Japan, however, remained dependent not only on imported iron ore but on oil as the nation shifted away from coal and hydroelectric power for energy. Private enterprise also played an indispensable role in Japan's emergence as an economic superpower, depending for long-term financing primarily on six large banks: Mitsui, Mitsubishi, Sumitomo, Fuji, Daiichi, and Sanwa. But by the 1960s thirteen city banks, controlling 60 percent of Japanese assets, were funding business and industrial growth. However, MITI remained the hub of decision making.

Stable political leadership was a crucial ingredient in Japan's formula for economic growth. Prime Minister Yoshida stocked the government with loyal bureaucrats, creating a "Yoshida School" of proponents of economic development. After its creation in 1955 the LDP advocated business interests, although it relied for its political power just as much on farmers, small businesses, and the financing of regional projects. The LDP majority in the Diet provided MITI with indirect means to boost economic growth, allowing it to grant generous depreciation allowances, approve tax write-offs for the costs of opening foreign branches, and maintain contingency funds to pay for bad debt contracts. It also organized "cooperative behavior" within designated "depressed industries" to regulate production and sales and lower costs while promoting exports in promising industries. MITI bureaucrats also took advantage of personal contacts dating from university days or earlier to enact industrial policy. More than in other ministries, they also engaged in the practice known as *amakudari* ("descent from heaven"), or retiring from government to a top job in private business whereby the bureaucrats, usually in their fifties, formed a partnership with those left behind for informal policy coordination and cooperation.

Hatoyama Ichiro, after replacing Yoshida as prime minister late in 1954, adopted a plan to achieve full employment and economic self-sufficiency that called for modernizing industrial plants, raising exports to balance imports, and suppressing consumption to spur savings. Several years later, during the prime ministership of Kishi Nobusuke, a strike at Mitsui's Miike Coal Mine in Kyushu over layoffs and technological changes had a decisive impact on the future of Japanese economic development. In August 1959, the coal miners union accepted Mitsui's plan to encourage the voluntary retirement of 5,000 employees with severance allowances. The Miike local fiercely opposed the plan, and a strike began in November when Mitsui arbitrarily fired 1,200 Miike workers, including 300 union activists. The striking workers sought arbitration through the Central Labor Relations Commission, which upheld the company's position. Strikers refused to return to work until the new administration, under Ikeda Hayato, devised a revised mediation plan in August 1960. Those workers who had been discharged would receive a bonus and retraining if they resigned voluntarily. Resolution of the strike removed the last barrier to Japan's emergence as an economic superpower because it signaled a national decision to place a priority on the growth of export industries that implied an increasing reliance on oil and coal imports, rather than national resource development.

AN ECONOMIC OFFENSIVE

Japan's leaders acted to exploit growing consumer power in the 1950s. In 1956 MITI announced the inauguration of the "citizen's car project" to replace the prevailing pattern in the vehicle industry of building trucks and buses. In 1959 the appearance of the Datsun Bluebird marked the opening of a new era of commercialized mass culture in Japan, as well as production of autos for export (especially to the United States). Among Japan's leading carmakers was Honda Soichiro, who in 1950 was producing motorcycles. His company's output increased from 300 units per month in that year to 18,000 units in 1958. In 1954 Honda had traveled to Germany, England, and Italy, studying motorcycle manufacturing methods and buying parts. In 1960 he built the world's largest motorcycle plant and began making new models with a more powerful design. Honda already had shifted his focus to exports, laying the groundwork for his company to be the world's largest motorcycle producer. Millions of people in the Third World were eager to purchase an inexpensive and efficient form of transportation. His marketing also focused on selling motorcycles to middle-class foreigners as a leisure activity, using the slogan "You meet the nicest people on a Honda." Overcoming initial government opposition, by the mid-1960s Honda had captured half the U.S. market in motorcycles, selling 300,000 units to Americans in 1966 alone.

In 1963 Honda Motors entered the automobile market, selling at first a few small, sleek, two-seat sports cars in Japan. This occurred after Honda infuriated powerful bureaucrats when he rejected orders to keep making motorcycles in compliance with government plans for Japan to have only a handful of automakers. Nor would he merge his operation with other auto companies. A series of innovative designs—especially the low-pollution and highly efficient four-cylinder engine whose exhaust gases did not require a catalytic converter for cleaning—helped Honda become a major car producer. Newer plants and harmonious labor relations were other factors explaining Honda's succcess. Honda workers received an array of benefits including insurance, free use of a company gymnasium and family swimming pool, half-price lunches, paid commuting costs, dormitory rooms, low-interest housing loans, and interest-free installment plans to buy Honda products. Cash awards and travel incentives encouraged suggestions for improvements. Honda also created a separate company research arm, convinced that engineers would be more innovative if unfettered by administrative procedures. Junior engineers worked on special teams without interruption on high-priority development projects. One of these teams created the City Car, or Civic, a small model with a boxy design that became popular in Japan and later in the United States.

Another pillar at the foundation of Japan's economic development was electronics. Morita Akio, co-founder of Sony Corporation, purchased transistor technology in the United States in 1955 that led to the marketing of the first pocket-sized transistor radios. Sony then made an all-transistor television set in 1959 and a transistorized video tape recorder in 1960. Meanwhile, Morita had been studying consumer markets and marketing techniques in North America and Europe. He lived in New York City for fifteen months, traveling around the United States to meet with department store executives and designers. Morita hired a U.S. advertising agency that initiated a publicity campaign featuring low-key ads that never hinted at the company's foreign base. Under his direction, from 1965 to 1968 Sony marketed the first affordable video tape recorder; a color video tape recorder; the first integrated circuit radio; a portable, battery-operated video recorder and camera; an integrated circuit television with a 1-inch screen; and the first 17-inch color television set. In 1969 Sony introduced its home color video tape player, marketing an adapter to record television programs off the air. From this technology came Betamax, a videocassette the size of a paperback book.

Sony's research and development in the 1960s perfected the Chromatron color television tube after buying the rights to the process from Paramount Pictures. It introduced the Chromatron tube in its Trinitron television set in 1969. By then Japanese sales in the United States had leveled at a total exceeding $1 billion, with Sony's annual portion at $300 million. Sony was Japan's first company to sell stock in the United States and the first to be listed on the New York Stock Exchange. With a net income in 1970 of $23 million, its common stocks were worth more than $13,000 per share as compared to 15 cents when the company started. In contrast to the typical Japanese company that depended on loans for 80 percent of its capital, Sony relied more on stock, with over 40 percent of sales to overseas investors in 1973. Morita set aside 5 percent of profits for research and development but ensured the commitment of generous funds to marketing as well. Targeting products for specific markets was one of his special talents. For example, in 1971 Sony began marketing in Britain a 13-inch Trinitron television set for $480, as compared to a 19-inch British model that sold for $600. By 1970 Sony's sales had reached $414 million, half from exports.

Government policy encouraged the private entrepreneurship that helped achieve Japan's tremendous economic growth after 1960. Prime Minister Ikeda's Income Doubling Plan set as its goal raising the domestic standard of living that had not matched economic expansion to increase consumption. The plan also sought to phase out old industries while fostering those that were competitive in world trade, particularly steel, chemicals, shipbuilding, oil refining, and petrochemicals. Another objective stressed the production of cost-effective and technology-intensive durable goods, notably cars, plastics, electrical goods, and synthetic fibers. Ikeda's government also encouraged the expansion of small producers, further stimulating economic growth. Economic gains in the 1960s exceeded expectations, as Japan rose from fifth in total GNP to third (behind the United States and the Soviet Union), with its annual growth rate exceeding 10 percent. Only a few Japanese could aspire to white-collar salaried jobs during the 1950s, but by 1970 employment as a *saririman* was no longer the exception but the rule. By 1965 Japan had an export surplus, and its share of world export trade rose from just 2 percent in 1955 to more than 7 percent early in the 1970s. In 1964 the Summer Olympic Games in Tokyo showcased the arrival of Japan as an economic power, with visitors marveling at its subways, monorails, elevated highways, and bullet train. That same year, the International Monetary Fund (IMF) and the World Bank held meetings in Tokyo, also spotlighting Japan's prominent international status.

SUPERPOWER UNDER ASSAULT

Japan's remarkable postwar economic growth was in part the result of the government's decision to finance development rather than social welfare programs, although Prime Minister Kishi secured the passage of a National Pension Law and Prime Minister Ikeda a universal health care bill. Ironically, a productive economy gradually eroded traditional values of sacrifice and self-denial, causing many Japanese to demand a quality of life like that of a genuine economic superpower. A government report in 1965 determined that Japanese educational, cultural, and public health facilities were equal to those in Western Europe but that housing, food, and sewage services were inferior. Car accidents were more numerous in Japan than in all of Western Europe. Housing prices rose in 1965 by 17.9 percent, and prices for rice grew at roughly the same rate, keeping pace with wage increases. That year, Prime Minister Sato Eisaku's measures to halt inflation caused a recession, resulting in a wave of bankruptcies as banks refused to renew loans. But the United States once again helped Japan recover from its economic troubles as a result of its intervention in Vietnam. By 1970 U.S. spending in Japan exceeded $450 million. The Vietnam War had a negative indirect impact on Japan's ability to sustain economic growth, however, because it destabilized the U.S. economy, contributing to the widening trade deficit with Japan that led to intense bilateral friction for at least the next two decades.

The war in Vietnam created major indirect economic benefits for Japan, which increased its exports of materials and components to South Korea, Taiwan, and various Southeast Asian nations, each having their own U.S. procurement contracts to fulfill. This period also witnessed a marked rise in

Japanese exports of televisions, auto parts, chemicals, and machinery to the United States to satisfy a consumer demand that U.S. firms could not, partly because of conversion to war-related production. Among the signs of Japan's prosperity in 1970 were 64 million visitors to the World Exposition in Osaka and the launching of the first Japanese satellite. That year, 90 percent of Japanese saw themselves as members of the middle class or better, and just 7 percent lived below the poverty level. By July 1971, Japan's foreign exchange reserve had risen from $2 billion in 1968 to $7 billion. But then came the Nixon Shocks. A month after announcing his impending visit to China, President Richard Nixon, in August 1971, made public the U.S. government's decisions to impose a 10 percent surcharge on imports and abandon fixed currency exchange rates. Nixon lifted the surcharge only after Tokyo revalued the yen upward nearly 17 percent and agreed to accept a voluntary reduction of 9.2 percent on Japan's synthetic textile and apparel exports to the United States. In February 1972, Prime Minister Sato also signed an agreement promising greater access for U.S. imports to Japan.

Despite economic friction, Sato's government consistently supported the U.S. war in Vietnam, in defiance of angry criticism from leftists and average citizens as well. After 1970 protests grew because of rising disillusionment with the government's economic policies. By 1972 new public activism resulted in the emergence of approximately 3,000 single-issue political movements, 60 percent dealing with ecology and 40 percent with peace or pragmatic local issues. According to political scientist Lawrence W. Beer, "environmental pollution (*kogai*) became a consensus enemy."[3] Ordinary citizens filed suit against polluters and signed petitions for environmental protection legislation. But the most dramatic of the citizens movements concerned opposition to construction of Narita International Airport. In 1962 the government decided a new airport for Tokyo was vital for economic development, and in 1966 a site was identified. Farmers on 20 percent of the land at the airport site acted to prevent construction of the airport, welcoming help from leftists who linked Narita with growing U.S. reliance on Japan for waging war in Vietnam. Protesters at first staged sit-ins, wrote letters, and distributed pamphlets, but in 1967 they began to organize large demonstrations. Leftists used guerrilla tactics, declaring an intention to kill policemen. In 1971 there were 1,800 injured and 500 arrested, and three policemen were killed. Narita International Airport finally opened in 1978, seven years behind schedule.

Although it refused to retreat on the issue of Narita, Japan's government was responsive on other social welfare issues. After passing a Consumer Protection Law in 1968, the Diet enacted 14 anti-pollution measures in 1970 alone and approved the creation of an Environmental Protection Agency in

July 1971. The government also developed new mechanisms to identify, mediate with, and compensate victims in pollution disputes. Japan's spending to fight pollution soon exceeded that of any other industrialized nation. But popular displeasure with Sato's failure to lower inflation, reduce housing shortages, expand health care, and resist U.S. dictates caused his approval rating to drop to 17.3 percent in June 1972, forcing him to resign the following month. Prime Minister Tanaka Kakuei's subsequent plan to revive economic growth called for massive spending on the domestic infrastructure. He also increased welfare services such as free medical care for the elderly and the provision of child allowances in 1972 and the indexing of pensions to the inflation rate in 1973. The sharp rise in government expenditures under Tanaka created a serious strain on the budget. Nonetheless, subsequent governments continued to finance social programs.

Then, in October 1973, the Yom Kippur War led Arab leaders to threaten Japan and other oil-importing countries with the same embargo imposed on the United States for its pro-Israel stance unless they demonstrated support for the Arab cause. In addition to implementing rationing and price controls, MITI ordered a 10 percent reduction in the industrial consumption of energy, creating serious distress for large industries (notably steel, copper, paper, synthetics, chemical fertilizers, and petrochemicals). The government also sought to lessen dependence on oil, by (1) providing financial incentives for using or developing alternate sources of energy, and (2) accelerating the nation's nuclear energy program. Overall, Japan's dependence on oil for energy declined from 80.3 percent in 1972 to 61 percent in 1983. The Keidanren federation, speaking for large firms in manufacturing, finance, and world trade, argued against the government's economizing measures, wanting to protect such noncompetitive industries as mineral smelting, synthetic textiles, and food processing. Just as upsetting to big business was the government's action in support of small companies, as it provided credits and loans to these firms as well as a lower tax rate than it imposed on large corporations. Tanaka, for example, endorsed a no-collateral loan program in 1973 for small business that provided funds to local chambers of commerce for low interest loans through the state-run People's Finance Corporation. In 1977 the program was extended to small retail and service industries.

Government no longer could dictate industrial policy after 1970. Court decisions and a rejuvenated Federal Trade Commission blocked MITI from playing a direct role in the decisions of private firms, forcing producers to react to the oil crisis without government help and supervision. Japan's shipping industry, for example, was first in the world in 1974, as 60 firms provided 50 percent of global commercial tonnage. By the late 1970s, however, the shipbuilders had scrapped 35 percent of capacity, with the government acting to provide wage subsidies, retraining allowances, and relocation for jobless workers. There had been a huge expansion from 1965 to 1974 in such heavy industries as crude steel, pig iron, and chemicals. Despite a dramatic decrease in dependence on oil, Japan's industrial production rose by 40 percent from 1974 to 1983. Exports of cars had increased from 117,809 in 1965 to 6.11 million in 1980, and the 1977 foreign exchange surplus reached $23.2 million. One explanation for this rebound was that even though the revalued yen made Japanese goods more costly, it made imported raw materials less costly. However, rising government indebtedness left less money for investment. Finally, the Arab oil embargo intimidated Japanese consumers, causing domestic spending to stagnate.

REVIVAL AND RESURGENCE

Three decades after World War II, Japan could boast of economic parity with the West, but recent events refocused attention on its vulnerability. Beginning in 1974, the Japanese government placed a priority on increasing productivity in knowledge-intensive and energy-efficient industries that had export potential as the primary means to resume economic growth. Japan's growing trade surplus caused greatly increased tensions with the United States. In 1965 Washington had forced Tokyo to limit the U.S. share of Japan's total steel exports, as it already had done with textiles. To avoid tariff retaliation, Japan imposed voluntary quotas on exports to the United States of specialty steel in 1974 and color television sets in 1977. But U.S. leaders remained dissatisfied because an elaborate system limited access to Japan's domestic market. Non-tariff barriers included quotas on more than two dozen types of imports, "buy Japanese" government procurement policies, arbitrary and burdensome customs procedures, discriminatory certification standards and design requirements involving costly tests, convoluted distribution channels, and a complex method of payment for foreign goods. U.S. complaints about Japanese tariffs and import quotas grew during the Ford administration, as the U.S. economy was mired in recession. Then, in 1975, Japan experienced the worst economic downturn since the U.S. Occupation, making it difficult for Tokyo to address and resolve American grievances.

Honda was among those responsible for maintaining Japanese economic growth. His sales target was not Japan, where three other automakers were larger than his company in 1977, but the United States. He sold his first car there in 1970, a snappy midget sedan that Honda saw American men buying as "a third car, just like a third mistress." Honda was Canada's most popular

Postwar Japan drops consumer goods instead of bombs in economic war against the West. *Far Eastern Economic Review*, Feburary 3, 1978.

foreign car in 1976, nearly matching this status in the United States. In the following year, Honda's stock began trading on the New York Stock Exchange. By then the company was making motorbikes, motorcycles, engine parts, autos, trucks, lawn mowers, farm machinery, and generators. It also owned amusement parks, an airport, and a fleet of ships to carry Honda cars to North America. Anticipating tariff retaliation as U.S. sales skyrocketed, Honda Motors was Japan's first automaker to build a factory in the United States (it started to assemble cars in Ohio in 1982). Its revenues reached $995 million, with 28,000 employees in 38 plants in 29 nations. Young Americans were drawn to the fuel efficiency and low emissions of Honda engines. During the 1980s the Civic and Accord became the basic family car for millions of Americans. Others drove cars that Toyota and Nissan made after imitating Honda in marketing methods, car types, and building plants in the United States.

Electronics joined automobiles in fueling Japan's economic resurgence after the oil crisis. Sony became a popular brand name in the United States during the 1970s; the company marketed cassettes, walkie-talkies, 23-band transistor radios, eight-track tape cartridges, dictating and transcribing machines, clock radios, and calculators with printout attachments. An electronics giant that smothered top American rivals Zenith, RCA, and Motorola, Sony saw U.S. astronauts carry its video recorders on the Apollo moon missions. Profits started to decline late in the 1970s, as U.S. consumers began favoring Matsushita's VCR technology over Betamax. Morita then marketed the Walkman radio, with annual sales soon reaching over 7 million units. During the 1980s Sony introduced a hi-fi video, audio disk, and compact home video camera, but competitors in Taiwan, South Korea, and Japan made the same products with comparable quality at lower prices. And in the United States, the flood of Japanese radios, tape recorders, and televisions resulted in U.S. restrictions on imports. In response, Sony built a television assembly factory near San Diego and a plant in Alabama to make tapes and casettes, later constructing factories in Barcelona, Stuttgart, and Wales. Sales of Sony's personal computer were not strong, but the American National Standards Institute adopted its floppy disk format. By the end of the 1980s, Sony was the world's most registered brand name.

By 1980 Japan's economy had recovered from the oil crisis, causing one observer to write that Japan had "the most efficient, effective, and adaptive economy in history from a semi-corrupt and factionalized political base."[4] For the next five years no nation matched Japan's growth rate, as it became the largest creditor in the world as well. Economic resurgence in the early 1980s transformed Japan from fourth in 1965 to first in the manufacture of motor vehicles, commanding 28.5 percent of the world market. Moreover, Japan "outproduced or challenged the supremacy of other major industrial nations in [the production for export of] electronic cameras, radios, quartz watches, televisions, calculators, home videos, cassettes, computers, silicon memory chips, and genetic engineering."[5] Of Japan's 25 biggest firms, 14 were in autos and electronics. Electronics firms used the domestic market to test innovations and lower costs, and carmakers added to export models special accessories and safety devices to enhance consumer appeal. Countless small companies supplied the automobile, electronics, and other industries, following strict guidelines and timetables. These small firms exploited new products, processes, technologies, and demands in ceramics, biotechnics, robotics, and office automation while creating thousands of new jobs.

Small business thus assumed a key role in Japan's economy in the 1970s. By 1980 small firms employed 72 percent of the work force. As the number of large companies fell in the late 1970s, the prevalence of lifetime jobs and enterprise unions declined. A merit system increasingly replaced seniority, linking wage increases to performance even in large corporations. In 1979 big business employed under the old system only about 25 percent of white-collar, male workers. Educated and talented young people were in very high demand, with 10 jobs for each applicant. Companies encouraged their older workers to retire, especially in shipbuilding, textiles, iron and

steel, lumber, chemicals, and nonferrous metal. Staying competitive required businesses to promise raises and rank to attract and now retain the
best workers. Also, women had entered the work force in substantial numbers during the 1970s, working in both manufacturing and the service sector. Many were returning to work after raising children, accepting part-time
employment at lower pay and with few benefits or opportunities for advancement. Despite continuing discrimination in hiring practices, by 1980
an increasing number of women were securing professional, technical, and
managerial positions. In 1985 an Equal Employment Opportunity Act required that employers refrain from practicing discrimination, but the legislation included no enforcement provisions.

Progress toward achieving gender equality slowed after 1980 because of
Japan's aging population. Conservative leaders now argued that women
had to stay home to care for elderly parents. Moreover, the government's attempt to shift welfare responsibilities to the family led to the ending of free
health care in 1982, with a law imposing patient fees. Indeed, excessive
government spending on social programs had contributed to the national
debt rising from 5 percent of the GNP in 1979 to 40 percent in 1983. And
economic recovery from the oil crisis did not result in the abandonment of
efforts at financial retrenchment. In 1980 the government adopted the zero
ceiling formula for the 1981 budget whereby ministries were not to spend
more than they had received for the prior year, although defense and foreign
aid were exempt. Prime Minister Nakasone Yasuhiro reduced government
spending in 1983 for the first time in 28 years. His search for new ways to
achieve a balanced budget led to his appointment of a study group to examine trade and agricultural policy, with Maekwa Haruo, former governor of
the Bank of Japan, as chair. In its 1986 report, the study group proposed tax
reductions and increased public works expenditures to boost domestic consumption. This would promote economic expansion, creating more jobs
and generating increased tax revenue.

Nakasone responded positively to the Maekwa Report, not least because
it would expand the purchase of imports, resulting in a reduction of trade
friction with the United States. Already he had approved measures to open
Japan's market through the simplifying of testing and inspection procedures. The government also acted to further liberalize financial markets and
to allow foreign participation on the Tokyo Stock Exchange. Nakasone's
tax reform package in 1987 called for reducing income tax levels, but imposing a 5 percent sales tax to cover lost revenue. Fierce opposition from organized labor, small business, and consumers forced him to withdraw the
proposal. However, Nakasone successfully pursued structural reform to
balance the budget. First, he lowered agricultural price supports, reducing

the gap between the producer and the consumer price of food. But beef, rice, citrus, and tobacco stayed protected from foreign competition. Second, Nakasone dramatically moved toward privatization, defying labor unions in returning the state-run Nippon Telephone and Telegraph and Japan National Railways to private ownership in 1985 and 1987, respectively. This further reduced union membership that already was declining because of the proliferation of small companies. Older unions disbanded, as firms offered generous benefits to attract and retain workers who were interested in their own socioeconomic status, not politics. In 1987 union leaders formed Rengo as an umbrella organization to represent a new work force.

In 1989 the end of the Cold War opened a new era for Japan that the last chapter will cover. After World War II, Japanese conservatives gambled that economic growth combined with U.S. protection would restore Japan to a prominent place in world affairs. Success was apparent in the 1960s, with Japan's emergence as an economic superpower. New problems arose in the 1970s, including denial of access to cheap technology, skyrocketing gas and oil prices, an end to low labor costs, and growing public spending on social welfare. The Japanese addressed and overcame these problems after 1980, restoring prosperity largely through the exploitation of consumer power. Japanese foreign trade continued to grow because of low prices for raw materials and falling energy costs, resulting in an increase of the foreign exchange surplus. But Japan's foreign trade constituted 22 percent of the GNP in 1985, whereas for the decade Britain's rate was 29 percent and West Germany's 31 percent. Japanese companies generated 5 percent of production overseas, whereas the rate for U.S. firms was 20 percent and Western Europe 15 percent. Prime Minister Nakasone thus could talk about the need for "internationalization" without creating fears of Japanese economic imperialism. He initiated this process through major reforms and a campaign for spiritual renewal emphasizing patriotism and national pride to create a New Japan able to fulfill an expanded, positive role in world affairs.

NOTES

1. Mikiso Hane, *Modern Japan: A Historical Survey* (Boulder, CO: Westview Press, 1986), 376.

2. Hans H. Baerwald, "Parliament and Parliamentarians in Japan," *Pacific Affairs* 37 (Fall 1964): 272.

3. Lawrence W. Beer, "Japan: Turning the Corner," *Asian Survey* 11 (January 1971): 81.

3

Cold War Client

Japan's economic development after World War II promoted the revival of national confidence and pride. The United States provided the security and protection that made this possible, but military dependence also was a consistent source of frustration and political discord. Washington dictated for the most part Tokyo's defense and foreign policy after 1952 until the Cold War ended with the fall of the Soviet Union late in 1991. Moreover, U.S. leaders wanted Japan to assume a greater share of the responsibility for building regional security and deterring the perceived threat of Communist expansion in Northeast Asia by strengthening its military capabilities. Yet postwar Japanese embraced pacifism. In fact, World War II permanently tarnished the image of the nation's military, which became the target of distrust, suspicion, and outright antagonism. Soon, Japanese people referred to military leaders derisively as *zeiken dorobo*, or "tax thieves." Conservative leaders tried without much success to weaken this pacifist consensus, promoting unpopular policies to preserve Japan's alliance with the United States.

REALIGNMENT AND REARMAMENT

Serious debate about the nature and scope of Japan's role in protecting itself and promoting regional security began as early as the spring of 1947, when the Truman administration's adoption of the containment policy ignited a war scare in Japan. At first, the Japanese with very few exceptions wanted to focus on economic recovery and reform, while relying entirely on the United States to provide protection. In 1948, however, fears grew that

U.S. officials had decided that Japan would be expendable in the event of a new international conflict. Then the Soviet Union signed an alliance with the new Communist government in China early in 1950 that Japan viewed as a direct threat to its security. A dilemma now faced Japanese leaders about how to remain disarmed to maintain peace and democracy, while at the same time ensuring protection against outside aggression. Article 9 of the Constitution, however, seemed to preclude rearmament, because it prohibited maintenance of "land, sea, and air forces, as well as other war potential" for all time. But Japan's conservatives increasingly argued that Article 9 meant renouncing war only to settle international disputes; they argued that the article did not preclude the creation and maintenance of armed forces for Japan's self-defense.

American intelligence and military advisors advocated at least limited Japanese rearmament from the outset of the U.S. occupation. As Cold War tensions grew, Washington came to see Japan as an ally to rebuild militarily, rather than as an enemy to punish. Adoption of the "reverse course" (*gyaksu kosu*) in 1948 installed this position as U.S. policy, as Washington pressed Japan to form a national police reserve. By April 1950, political scientist Kawai Kazuo would write that Japan's commitment to forsake rearmament "no longer depends primarily on whether or not the Japanese are willing to abide by it, but upon whether the Allied Powers will be able to agree to allow Japan to retain it."[1] The Socialist and Communist parties both strenuously opposed even partial rearmament, demanding strict pacifism and neutrality. Revival of militarism would waste resources and threaten democracy, they warned, while limiting trade opportunities in a frightened Asia. Evidence of the Japanese reluctance to rearm reinforced the position of U.S. military leaders in support of delaying Japan's sovereignty and keeping military bases after independence. Already, the United States had reaffirmed control of Okinawa in the Ryukyus, which had been under military occupation since the end of World War II. During early 1950 the U.S. State Department moved closer to the military's position and supported limited rearmament, U.S. bases in Japan, and a bilateral defense agreement.

Prime Minister Yoshida acted to exploit growing U.S. security concerns. He proposed Japan's rejection of neutrality in favor of an alliance with the United States, including military bases in Japan, in return for an early peace settlement restoring Japan's sovereignty. President Harry S. Truman readily agreed, instructing John Foster Dulles, his special representative, to work out the details. Dulles tried in subsequent negotiations to gain a promise of full rearmament, but Yoshida resisted this pressure, stating flatly, "Don't talk nonsense." Three days before the start of the Korean War, Tokyo received Washington's latest request to rearm. North Korea's attack in June 1950 weakened Yoshida's resolve, as most Japanese citizens accepted gradual and limited rearmament. This was because the U.S. Eighth Army left Japan to prevent Communist conquest of the Korean peninsula. Yoshida, in July 1950, agreed to establish a National Police Reserve (NPR), persuading the Diet to approve the creation of a force of 75,000. The United States then provided training and equipment for the NPR, with its mission being to control domestic order. In June 1954 the NPR became the Self-Defense Forces (SDF) equipped with artillery and tanks. Blocking major increases in the number of Japanese under arms, Yoshida kept the total below 180,000, or half what Washington now wanted. By 1954, however, he had abandoned his initial interpretation of Article 9, arguing that Japan could maintain a "military without war potential."

Meanwhile, Dulles concluded negotiations with Yoshida that would result in 48 nations signing the Japanese Peace Treaty in September 1951 at the San Francisco Conference (the treaty became effective later, in April 1952). The Soviet Union did not sign, and the United States and Britain could not agree on whether to invite the People's Republic of China (PRC) or the Republic of China (ROC) on Taiwan, so China had no representation. Burma and India refused to sign, the former viewing the terms as too lenient and the latter as too harsh. It is significant that the treaty recognized Japan's right of self-defense. However, to regain its sovereignty Japan had to approve a bilateral security treaty with the United States, forcing continued acceptance of U.S. military bases in Japan. Washington had obtained advance agreement from Japanese leaders for this U.S.-Japan Security Treaty of 1951 that provided the foundation for postwar Japanese-American partnership in world affairs. Signed on the same day as the peace treaty, it authorized the United States to use its bases in Japan for military operations elsewhere in Asia without consulting the Japanese government. After 1952, 260,000 U.S. troops remained on 2,824 military bases with authority to suppress internal disturbances.

By the time Yoshida resigned as prime minister in December 1954, he had filled out the details of Japan's Cold War alliance with the United States. In February 1952 an Administrative Agreement granted the United States power to garrison specified areas, remove buildings, acquire rights of way, and even arrest Japanese citizens committing disturbances outside U.S. military bases. Any American personnel committing crimes in Japan came under U.S. jurdisdiction. Tokyo negotiated the U.S.-Japan Mutual Defense Assistance Agreement of March 1954, which allocated $150 million in weapons and equipment, as well as $100 million in offshore procurements, on the condition that Japan increase its own defense capabilities. This Cold War alignment with the United States stirred profound fears of revived militarism among the Japanese people. For example, the Diet approved the creation of the SDF only after agreeing that its mission was to combat "direct or indirect aggression" that threatened Japan's peace and independence. The Japan Socialist Party (JSP) led a coalition of representatives in preventing the establishment of a Ministry of Defense in September 1954, portraying the legislation as inviting militarist adventures and imperialism. Instead, the Diet set up a Japan Defense Agency under a civilian director general who was responsible to the prime minister. To ensure civilian control, the Diet prohibited military officers from holding command positions in the Agency. The Diet had to approve all operations, barring actions outside of Japan.

Leftist politicians condemned Japan's Cold War alliance with the United States, demanding a peace treaty that all former Allied nations would agree to accept, permanent neutrality, and no foreign bases in Japan, while denouncing steps toward rearmament. But right-wing groups advocated fuller remilitarization, criticizing the NPR as an overpaid and coddled mercenary force that lacked traditional training and rigorous discipline. Attitudes on the right changed in October 1951 when the government enlisted 400 previously ostracized prewar army officers to serve as trainers in the NPR. In February and March 1952 a massive "depurge" led to the return to service of all but 5,500 military leaders who had fought in World War II, many then traveling to the United States for training in tactics and weapons. Often members of postwar private militarist groups, or *kikan*, these new SDF officers stressed discipline, obedience to command, and sacrifice, relying on indoctrination techniques reminiscent of prewar service to the emperor. Many were disgruntled because the SDF was a "less than genuine Army, Navy and Air Force than an inflated riot squad incapable of any effective combat on the field of battle."[2] The Diet ensured, however, that the SDF concentrated its efforts on relief and rehabilitation projects in response to natural disasters. By 1965 it had won broad popular respect and support after participation in over 4,000 such operations.

CONSOLIDATION AND CRISIS

Japan was a fully dependent partner of the United States when Hatoyama Ichiro became prime minister in December 1954. By then a consensus was firmly in place supporting what observers labeled the Yoshida Doctrine of relying on U.S. protection and following Washington's lead in foreign policy. Nevertheless, Japan's relationship with the United States remained a source of heated controversy, constituting by far the most divisive force in domestic politics for the rest of the decade. Conservatives denounced the security treaty because it infringed on Japanese sovereignty, and leftist politicians condemned Japan's alignment with the United States against the Soviet Union and partial rearmament as risking a return to war. Public opinion polls regularly found half of respondents holding no firm stand on the issue. Washington made plain its expectation that a now sovereign Japan would assume greater responsibility for its own defense and integrate itself more fully into the U.S. defense system in Asia. But most Japanese wanted to avoid foreign policy initiatives, fearing the costs and appearance of being provocative. Japanese governments therefore were reluctant to risk a hostile reaction to signs of revived militarism at home and among prewar victims of imperialism abroad. Politicians also resisted diverting any funds from economic development.

Close ties developed between Japan's SDF and the U.S. military following 1954. At first, Washington envisioned a small Japanese force able to hold off an outside attack for 90 days, but it adopted a more grandiose plan during the Korean War that more conservative Japanese endorsed. Hatoyama's hawkish stand against Yoshida's resistance to U.S. pressure for full-scale rearmament helped win him the prime ministership, but he could not build a consensus behind remilitarization. The U.S. government reluctantly adjusted to these limitations, providing Japan by 1962 with 98 percent of its weaponry and 82 percent of its communications equipment. U.S.-Japan security cooperation also extended to major defense industries in both countries, although military production averaged only 1.2 percent of total industrial output in Japan between 1954 and 1960. However, pacifism remained strong not least because of an anti-nuclear movement that had its origins in public horror after the atomic attacks on Hiroshima and Nagasaki. Opposition to nuclear weapons intensified in 1954 after radioactivity from an American H-bomb test on Bikini atoll showered a Japanese fishing boat, the *Lucky Dragon*, causing one death. Responding to public protests, the Socialists reunited in 1955 over an agreement to advocate "self-reliant independence" rather than "neutralism." JSP gains in elections that year motivated conservatives to form the Liberal Democratic Party (LDP), reinforcing political support behind the Yoshida Doctrine.

Japan entered a period of profound political disruption in February 1957 when Kishi Nobusuke became prime minister. He was a vocal proponent of the elimination of Article 9, rearmament, and close alignment with the United States, as well as reversing occupation reforms. Students, leftist politicians, and intellectuals detested Kishi because of these views as well as his staunch anti-communism, which added to their view of him as an unreconstructed fascist. Kishi quickly confirmed his critics' fears when he acted to reinstitute moral education, or *shushin*, which required the teaching of ethics classes to develop in students honesty, politeness, and respect as well as obedience and loyalty in defending the nation. In September 1958 the Japan Teachers Union, or Kikkyoso, held pickets to block teachers from attending training sessions on *shushin*. "It's the people who support moral education that I don't like," said one student. "Why should politicians who spend their time drinking in geisha houses at the taxpayers' expense start talking about the need to teach children ethics? A lot they know about ethics! What they want is to recover the power they used to have and to make us all obedient again."[3] But Kishi's determination to renew the U.S.-Japan Security Treaty would ignite a much bigger crisis.

In 1955 the United States had resumed pressure on Japan to expand the overseas role of the SDF in negotiations for revision of the security treaty. A joint communiqué emerging from the talks enraged many Japanese because it seemed to suggest that Japan might undertake military commitments in the Pacific in return for treaty revision. Anticipating opposition to renewal, Kishi wanted changes that would restore Japan's diplomatic independence. After negotiations for a new accord resumed in September 1958, opponents established the People's Council for Preventing Revision of the Security Treaty (Ampo joyaku kaitei shoshi kokumin kaigi), a coalition consisting of Socialists, Communists, and the All-Japan Federation of Student Self-Government Associations or Zengakuren (created in 1948 and claiming 300,000 members by 1959). In March 1959 at its first meeting Ampo affirmed opposition to nuclear weapons, foreign military bases in Japan, and rearmament. But moderates in the JSP who backed the security pact bolted to form the Democratic Socialist Party (DSP) in January 1960.

In January 1960, Kishi left for Washington amid huge demonstrations against revision. There, he signed a revised treaty providing for a positive guarantee of U.S. protection and a more equitable partnership. The two nations agreed "to meet the common danger" in case of armed attack on either party in territories under Japanese jurisdiction, a pledge for mutual consultations in the event that the peace and security of Japan or East Asia were threatened, and a virtual veto over the deployment of nuclear weapons in Japan. A new administrative agreement relieved Tokyo of the obligation to help maintain U.S. military personnel in Japan. Fierce opposition to Kishi's treaty was certain because it extended for ten more years the U.S. base rights in Japan. Critics pointed out that the United States had imposed the security treaty on Japan but that the consent for renewal would make continued dependence a free choice. As the Diet debated ratification, demonstrations and political disruptions occurred outside, with protesters even staging a mass urination on the building. The Socialists staged a sit-in outside the speaker's office to block him from opening the session, almost strangling him upon his release. Kishi ordered the police to enter the building in force and eject protesting Socialist members. The Diet then convened, and the LDP members ratified the treaty after midnight in the absence of the boycotting dissenters.

Kishi's actions set off a series of angry protests, with thousands of housewives, shopkeepers, professors, and pacifists joining in organized, riotous snakedancing street demonstrations. Some students even shouted "Kill Kishi!" On June 4, 1960, a communications workers stoppage idled over five million, while more than 13 million people signed petitions demanding new elections. Adding to popular unrest was the collapse of the Paris Summit in May 1960, when many observers of international affairs had anticipated Soviet-American progress toward ending the Cold War. But when the Soviet Union shot down an American U-2 reconnaissance plane over its airspace a few days before the conference, Moscow angrily ended the talks because the Eisenhower administration refused to apologize or end the flights. Critics pointed to U.S. president Eisenhower's visit as yet another provocative act to alert the Soviets of U.S. war readiness, not to mention the belief that the U-2 spy planes came from bases in Japan. On June 10, an angry crowd surrounded the U.S. president's press secretary when he arrived at Tokyo's Haneda Airport to prepare for Eisenhower's visit. Five days later, a police advance on protesters outside the Diet injured 600 students, and fleeing demonstrators trampled a woman to death. As a result, Eisenhower cancelled his visit. On June 25, a strike involving six million workers caused Kishi to consider seriously but then abandon plans to mobilize SDF forces to silence further protests. Denunciations of his undemocratic behavior and loss of face after Eisenhower's cancellation forced Kishi to resign in July 1960.

AN ALLIANCE UNDER ASSAULT

Prime Minister Ikeda adopted a "low posture" in foreign policy to avoid the nasty confrontations with the Diet that had discredited Kishi. Ikeda named Ohira Masayoshi as foreign minister in 1962, and Ohira proceeded to implement more fully Ikeda's approach. Ohira admitted shortly after his appointment that "I am an amateur as far as foreign policy is concerned and I fully realize the limitations of my ability." Critics charged that reaching out for cooperation with the JSP, rather than ramming unpopular policies through the Diet, led to unnecessary concessions. But Ohira believed that achieving domestic political unity and strength was essential before Japan could perform a more active world role. He developed a plan to expand exports as a means to boost economic growth, which required maintaining close commercial ties with the United States. In December 1962, he led Japan's delegation at the second annual meeting of the Joint U.S.-Japan Committee on Trade and Economic Affairs, working to open markets for Japan's goods in the United States. Reflecting a new consensus in the LDP, Ohira was a moderate on increases in defense spending, but he favored Japan assuming a greater share of responsibility for its military protection. He also believed Japan could best influence Communist China by providing a forceful example of a successfully operating democracy in Asia. Other nations in Southeast Asia also would follow the example.

Meanwhile, John F. Kennedy had become president of the United States, developing a cordial relationship with Ikeda when Japan's prime minister visited Washington for talks in June 1961. Attorney General Robert Kennedy reciprocated in 1962, traveling to Japan again in 1964. But the Kennedy administration, like its predecessor, had trouble understanding the reasons for pacifism in Japan. Edwin O. Reischauer, the new ambassador and noted specialist on Japanese history, questioned the basis for opposition to fuller rearmament in his first speech in May 1961. A public opinion poll still found a plurality of Japanese against remilitarization, the first of five reasons being fear of renewed war. Some observers anticipated a foreign policy shift when Sato Eisaku replaced Ikeda as prime minister in November 1964. In his acceptance speech, Sato called for an expanded international role for Japan commensurate with its status as a global economic power. "I think that unarmed nations and non-nuclear nations, such as Japan," he stated, "should express a more positive voice for the maintenance of peace." But just three days after taking office, his refusal to prevent the U.S. nuclear submarine *Sea Dragon* from visiting Sasebo naval base ignited pacifist and leftist protests that led to urban riots and dozens of injuries. Sato ignored these demonstrations. Before the Diet, he declared his firm support for close ties with the United States.

U.S. bases in Japan remained a contentious issue. Indeed, a November 1966 poll found that only 18 percent of respondents held positive views toward the U.S. presence, whereas 38 percent wanted U.S. troops to leave. Opposition had been growing since 1954 because of a succession of incidents involving American military personnel. A 1957 report noted that stray bullets or shells from U.S. firing ranges had killed or wounded 150 Japanese. Also, several legal attempts to have the security treaty of 1951 declared unconstitutional had failed. For example, in 1959 the Tokyo District Court acquitted seven defendants who had been charged in 1957 with breaking into the U.S. Air Force base west of Tokyo to block the extension of the runway onto agricultural land. Because of Japan's Administrative Agreement with the United States, the protesters faced more punitive penalties than those imposed for trespass on other property. The court acquitted the men after finding that the security treaty was illegal under Article 9. But then the Japanese Supreme Court overturned the ruling in 1962, arguing that a treaty was a "political question" that only the Diet could consider. By 1968 a poll revealed that 56 percent of respondents wanted the removal of U.S. bases. This undoubtedly reflected a steady stream of troublesome incidents, the worst being in May 1968 when the U.S.S. *Swordfish* docked at Sasebo. Four days after its arrival, the Maritime Safety Agency determined that radiation levels in air and water were ten to twenty times above normal rates, bringing charges that the vessel had discharged nuclear coolants into the harbor.

It was the Vietnam War, however, that under Sato transformed the U.S. military presence in Japan into an incendiary issue. During a meeting with President Lyndon Johnson in January 1965, Sato defended the U.S. bombing of North Vietnam. This galvanized an antiwar movement in Japan that drew widespread public support. In June, Tokyo and Osaka were centers of the first nationwide protest against the Vietnam War, attracting over 100,000 intellectuals, socialists, labor activists, religious leaders, and students. That same year, the Citizens' Federation for Peace in Vietnam (Beheiren) mounted a campaign condemning U.S. military action in Indochina. Protests against Vietnam were a major headache for Sato because Japan had formal relations with South Vietnam and by 1965 had paid it $39 million in reparations for its wartime occupation of Indochina. But Sato also wanted to support U.S. efforts to combat Communist expansion. Bowing to U.S. pressure in 1965, Japan reduced the level of its unofficial trade with North Vietnam. Not only did U.S. bases in Japan become vital staging areas for military operations in Vietnam, but for the first half of 1966 the U.S. procurement contracts totaled $50 million. By 1967 over 1,500 Japanese civilians were working for the U.S. military sea transport service in Vietnam and in other Pacific locations, shipping boots, food, napalm, and vehicles. Sato also allowed the United States to recruit captains and crews in Japan to operate landing craft in Vietnam.

Sato defended these steps, arguing that the Vietnam War might threaten Japan's peace and security. Prior consultation was unnecessary, he claimed, because U.S. troops were using bases in Japan for noncombat purposes. But antiwar activists rejected Sato's arguments. Student protesters blocked his departure from a dinner engagement in August 1965, forcing him to sneak out a side entrance. That year, members of weaker factions in the LDP began pressing Sato to take the initiative and call for a cease-fire in Vietnam. Sato's refusal to alter his unwavering support of U.S. policy meant that political unrest would continue. In October 1967, he visited

South Vietnam, defying student efforts to block his visit, but demonstrators were there to protest his return. Before leaving Southeast Asia, Sato declared that an end to the U.S. bombing of North Vietnam would not bring peace. When he left to meet with President Johnson, massive student demonstrations took place at Haneda Airport. In Washington, Sato promised renewal of the security treaty in return for U.S. restoration of Japan's control over the Bonin islands, with the transfer to occur in November 1968. Shortly after his return, over 250,000 workers joined in antiwar strikes. Surprising many, Sato issued in December 1967 his famed Three Non-Nuclear Principles, forswearing the manufacture, possession, and introduction of nuclear weapons in Japan, but this did not pacify his critics.

Reporting on the year 1968, one writer concluded that because of "the dynamic, mass consumption prosperity of [Japan's] domestic economy, the only really controversial issues are in foreign policy."[4] Popular opposition to the Vietnam War derived from a troubling realization that Japan's prosperity and peace were being purchased at the cost of war and repression of democracy elsewhere. The conflict in Vietnam also intensified postwar fears that Japanese militarism would invite a return to war, having an adverse effect on the SDF. In 1966 Japan had the second largest army in Asia, but its ground force rarely exceeded more than 141,000. The government then set a new target of 171,000 in 1967, but a huge enlistment campaign failed to expand recruitment. That year, the five-year Second Defense Plan providing for "modernization of equipment" was completed, arming the SDF with a variety of sophisticated weapons that included anti-tank rockets, destroyers, fighter aircraft, and diesel-powered submarines. Beheiren not only opposed this military expansion in 1968, but demanded the termination of the security treaty and the return of Okinawa. Protests against the war in Vietnam climaxed on antiwar day, October 21, when police arrested thousands of demonstrators. That year, only 14 percent in one poll supported the U.S. defense of South Vietnam and 2 percent approved the bombing of North Vietnam. Over the next three years, Beheiren sponsored a series of peaceful rallies and demonstrations involving nearly 19 million people.

A PARTNERSHIP IN TRANSITION

Japan's pursuit after 1969 of more independence in foreign and defense policy led to its insistence on regaining control over Okinawa. Since 1949, Okinawans had wanted the United States to end the military occupation of their island. Reacting to rising criticism, President Eisenhower in 1957 publicly promised to return Okinawa, acknowledging that Japan had "residual sovereignty." In 1961 Okinawans expected the Kennedy administration to take steps toward this end, but they were disappointed. Construction of missile sites that spring brought protests from Okinawa's elected legislature, as well as charges that Tokyo was silent because this would avoid placement of the sites in Japan proper. Then, after passage of a UN resolution denouncing colonialism, Okinawa's assembly unanimously approved and sent to the United Nations a petition pointing to the U.S. presence as an example of continued colonial rule and demanding the U.S. departure before February 1, 1962. In March 1962, President John F. Kennedy publicly declared that the Ryukyus were a part of Japan, but he said he would not consider returning Okinawa before tensions subsided in East Asia. In 1966 the United States spent $240 million in aid and expenditures on Okinawa. Because one-seventh of Japanese dollar credits came from Okinawa, Tokyo applied little pressure on the United States for reversion.

American military operations in Vietnam caused Okinawa's reversion to become a heated issue in Japanese politics. Washington could use bases on Okinawa for direct combat without prior consultations with Japan because the 1960 treaty did not apply to the island of Okinawa. U.S. troops later stored poison chemicals there and established a training center for military personnel from South Korea, South Vietnam, and the Philippines. Rising popular demands for reversion prompted Ambassador Reischauer, in January 1967, to refer to Okinawa as "the gravest single problem in Japanese-American relations." By 1969 when Richard Nixon became president, even those Japanese favoring U.S. policy on Vietnam and Taiwan wanted the United States out of Okinawa. On April 28 of that year, "Okinawa Day" witnessed the largest and most violent demonstrations to date demanding immediate reversion. Sato's visit to Washington in November ignited the biggest demonstration ever, with 1,700 arrests and countless injuries. In the Sato-Nixon communiqué of November 21, Nixon agreed to take rapid steps for restoring Japan's administrative control "with a view to accomplishing reversion in 1972." Provisions of the security treaties would apply, but the United States agreed to withdraw all its nuclear weapons "consistent with the policy of the Japanese government." Signing on June 17, 1971, both sides ratified the Okinawa Reversion Treaty during November. Japan regained administrative control on May 15, 1972.

Resolution of the Okinawa issue removed the last cause of friction remaining from World War II, enabling Japan and the United States to address directly emerging problems that would dominate their relationship for the next two decades. In the Sato-Nixon communiqué, Sato agreed to automatic renewal of the security treaties, which were open to renegotiation or abrogation in 1970. He also invited angry protests when he approved inclusion of Japan's understanding for the first time that South Korea's security was "essential" and that Taiwan was "a most important factor" for Japan's security. Moreover, the communiqué stressed the need for joint action to strengthen the world economic system, promote balanced and free trade, contribute to economic development in Asia, and control inflation. Questions remained, however, about the value of U.S. pledges of military protection after enunciation of the Nixon Doctrine in 1969, which ruled out future U.S. ground combat operations in Asia. Sato, in a February 1970 speech, said that Japan had to provide for its own defense first and rely secondarily on the United States. Most Japanese, an observer reported in 1970, would accept modest expansion of the SDF to encourage the closing of U.S. bases, but only if it "remains tactical, non-nuclear, and limited to purely defensive functions."[5] Despite demonstrations, a boycott, and a shoving match, the Diet renewed the security treaties in June 1970.

U.S. withdrawal from Vietnam caused Sato's government to place more importance on developing the capacity for self-defense while hesitating to assume new commitments abroad. In 1970 Sato named avowed nationalist and rearmament advocate Nakasone Yasuhiro as the director general of the Defense Agency. Nakasone had supported the transfer of U.S. bases to a Japan with an independent nuclear capability, but he worked closely with Washington to arrange for nonproliferation of nuclear weapons and joint use of military installations. Justifying his new stance as necessary for developing a national consensus on defense and security issues, he persuaded the United States to share nuclear technology with Japan to power electricity plants. Nakasone also developed as government policy the five principles of national defense, calling for protection of Japan's constitution and territory, pursuit of global harmony in diplomacy, civilian control of the military, enforcement of the Three Non-Nuclear Principles, and reliance on the security treaties only as a supplement for defense. He changed the insignia of the SDF from the dove of peace to the cherry blossom, which was the emblem of samurai warriors in feudal Japan. Under his direction, the proposed Fourth National Defense Plan called for doubling defense spending from 1972 to 1976. Under Sato, Japan thus moved toward accepting more responsibility for its own defense, resulting in the highest increase in military spending in the world.

EMERGENCE FROM THE SHADOW

Tanaka Kakuei, Sato's replacement, would be the first prime minister to lead Japan in the search for an alternative to the Yoshida Doctrine. While head of MITI under Sato, he had skillfully negotiated an agreement with the United States averting U.S. imposition of a surcharge on Japanese textiles.

Trade friction worsened under Tanaka, but the Vietnam War ceased to be a source of acrimony when, in January 1973, the Paris Peace Accords ended U.S. involvement there. Japanese-American relations remained frosty in 1974, even though Gerald R. Ford, Nixon's successor, was the first U.S. president to visit Japan. Newly elected prime minister Miki Takeo then attended the Group of Seven (G-7) Summit in France to seek cooperation among the industrialized nations for economic and monetary stabilization. While trade disputes with the United States intensified under Miki, American criticism of Japan's limits on defense spending became an increasingly contentious issue. Miki decided in 1976 that no more than 1 percent of Japan's GNP was to be spent on defense, a ceiling adhered to until 1987, that received strong support in Japan and sharp criticism in the United States. Meanwhile, the Diet resisted pressure to ratify the Nuclear Non-Proliferation Treaty while criticizing Miki's policy of establishing diplomatic contacts with North Korea.

Jimmy Carter's election as president troubled the new government of Fukuda Takeo late in 1976 because of Carter's proposal to withdraw U.S. troops from South Korea. This caused Japan to expand its naval power, deciding in December to purchase 45 anti-submarine planes from Lockheed and extend its territorial limit to 200 miles out to sea—ostensibly for security reasons. But Japan also wanted to protect its fishing rights against growing U.S. pressure to limit catch totals. Economic friction also would continue to undermine the U.S.-Japanese partnership after Ohira became prime minister in 1978, but Washington's anger with Japan grew after the Islamic revolution in Iran led to a second oil crisis that year. In defiance of U.S. pressure, Tokyo refused to unite with industrialized countries in reducing oil imports in response to the decision of oil-producing nations to raise prices. In 1979 Washington voiced displeasure with Japan during the Iran hostage crisis for not only refusing to join an oil embargo but also providing loans to Teheran. Iran ultimately ended oil supplies to Japan in April 1980, when Tokyo refused to pay higher prices. By then Ohira was cooperating with U.S. actions to punish the Soviet Union for invading Afghanistan late in 1979, as Japan joined in the imposition of economic sanctions and the boycott of the Olympic Summer Games in Moscow.

Washington remained dissatisfied with the extent of Japan's contribution to preserving global peace and stability. What especially annoyed the Americans was a continued high level of U.S. spending on defense while its trade deficit with Japan steadily increased. In response, during a meeting in 1979 with Carter, Ohira agreed to open Japan's domestic market to more U.S. products. In January 1980, the United States pressed Japan's government to raise its military expenditures in reaction to what Washington thought was a renewed Soviet military threat. Most Japanese simply did not share the American anxiety about the possibility of a Soviet attack on Japan, although polls found that 80 percent disliked the Soviet Union and saw it as a threat to Japan's security. Yet harsh criticism of the security treaties revived when former ambassador Reischauer publicly admitted that U.S. nuclear-powered warships regularly visited Japan's ports. Public opinion polls showed that most Japanese were opposed to expanding the SDF and increasing defense spending, because this would siphon funds from social programs. Pacifist and neutralist attitudes still influenced the general public during the 1980s. By then a majority of Japanese no longer trusted the United States to defend Japan, expressing a preference for relying on the United Nations to resolve global disputes.

Prime Minister Nakasone Yasuhiro sought to end Japan's dependence on the United States while enhancing its strategic role as an equal partner in containing the Soviets. Understanding that this would require swift action to repair strained relations with the United States, one month after he took office in November 1982 he announced key concessions on trade and plans to visit Washington early the next year. During his first meeting with President Ronald Reagan, his statement that he viewed Japan as an "unsinkable aircraft carrier putting up a tremendous bulwark of defense against infiltration of the backfire bomber" in an overall strategy to deter the Soviets received harsh criticism in Japan. Before leaving Washington, he also committed Japan to protecting its "four straits" and defending sea lanes up to 1,000 miles from the home islands. Upon returning to Japan, Nakasone urged the Diet to pass a 6.5 percent increase in military expenditures for 1983 to provide Japan with the ability to fulfill his promise of expanded patrolling responsibilities in the Pacific. But domestic criticism and a $57 billion deficit forced him to abandon his goal of higher defense spending. In November 1983, Nakasone relied on executive powers to approve the sale of weapons technology to the United States under government supervision in the area of electronics and optics. His action undermined the general ban on all arms exports including military technology that had been in place since 1976.

Despite Nakasone's efforts, Japan's partnership with the United States did not experience fundamental changes during the 1980s. Although Ronald Reagan was the first U.S. president to address Japan's Diet, his reciprocal visits with Nakasone were mainly of symbolic value. For example, from 1982 to 1987 military expenditures grew from 5.2 percent to 6.5 percent of the general account budget, but this exceeded only slightly the limit of 1 percent of the GNP. The SDF ground forces remained well below 180,000 in total, as they had been since 1953. A dissatisfied U.S. House of Represen-

Prime Minister Nakasone Yasuhiro's response to public criticism of his policies to expand Japan's military capabilities. *Far Eastern Economic Review*, June 8, 1983.

tatives approved, in June 1987, an extraordinary resolution requiring the secretary of state to discuss with Tokyo the possibility of Japan raising its military spending to at least 3 percent of its GNP or provide the United States with a security fee of equal amount. That month, Washington imposed sanctions on the Toshiba Company after learning the Japanese firm had sold eight computer-guided multi-axis milling machines to the Soviet Union, providing the capability to make silent-running propellers for its submarines. Washington's pressure to close the trade imbalance then forced Japan, in October 1987, to approve a contract to buy the American-made FSX fighter plane to replace its F-15s, although a government report strongly favored domestic manufacture.

Japan's emergence as a global economic power undermined the logic of the Yoshida Doctrine that left all political and security matters subject to Washington's approval. During the 1980s critics still ridiculed Japan as an "abnormal," "effeminate," and "Peter Pan state" unwilling to defend itself.[6] And Nakasone's efforts to build Japan's military power and expand its global responsibilities ended when Takeshita Noboru replaced him as prime minister in October 1987. As minister of finance for Ohira and Nakasone, he had achieved world prominence as a key spokesman for Tokyo in clashes with the United States over a Japanese trade surplus that had reached $60 billion in 1987. Predictably, Takeshita concentrated on improving economic relations with the United States, ignoring the need as the

Cold War ended to reorder the military and security basis of the Japanese-American partnership. His policy proposals to raise imports, lower exports, spur consumption, reform the tax system, and balance the budget by 1990 were very unpopular, adding to the already hostile reaction of the Japanese people to U.S. criticism of Japan. Exposing the troubled state of the U.S.-Japan alliance after more than four decades of existence was an August 1987 newspaper survey of junior high students: 49 percent of these young Japanese declared that if Japan went to war again, the enemy would be the United States.[7]

NOTES

1. Kawai Kazuo, "Japanese Views on National Security," *Pacific Affairs* 23 (June 1950): 126.

2. I. I. Morris, "Signs of the Military in Post-War Japan," *Pacific Affairs* 31 (March 1958): 6.

3. Quoted in I. I. Morris, "Policeman and Student in Japanese Politics," *Pacific Affairs* 32 (March 1959): 15.

4. Douglas H. Mendel Jr., "Japanese Opinion on Key Foreign Policy Issues," *Asian Survey* 9 (August 1969): 638.

5. Douglas H. Mendel Jr., "Japan's Defense in the 1970s: The Public View," *Asian Survey* 10 (December 1970): 1069.

6. John K. Fairbank, Edwin O. Reischauer, and Albert M. Craig, *East Asia: Tradition and Transformation* (Boston: Houghton Mifflin, 1989), 873.

7. John Welfield, *An Empire in Eclipse: Japan in the Postwar Alliance System* (Atlantic Highlands, NJ: Athione Press, 1988): 448.

4

Contending with the Communists

China and Russia had played significant roles in the course of Japanese history before World War II. Following the Meiji Restoration in 1868, Japan fought wars with both countries to extend its empire in the Pacific, resulting in the establishment of colonial rule over such territories as Korea, Taiwan, and the Kurile Islands. China under Chiang Kai-shek and the Soviet Union under Joseph Stalin were allies of the United States in World War II, helping to defeat Japan. The Cold War between the Soviets and the Americans, especially after the Communist triumph in China, prevented Japan from developing an amicable and cooperative relationship with either China or Russia after the restoration of its sovereignty in 1952. Despite Washington's insistence on maintaining a united front, Japanese leaders tried to expand trade with both Communist nations, also seeking to resolve territorial and other disputes. But Japan's alliance with the United States and anxieties about the influence of Moscow and Beijing over Japanese leftist politicians made it difficult to attain even partial normalization of relations with the Soviet Union and China.

FOUNDATION FOR FRICTION

At the Moscow Conference in December 1945, the former Allies adopted an arrangement for theoretical international control over postwar Japan. A Far Eastern Commission comprised of the 11 nations that had fought against Japan would meet regularly in Washington to determine central policies. In Tokyo, an Allied Council composed of representatives from the "Big Four" (the United States, Britain, China, and the Soviet Union) would advise General Douglas MacArthur, the Supreme Commander of the Allied Powers (SCAP), on site. From the start, MacArthur exercised complete control over the U.S. occupation of Japan. Denied any direct role in the U.S. occupation, Moscow tried to influence developments in postwar Japan indirectly. It maintained a huge embassy in Tokyo, at its peak five times larger than that of any other nation. Soviet agents posing as interpreters and news analysts established ties with the Japan Communist Party (JCP) and other leftist groups, offering financial support and political guidance. Initial leftist support for U.S. reforms ended in January 1950 when an article in *Journal,* a publication of the Communist Information Bureau that the Soviet Union had created in 1947 to promote postwar expansion of communism, criticized the JCP for collaborating with the U.S. imperialists and demanded adoption of a new strategy emphasizing confrontation and violence. Following orders, the JCP attacked Yoshida's government for "selling out the nation" and "voluntarily offering the country as a base for United States operations."[1]

Leftist demonstrations and riots followed, becoming more frequent after the Korean War began. But strikes and acts of sabotage alienated many who sympathized with the left while terrifying average citizens who came to see the JCP as a tool of a hostile foreign power. For Prime Minister Yoshida, the JCP's efforts to undermine political and social stability were intolerable. In 1952 the Diet approved the Subversive Activities Prevention Bill, enhancing the power of the police to detect and punish Communists. More important, in June 1954, another law, reversing a key occupation reform, recentralized administration under a National Police Agency with regional branches. Also, a new National Public Safety Commission would appoint a chief of prefectural police, replacing previous municipal and local administration. Harsh Soviet criticism of these changes, combined with the growing desire of the Japanese to regain independence, persuaded President Truman to formulate and secure approval in September 1951 for the Japanese Peace Treaty without Moscow's or Beijing's participation or approval. The Soviet Union refused to recognize Japan's government after sovereignty was regained in April 1952; it also blocked admission of Japan to the United Nations.

Soviet refusal to recognize the Yoshida government made it impossible to settle unresolved disputes after World War II. For example, the Soviet Union had refused to release promptly an estimated 594,000 Japanese prisoners of war in Siberia, subjecting them instead to slave labor and political indoctrination. In December 1946, Moscow began a slow repatriation that by 1949 returned to Japan 70,880 captives. Tokyo claimed, however, that

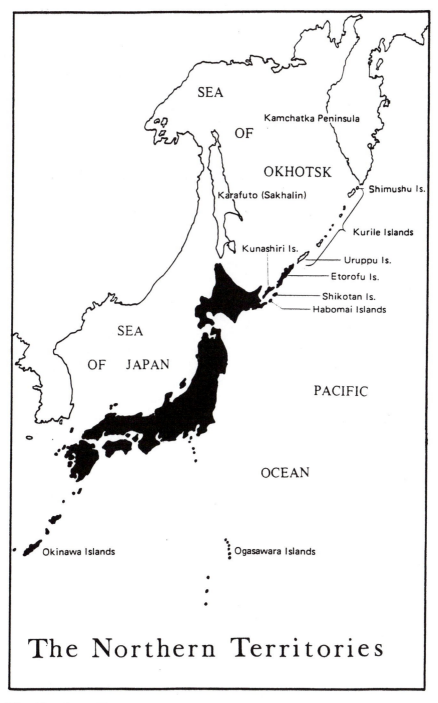

The Northern Territories

The Northern Territories
Source: Swearingen, *The Soviet Union and Postwar Japan*

an additional 95,000 Japanese still remained incarcerated in Siberia, alleging that the Soviets had executed 55,000 Japanese prisoners of war and subjected the remainder to inhumane treatment. Japan and the Soviet Union also clashed over fishing rights, as Japanese fishermen and ships returned to traditional waters in the northwestern Pacific and Sea of Okhotsk after 1945. By 1955 the Russian catch in these waters was twice that of 1940. Finally, the Soviets near the end of World War II had seized the islands of Etorofu, Kunashiri, Shikotan, and the Habomais, insisting that all were part of the Kurile Islands, which Japan had taken from Russia in 1905. Wartime agreements slated them for return to Moscow, but Tokyo rejected the Soviet claim to the "Northern Territories" because they were part of Hokkaido; indeed, Tokyo demanded their return.

Moscow's intransigence and leftist political agitation resulted in rising public hostility in Japan toward the Soviet Union. In response, the Soviets sought to regain political influence in Japan by supporting the peace movement. After the U.S. occupation ended, the JCP tried to persuade the Japanese people that the Soviet Union was a force for peace and that its policies against capitalist exploitation deserved enthusiastic support. Young people, intellectuals, women, trade unionists, and leftist politicians joined "Peace Committees" that developed action programs to mobilize opposition aimed increasingly at discrediting U.S. policies in the Cold War. By contrast, these mass organizations lauded Moscow for criticizing the Japanese Peace Treaty for not including sufficient safeguards against remilitarization. Despite these groups portraying the Soviet Union as a champion of neutralism, the vast majority of Japanese viewed Moscow as a threat and distrusted the JCP.

RECONCILIATION WITHOUT RESOLUTION

Japanese leaders understood that with the end of the U.S. occupation, Japan had to establish a stable relationship with the Soviet Union for security and economic reasons. Tokyo had to have diplomatic relations with the world's other superpower, especially if it hoped to resolve disputes over prisoners, fishing, and the "Northern Territories." Prime Minister Yoshida had maintained a policy of keeping the Soviet Union at a distance, thus strengthening Japan's Cold War alliance with the United States. But when Hatoyama Ichiro replaced him as prime minister in December 1954, he specifically announced his intention to normalize relations with the Soviet Union. His primary objectives were to gain Japan's admission to the United Nations and to demonstrate independence from the United States. Also, families and friends of Japanese nationals still detained in Siberia were putting pressure on the government to secure their return, which prompted a Red Cross investigation beginning in 1953. Hatoyama was willing to compromise on the "Northern Territories" issue, as well as the fishing rights dispute, to gain a peace treaty. But the Eisenhower administration warned against concessions in subsequent Soviet-Japanese negotiations, hoping to squelch the talks and prevent a reconciliation.

Adding urgency to the need for normalization of relations between Japan and the Soviet Union was the worsening clash over fishing rights. Moscow had acted systematically to limit Japanese fishing, such as declaring in 1955 that its territorial waters extended 12 miles from the Kurile Islands, to include the "Northern Territories" that Japan claimed. Enforcement led to frequent incidents with fishermen, as Japanese violators were seized, fined, and briefly imprisoned. Moscow also sought to drive Japan's fishermen from deeper waters. Tokyo and Moscow pursued a resolution of this issue before negotiating normalization, signing, in May 1956, the Soviet-Japanese Fishing Treaty that created a joint commission to regulate fishing activities in the northern waters. Thereafter, Moscow's representatives worked to impose limits on the Japanese catch to more restricted areas and smaller size. The fishing agreement cleared the way, however, for the Soviet Union and Japan to sign a treaty in October 1956 ending the state of war and normalizing relations between the two nations. It provided for the mutual exchange of diplomatic and consular personnel and the restoration of economic ties. In addition to waiving mutual reparation claims, the Soviets agreed to return all remaining Japanese prisoners of war. Repatriation was a critical provision, because public opinion polls found this to be a more important issue for most Japanese than the territorial dispute.

Subsequent negotiations to complete repatriation were very acrimonious, as Moscow claimed to hold far fewer Japanese than Tokyo insisted were still in Soviet hands. When the repatriation process ended in 1958, thousands of Japanese families believed their relatives were still being held in the Soviet Union. Anger over the repatriation issue contributed to anti-Soviet attitudes among most postwar Japanese. Adding further strain to Soviet-Japanese relations was Moscow's provocative behavior in denying Japanese fishermen access to Peter the Great Bay in 1957 and the Sea of Okhotsk in 1959. Japan reacted with outrage, dismissing the Soviet defense of these actions as necessary steps for conservation. Moscow suggested that agreements favorable to Japanese interests would be possible if Tokyo abandoned claims to the Kurile Islands, ended its alliance with the United States, and declared neutrality. Because Japan's economy and food supply depended on the fishing industry, pressure grew for concessions. In September 1958 the Great Japan Fishery Association urged the government to concede Soviet control over two of the disputed islands, but the vast majority of Japanese opposed trading land for fish. Seizures continued, reaching a total from 1946 to 1969 of 1,312 ships and 11,974 fishermen and leading to the death of 32 Japanese.

Many Japanese had opposed normalizing relations with the Soviet Union, but the business community hoped normalization would spur increased trade. After almost total extinction during the U.S. occupation, commercial relations in the Soviet Union resumed after Japan regained independence. Soviet suppliers shipped small amounts of coal, lumber, and various metal ores, but none of Japan's top trading firms showed much interest in establishing greater economic ties. This was in part the result of Moscow coupling prospects for more trade with political aims, hindering commerce with bureaucratic red tape, and not providing good port facilities. Even after signing its first trade agreement with Moscow in 1957, Tokyo not only resisted pressure for political concessions but followed the guidelines of the Coordinating Committee (COCOM) that the United States and Western Europe had created to restrict trade in strategic items with the Soviet bloc. Yet another barrier to improved economic relations was Moscow's testing of intercontinental ballistic missiles (ICBMs) with flights over Japan, as well as atomic test explosions showering Japan with fallout. Soviet resumption in 1961 of nuclear testing drew criticism even from the Japan Socialist Party (JSP). But the JCP announced that "since the Soviet Union is a peace force, nuclear tests are a natural defensive measure. . . . The main danger is not fallout, but that nuclear war will be unleashed by American imperialism."[2]

A STRAINED RELATIONSHIP

For "the vast majority of Japanese," one observer reported in 1961, the Soviet Union's "ideology has remained repulsive, its behavior aggressive and its general aspect frightening."[3] Prime Minister Ikeda Hayato, however, did not dismiss the possibility of exploiting the Soviet market for rising amounts of Japanese manufactured goods. In addition, he saw opportunities for joint ventures to develop Soviet natural gas, coal, iron ore, and copper. In 1962 he approved the visit to Moscow of a business delegation to discuss possible investment in Siberia, an area in which Japan had shown an economic interest for nearly a century. Soviet foreign minister Anastas Mikoyan visited Tokyo later that year, presenting a proposal to purchase $350 million in Japanese machinery if Tokyo agreed to defer payments for ten years. He offered as an incentive Japanese access to Siberian oil, but Ikeda rejected these terms. In 1964 Soviet premier Nikita Khrushchev offered to return Shikotan and the Habomais if U.S. troops withdrew from Japan and Okinawa. There was little chance of Japan accepting this offer after the pro-American Sato Eisaku became prime minister later that year. In July 1965, his foreign minister silenced optimists when he publicly expressed pessimism about increased trade with the Soviet Union.

Japanese protests against U.S. military operations in Vietnam prompted the Soviet Union to seek expanded influence in Japanese politics, although its split with the People's Republic of China (PRC) complicated these efforts. In August 1963, the JCP rejected a JSP resolution endorsing the recently signed Nuclear Test Ban Treaty at the Hiroshima Atomic Bomb Conference, instead supporting the PRC in denouncing it as a means to ensure Soviet and American domination of world affairs. The Soviet Union publicly praised the JSP for backing the Test Ban Treaty, opposing the Vietnam War, demanding the U.S. return of Okinawa, criticizing visits of U.S. nuclear submarines to Japan, and condemning the security treaties with the United States. Moscow and the JSP joined in creating the Japan-Soviet Friendship Society and the Society for Japanese-Soviet Relations in 1965. Thereafter, the JSP lobbied for talks to expand trade, as well as exploit opportunities for economic development in Siberia. In response, Sato backed the creation of the Japan-Soviet Economic Committee (JSEC) to meet annually to devise plans for expanding trade and fostering the economic development of Siberia. He then dispatched his foreign minister to Moscow in January 1966 for discussions resulting in the signing of a two-year civil aviation deal and a five-year trade agreement. Subsequent negotiations caused lowered expectations because the Soviets wanted more capital investment and longer repayment terms than Japan was prepared to grant.

Moscow sent a trade mission to Japan in January 1968 to resume talks on economic cooperation. Tokyo insisted on steps to end its adverse trade balance with the Soviet Union and the "Northern Territories" dispute while refusing to defer Soviet payments on the purchase of consumer goods. Although discussions stalled regarding oil and gas projects, in June 1968 negotiators signed the first agreement for Siberian development, providing for exploiting forest resources along the Amur River. Also, Japan agreed to a loan of $133 million with repayment over five years at 5.8 percent interest for Moscow to buy Japanese machinery, with Tokyo agreeing to spend an equal amount on Soviet lumber products. A new trade deal in March 1969 provided for more Soviet imports from Japan to close the trade gap, but COCOM restrictions against the Soviet Union limited the extent of its impact. Furthermore, differing expectations made significant major progress on joint Siberian economic development virtually impossible. "To the Soviets," U.S. foreign service officer David I. Hitchcock Jr. wrote at that time, "it appears to mean above all, very large, soft, capital loans, primarily to strengthen the Soviet economy and secondarily to help improve relations with Japan vis-à-vis both China and the U.S.; to the Japanese, it appears to mean more Soviet purchases of Japanese exports, improved prospects for the settlement of territorial and fishing disputes, and a foot in the door of Siberia, in case of future shortages of natural resources."[4]

Soviet-Japanese economic cooperation in the 1960s reflected the uneven pattern of postwar relations between Moscow and Tokyo. Starting in 1969, Japan identified the disputed "Northern Territories" on maps as Japanese territory. That year, Moscow approved Japanese air flights to Europe across Siberia, coinciding with the completion of cable service between Japan and Nahodka. Then in August the Soviets sank a Japanese boat, resulting in the death of 11 fishermen. Nevertheless, by 1971 Soviet-Japanese trade had reached $1 billion in value, although no major Japanese producer relied for success on access to Soviet raw materials or markets. Thereafter, Japan's interest in economic cooperation with the Soviet Union diminished not only because it saw Moscow as a bad risk but because it feared that Moscow would use profit from economic development to fund greater military capabilities. Indeed, Soviet military expansion in East Asia after U.S. withdrawal from Vietnam created growing anxiety in Japan. In 1978 Japan's normalization of relations with the PRC brought Soviet-Japanese relations to a new low when Tokyo spurned a Soviet offer to return Shikotan and the Habomais if it nullified the treaty. Moscow then increased the Soviet population and expanded military fortifications on the Kuriles. In response, Japan strengthened its defenses on Hokkaido.

Soviet-Japanese relations further deteriorated after Moscow's invasion of Afghanistan late in 1979, as the SDF participated in joint military exercises with the United States. Early in 1981 Japan's government named February 7 "Northern Territories Day" to apply pressure on the Soviets to return the disputed islands. Nakasone Yasuhiro, after becoming prime minister late in 1982, took united action with the United States against the Soviet Union in world affairs. Withholding funds for Siberian development, he even expelled Soviet diplomats on charges of spying. Nakasone reacted with caution after 1985 to reforms that new Soviet leader Mikhail Gorbachev enacted. Then in early 1986, for the first time in ten years, the Soviet foreign minister visited Toyko. He wanted a long-term trade deal, but because he would not discuss the "Northern Territories" dispute, Japan was unresponsive. Nor was there progress on trade or fisheries, but Moscow agreed to allow Japanese citizens to visit family grave sites in the Kuriles. Responding to a suggestion from Gorbachev for an exchange of visits, Nakasone invited him to come to Tokyo in March 1987, but turmoil after the Reykjavik summit conference forced postponement. Japan then distanced itself once again from Moscow after the

United States protested Toshiba Company's sale of military technology to the Soviets, leaving Japanese-Soviet relations more estranged than ever as the Cold War came to an end.

CHINESE CHECKER

Washington's decision to transform Japan into a bulwark in Asia against Communist expansion complicated an already troubled Sino-Japanese relationship. When Mao Zedong declared establishment, on October 1, 1949, of a Communist government in China, Prime Minister Yoshida resisted U.S. pressure to join in containing the PRC. Although they were openly critical of U.S. efforts to isolate Beijing, Yoshida and his political associates cooperated in creating an anti-Communist bloc that comprised Japan, the United States, and other pro-American governments in Southeast Asia. This accommodation brought criticism, particularly from opposition parties on the left. To pacify its critics, the Yoshida government relaxed trade restrictions on the PRC early in 1950, resulting by June in total value reaching $59.2 million and restoring Japan's prewar reliance on China for large amounts of iron ore, coal, soybeans, and salt. But then the start of the Korean War had a dramatic impact on Japan's relations with the PRC. After Chinese military intervention late in November 1950, the United States, coinciding with its decision to halt its own trade with China, began imposing restrictions on Sino-Japanese trade that lasted until the early 1970s. The Mutual Defense Assistance Control Act of 1951 denied U.S. aid to any nation not complying with these limitations.

During 1952 the United States organized the China Committee (CHINCOM) (an organization that paralleled COCOM, but with 200 more embargoed items) to supervise trade sanctions against the PRC. Washington made it a virtual condition for Japan to regain sovereignty that it not only comply with CHINCOM guidelines but also shun the PRC. In a letter to John Foster Dulles in December 1951, Yoshida formally agreed to the trade boycott. This contradicted his previously stated position that China's new government did not pose a threat to Japan. Also, he had seen China as Japan's natural market and trade with the PRC as a way to break its alliance with the Soviet Union. But under his new policies the value of Sino-Japanese trade declined by 1952 to an anemic $19.5 million. Angering Beijing, Japan then signed a treaty in April 1952 with the Republic of China (ROC) recognizing Chiang Kai-shek's Guomindang government that had fled to Taiwan late in 1949. Business leaders opposed recognition but wanted a restoration of economic ties with Mainland China. Many political leaders agreed, forming a Trade Promotion Dietmen's League to urge the relaxation of export limits and a liberalized travel policy. After half the Diet joined this group, in June 1952 Yoshida sanctioned the first private trade agreement between official PRC agencies and private Japanese trade associations. Beijing welcomed the chance to improve relations, hoping to promote economic recovery and to weaken Japanese links with Taiwan.

Two additional Sino-Japanese trade deals occurred in 1953 and 1954. Then prime minister Hatoyama acted positively to expand trade with the PRC. He dispatched leading industrialist Takasaki Tatsunosuke, his director of the Economic Planning Agency, to the Bandung Conference in 1955 to meet the PRC's foreign minister, Zhou Enlai. This resulted in agreements for the release of Japanese prisoners of war in China (even though Beijing classified them as war criminals), and on fishing rights. When Kishi became prime minister, he stated in 1957 his desire to expand trade with China, but without weakening the unity and security of the "Free World." He relaxed travel restrictions to Mainland China in July while removing from the embargoed list iron, steel, ships, machinery, rolling stock, and vehicles. That year, Japan's trade with the PRC reached a value of $144.7 million, compared to $147.8 million with Taiwan. Rising Cold War tensions made achieving a fourth private trade deal difficult, but negotiators reached agreement in March 1958 despite protests from the Guomindang legislature on Taiwan. Japan's refusal to retreat would result in Chiang's government ending trade talks with Tokyo and imposing an embargo in the same month. In response, Kishi's government pledged not to recognize the PRC or allow Beijing to open a trade agency or fly its flag in Japan. This satisfied Chiang, who ended the boycott. Resumption of the trade talks led to a one-year deal with Taiwan in May 1958.

Now it was Beijing's turn to condemn the Japanese government, both in government pronouncements and in the press. It might have been possible to avoid further deterioration of relations had another explosive incident not occurred. That spring, the Japan-China Friendship Society, which arranged for tourists and private companies to visit Mainland China, held a stamp and textile exhibit at a Nagasaki department store, flying the PRC's flag outside the building. On May 1, 1958, the Guomindang embassy protested the flying of the flag; and on the following day a Japanese draftsman, evidently acting on his own initiative, pulled it down. An outburst of nationalistic fury followed in China, with Beijing blaming this "vicious provocation" and the "desecration" of its flag on the Japanese government. On May 7 a PRC warship seized 14 Japanese fishing boats and 170 fishermen about 100 miles north of Taiwan. Exactly one week after the flag incident, new Foreign Minister Chen Yi announced that Beijing did not need trade with Japan and was cancelling the March trade deal and all contracts with Japanese firms.

The trade suspension led to the value of Sino-Japanese trade plummeting to $23.4 million in 1960. Most Japanese thought trade with Mainland China was beneficial, but not at the expense of damaging Japan's ties to the United States and Taiwan.

TRADING WITH THE ENEMY

Toyko's relationship with Beijing remained chilly. Among those working to improve relations was Takasaki Tatsunosuke and LDP leader Matsumura Kenjo, who both wanted to expand trade looking toward the creation of an economic bloc in East Asia. "To them," one observer explained at the time, "China is China, revolutionary Marxism notwithstanding."[5] During their visit to Beijing in 1960, they stressed the profound sense of guilt Japan felt for waging war against China. This set the stage for private Japanese firms to negotiate unofficial or semi-official trade deals with the PRC. But Beijing required these companies to accept Zhou's three principles of (1) refusing to adopt policies hostile to China, (2) not accepting the two-China concept, and (3) urging Japan's recognition of the PRC. At first, Beijing named 48 "friendly" firms in 1960, adding 19 more in 1961 and then reaching a total of 108 in 1962. Ikeda naturally embraced this method for expanding Sino-Japanese trade because his main aim was to create outlets for Japan's rising industrial production. At his first press conference as prime minister, he urged less dependence on the United States and more open relations with the PRC.

U.S. president John F. Kennedy's opposition to Japanese moves toward recognizing the PRC, as well as criticism in Ikeda's own party from those who backed Taiwan, caused Ikeda to follow a policy toward China of *seikei bunri*, or consciously separating politics from economics. During 1961 the Ikeda government co-sponsored a U.S. resolution to block action on whether the PRC should join the United Nations, making the decision an "important question" requiring a two-thirds vote from UN members. After calling on the PRC to become a peace-loving nation, Ikeda dispatched representatives to Taiwan to reassure the Guomindang government that he would support only trade with Mainland China. But that same year, Japan's ambassador to the United Nations stated that Taiwan had no political control on the mainland, reflecting Japan's tacit adoption of a two-China policy. Ikeda's avoidance of confrontation with opposition parties contributed to leftist political leaders accepting what amounted to de facto normalization. Nevertheless, new JSP chair, Eda Saburo, still pressed for closer relations with the PRC. But most Japanese were noncommittal, ranking Beijing behind only the Soviets as most unfriendly toward Japan and opposing the return of Taiwan to the PRC.

Just before the Cuban Missile Crisis in October 1962, when a U.S. block-ade persuaded Moscow to remove its missiles from Cuba to avoid igniting a Soviet-American nuclear war, Ikeda invited Zhou Enlai to visit Japan. Beijing accepted, hoping to weaken Tokyo's reliance on Washington with prospects for expanded trade. In Tokyo, Zhou specified as conditions for a trade deal that Japan sever its ties with Chiang's regime and end its alliance with the United States. But evidently the world's brush with nuclear war persuaded Beijing to moderate its stand. In November 1962 an unofficial Japanese delegation visited Beijing and signed the Liao-Takasaki Memo-randum, a five-year trade agreement worth $450 million. In 1963 the largest Japanese trade fair ever was held in China. During the next decade alone, eight trade delegations visited the PRC, promoting renewed Japanese inter-est in investing in Mainland China. For example, Ohara Soichiro, owner of Kurashiki Rayon Company, negotiated a vinylon plant export deal with the PRC worth $22 million in August 1963. A motive for him was to compen-sate for the devastations of World War II, having been a veteran of the fight-ing in China. The ROC in Taipei immediately protested, threatening to cut off all economic and political ties with Japan. Yoshida, on his own initia-tive, then wrote a letter to the Guomindang government on May 30, 1964, promising that Japan would not approve Export-Import Bank loans to the PRC. Unable to pay in cash, the PRC canceled the vinylon deal after newly elected prime minister Sato Eisaku refused to reverse the decision to deny Beijing's credit request.

Sato, during his meeting with U.S. president Lyndon Johnson in 1965, discussed his desire to expand Japanese trade with the PRC, trying to act in accordance with an emerging consensus behind *jishu gaiko*, or independent diplomacy. Japan's prime minister therefore included in the Sato-Johnson communiqué of January 13, 1965, a statement of his policy commitment to separate politics and economics regarding China, meaning to retain friendly relations with Taiwan, but pursue more private ties with the PRC, especially in trade. This differed from Johnson's statement of a U.S. policy thoroughly supporting Taiwan and expressing concerns about the PRC's aspirations for expansion in Asia. Sato had distanced Japan for the first time publicly from the United States, as well as endorsing Asian nationalism. But he did reassure Johnson that Japan would not recognize the PRC. That same month, Sato declared his desire for more exchanges and greater friendship between the PRC and Japan, stating that he would pursue these objectives with prudence and without haste. But the PRC, furious with Sato's support of U.S. policy in Vietnam, made it clear that there could be no normalization with Sato or any of his followers leading Japan's government. In April 1965, Beijing publicly condemned Japan as a tool of U.S. imperialism and an enemy of China.

Despite Chinese denunciations peaking that summer, Miki Takeo, Sato's foreign minister, announced in August that approval of Export-Import Bank loans would occur on a case-by-case basis. Tokyo then approved the PRC's request for credit, allowing for completion of the vinylon plant agreement, Japan's first postwar project in China. Soon thereafter, this source of credit financed 15 percent of all Sino-Japanese trade, elevating the PRC from Japan's twenty-fifth largest trading partner in 1946 to fourth in 1965. That year, Beijing greeted Japanese economic delegations, technical experts, industrial exhibits, and cultural missions while the Sato government approved creation of a special travel agency in Tokyo specifically to arrange tours to China. Pressure from businessmen and even conservatives for greater trade with the PRC brought more active discussion of the need to recognize the PRC. But Sato's success in separating politics from economics prompted one writer in January 1966 to observe that for Japan, diplomatic normalization with the PRC "needs no immediate solution nor should it be solved hastily."[6] In 1966, however, the Great Proletarian Cultural Revolution in China ended progress toward better relations. When Sato sent his foreign minister to Beijing, Zhou made further economic cooperation contingent on Japan halting trade and investment in Taiwan and South Korea, barring arms exports to the United States for use in Vietnam, and prohibiting joint ventures with U.S. companies.

Sato's response to Chinese militancy was predictable. Before the Diet, he reiterated his firm support for close ties with the United States and urged the PRC to stop its testing of nuclear weapons. During his trip to the United States in 1967, Sato declared publicly that the PRC was a common enemy of Japan and the United States. That year, he stopped in Taiwan as part of his tour of Southeast Asia, bringing denunciations from Beijing. This made the negotiation of a one-year extension of the Sino-Japanese trade deal difficult, especially after the PRC arrested Japanese journalists and businessmen in China, allegedly for spying. Beijing then cancelled 40 Japanese economic development projects, including proposals for a textile and a fertilizer plant. During the Cultural Revolution the number of Japanese trade representatives working in China declined from 100 to 20. In 1967 Beijing charged Japan with joining the United States and the Soviet Union in a plot to control Asia after Tokyo acquired nuclear weapons. That year, a majority of the Japanese people named the PRC as the nation they disliked most in the world.

NORMALIZATION OF RELATIONS

Washington's decision to deescalate military operations in Vietnam after 1968 combined with the end of China's Cultural Revolution to help restore stability in Sino-Japanese relations. Sato's departure removed an important barrier to Japan's normalization of relations with the PRC. More important was President Richard M. Nixon's decision to reverse the Cold War policy of isolating Beijing and backing Chiang's government on Taiwan. In July 1971, Nixon announced that he would visit the PRC in 1972, hoping to gain Beijing's cooperation in an orderly U.S. withdrawal from Vietnam and to exploit the Sino-Soviet split for Washington's advantage. This embarrassed Sato because Nixon had not informed him of his plans to seek a reconciliation. But Tokyo should not have been surprised, because Washington had been moving toward relaxing relations, abandoning references to "Red China," and supporting a two-China solution at the United Nations. Many Japanese shared the view of one writer that "Washington and Peking played ping pong diplomacy while an inflexible Sato was still searching for a paddle."[7] Business interests were vocal in pressing the Sato government to follow Washington's lead.

In September 1972 the newly elected prime minister, Tanaka Kakuei, made a historic five-day visit to China. Upon his arrival in Beijing, he offered a vague apology for the "great inconvenience" that the Japanese had inflicted in the past on the Chinese people. This fell far short of what China expected as atonement for Japan's many acts of aggression and wartime atrocities. Tanaka then signed, however, a communiqué establishing formal diplomatic relations with the PRC while promising to terminate ties with the ROC on Taiwan. He also stated that Japan "understands and respects" Beijing's position that Taiwan was a part of China. In return, Zhou agreed that the communiqué would not mention either Japan's treaty or its trade links with Taiwan. Both nations agreed to negotiations for a future treaty of peace and friendship. Tanaka's achievement of reconciliation with Beijing silenced critics of Sato's China policy and also gained leverage for Japan in negotiations with the Soviet Union. Japan closed its embassy in Taipei in November. Tokyo opened an office in Beijing in January 1973, with the PRC reciprocating in Tokyo the following month. After approval of Export-Import Bank loans and an oil import agreement with PRC, Sino-Japanese trade grew in value by 83 percent from 1972 to 1973 and exceeded $2 billion in value, an amount now larger than that with Taiwan. But Sino-Japanese talks for full normalization proceeded slowly, largely because Tokyo refused to cut all its ties with Taiwan as Beijing demanded.

Soviet leader Leonid Brezhnev and Chinese leader Mao Zedong compete for economic development aid from Japan. *Far Eastern Economic Review*, March 19, 1973.

A major reason for Tanaka's reluctance to sever contacts with Taipei was that Japanese trade with Taiwan during the 1960s had averaged about $500 million annually. Also, he did not want to lose either the financial returns Taiwan generated for Japan from tourism or the profits for Japan Airlines (JAL). Growing charges of corruption against Tanaka also meant that he could not afford to alienate supporters of the Guomindang in the Diet. After Tanaka returned from Beijing in the fall of 1972, Foreign Minister Ohira Masayoshi declared that Taiwan's flag no longer represented a government, bringing an immediate protest from Taipei. His efforts to appease the ROC led early in 1974 to Ohira arranging a compromise providing for Taiwan to operate in Japan under a private designation, but Taipei rejected this plan and insisted on recognition as a government. To force compliance, Chiang's government threatened to end all airline flights between Japan and Taiwan. When Tanaka stood firm, the ROC terminated air rights in April 1974, resulting in losses to JAL of $33.3 million during the next year. Taiwan thus had reemerged in 1975 as a "major divisive issue"[8] for the LDP, forcing Tanaka, then under attack for corruption, to initiate a frantic search for a solution. Japan's issuance of a careful statement that the flag of Taiwan represented a country, rather than a government, brought resumption of air service in September 1975. Trade, investment, and tourism with Taiwan boomed for the rest of the decade.

Tokyo and Beijing negotiated a number of new plant and technology deals following normalization that resulted in fuller exploitation of complementary economies. After mutually granting most-favored-nation status in trade, the PRC and Japan signed cooperative agreements covering airflights, shipping, and fishing rights. To meet its energy needs, Japan wanted to exploit the PRC's offshore oil resources, but an emerging dispute over the disposition of the Senkaku Islands northeast of Taiwan slowed progress toward an oil deal. Another problem was Beijing's insistence on including in a treaty of peace and friendship with Tokyo a clause condemning the alleged Soviet drive for "hegemony," or domination, in the Pacific. Beijing showed its desire for an agreement when it accepted Japan's control over the Senkakus. To further isolate the Soviet Union and enhance the PRC's influence in Northeast Asia, Beijing's new leader, Deng Xiaoping, dropped his hostile rhetoric toward new Japanese prime minister Fukuda Takeo and assumed a flexible stand on the anti-hegemony clause. Trade talks resumed, and, on February 16, 1978, Japan and the PRC signed an eight-year, $20 billion trade deal for the construction of industrial factories, the sharing of technical knowledge, and the purchase of construction machinery with low-interest loans for China to exploit its coke, oil, and steam coal resources. Another agreement finalized during the next year provided for extracting offshore oil in and around the Senkakus.

Meanwhile, former prime minister Kishi mobilized supporters of Taiwan in the Diet behind a demand for resolving the Senkakus issue as part of the peace and friendship treaty. Irritated and embarrassed about Tokyo raising the issue, the PRC sent 80 armed fishing boats to the Senkakus in April 1978, resulting in another suspension of negotiations. When Japan refused to be intimidated, Beijing withdrew most of the ships. Fukuda minimized the importance of the clash, and Deng sent an apology for this "accident" to Tokyo. Sino-Japanese negotiations reopened in July, and on August 12, 1978, the PRC and Japan signed a Treaty of Peace and Friendship, thereby completing the normalization process. A key provision of the accord stated that both nations opposed attempts for hegemony in Asia and did not seek this objective. Thereafter, the two nations negotiated deals for Japanese construction of a steel plant in China and help in modernizing oil refineries, power plants, and rail and port facilities there. The value of trade increased from $3.4 billion in 1977 to $5 billion in 1978, largely the result of greater Japanese purchases of oil from the PRC. Tokyo had calculated that Moscow so urgently needed economic ties with Japan that it would not act on its threats of retaliation. Japan's gamble succeeded, as the Sino-Japanese treaty had no negative impact on Soviet-Japan relations, although Moscow did continue its expansion of Soviet military power in Asia and the Pacific.

SEARCH FOR STABILITY

Ogata Sadako, an authority on Japan's role in world affairs, wrote in 1965 that the Japanese attitude toward China was "a mixture of fear, disdain, and a sense of kinship."[9] By then the PRC was a united and powerful state bent on gaining industrial power to complement its military strength and extend China's political influence throughout Asia. Yet many Japanese still referred to the Chinese as *chankoro*, or "pigtailed fellows," reflecting attitudes of racial superiority. China, however, was neither a foreign nor an alien land, but a nation that had close geographic and cultural ties with Japan. Naturally, the political disruptions of the Cultural Revolution in China troubled the Japanese, who feared the spread of political radicalism to Japan. Anxiety grew in the late 1960s as Communist leaders of the Zengakuren, a student organization, persuaded its members to participate in a series of demonstrations against U.S. military action in Vietnam. Student uprisings occurred on many college campuses, including a five-month strike at Waseda University. In January 1969 the government sent police to restore order at Tokyo University.

Student radicals eventually became frustrated with their ineffectiveness in changing Japan's political system, causing many to embrace more direct and dramatic forms of violent protest. Left-wing terrorist groups had been active in Japan after the end of U.S. occupation, attempting to overturn the postwar system and align Japan with the Communist world. These terrorist groups joined to form the Red Army Faction, which emerged in 1968 as a branch of the Zengakuren. In the following year it became independent and changed its name to the United Red Army, or Sekigunha. Seeking a world Communist revolution, the vast majority of its members would follow rules without any questions. In 1971 and 1972 the United Red Army attracted elite university students and resorted to violent attacks against the state, such as bombings, post office and bank robberies, and airplane highjackings. Another terrorist group, the Japanese Red Army (Nihon Sekigun), split from the United Red Army in 1972. Young members would receive training in Beirut, Lebanon, on how to become revolutionaries, learning after seven weeks of instruction how to die for their cause. The Japanese Red Army developed close ties with the Palestinian Popular Front for the Liberation of Palestine, remaining active for the remainder of the decade.

These Red Army groups saw themselves as operating in a global context, claiming to be a part of the international vanguard for world revolution. The Red Army highjacked a JAL plane in November 1970, forcing it to land in North Korea. The group staged another highjacking during 1973. On May 30, 1972, three members of the Japanese Red Army launched a grenade and machine gun attack at the Lod Airport in Israel, resulting in the killing of 26 people and the wounding of 70 others. The Red Army's domestic network suffered a major blow that year, when government agents surrounded a number of its members in a mountain redoubt about 100 miles north of Tokyo and forced them to surrender. Thereafter, factionalism divided the group, as many of its adherents shifted activities to fighting pollution. When members of the Japanese Red Army tortured and killed 14 innocent Japanese, this terrorist group seemed comprised of lunatics in pursuit of unrealistic political goals. In 1974 Japanese terrorists highjacked a ferry in Singapore and seized the French embassy in The Hague. The Japanese Red Army's subsequent terrorist acts included the occupation in 1975 of the U.S. and Swedish embassies in Kuala Lumpur, Malaysia. The group's highjacking of a JAL plane in Bombay in 1977 sought to secure the release of the group's imprisoned comrades in Japan. But its efforts only discredited radicalism in Japan.

Japan's government downplayed allegations that Beijing had encouraged the activities of these terrorist groups. Instead, Tokyo focused attention on other signals of the PRC's desire for closer economic cooperation, such as Deng's visit to Japan in October 1978. Japan also lauded Beijing's decision not to renew its 1950 treaty with the Soviet Union in 1979. By then, Japan had committed private and official means to assist the PRC with capital and technology to implement its modernization plans. Designating the PRC as an investment priority in 1979, Japan extended credit mainly for railroad and port construction. Beijing also secured loans for a petrochemical plant at Daqing, an iron mill at Baoshan, a hospital in Beijing, and an agricultural technical assistance project in northeastern China. Annual trade now topped $9 billion, as China provided Japan with oil, coal, and other resources. But then, as a result of disagreement within the Communist Party leadership regarding the pace of economic liberalization, China voided its trade agreement with Japan, canceling some of its economic development projects. It also suspended orders with Japan for equipment and plant construction vital to the success of the PRC's ten-year economic development program. Beijing's inability to pay for its grandiose economic plans led to disappointment and dismay in Japan's business community. Renegotiation efforts ceased in January 1981 after Tokyo refused to make concessions that Beijing demanded for trade and investment in China.

New prime minister Suzuki Zenko attended three summits with Beijing's leaders after taking office in July 1980, resulting in the resumption of talks about the Senkakus. Reflecting improved relations, the PRC secured modest government and private loans from Japan and accepted foreign aid. In 1982 the PRC was Japan's top recipient of Office of Development Assistance (ODA). But that year, a new dispute threatened Sino-Japanese cooperation when a Tokyo newspaper reported that the Japanese Ministry of Education was planning to approve a textbook revision referring to Japan's invasion of China in 1937 as an "all round advance into China" while attributing the Nanjing Massacre of 1938 (when occupying Japanese soldiers killed thousands of Chinese civilians) to the "stubborn resistance of the Chinese troops." In response, Beijing sent angry official protests to Tokyo and initiated a media campaign in China criticizing Japanese "reactionaries" for distorting the historical record. After Japanese publishers withdrew the revisions in September 1982 the controversy died down, but it resumed in June 1985 when a new Japanese textbook claimed that it was the Chinese government's provocation in 1937 that had ignited the Sino-Japanese War. Then, one year later, the Minister of Education stated publicly that during the War Crimes Trials after World War II, the Allied Tribunal's conviction of wartime Prime Minister Tojo Hideki as a war criminal was wrong and that the Nanjing Massacre was merely a consequence of war. These events sparked new anti-Japanese student demonstrations in China.

Prime Minister Nakasone quickly acted to repair the damage, cancelling his scheduled visit to the Yasukuni Shrine where Japan's military war dead were enshrined, removing his education minister, and promising no further textbook revisions. But he invited the harsh press criticism he then received for this retreat because he had been urging the Japanese to acknowledge openly not only Japan's economic power but its need to play a more active role in world politics. Beijing was not alone in raising objections. If Japan wanted to attain genuine status as a world leader, critics argued, it had to accept responsibility for its previous acts of aggression, imperialism, and war. Despite this and other acrimonious incidents, including Beijing's expulsion of Kyodo News Agency, student exchanges and tourism increased in the 1980s. The PRC also tolerated a huge trade imbalance with Japan, with deficits reaching $5.22 billion in 1985 and $5.13 billion in 1986. The situation worsened for the PRC with the fall in oil prices, its leading export. Beijing complained that Japan was happy to export its manufactured goods but was reluctant to share its technology. At one student demonstration in China, protesters referred to a "second Japanese invasion" with a character poster at Beijing University that reportedly depicted a Japanese as declaring "I used to be a Japanese imperialist, decapitating fifty people in Shenyang [during World War II], but now I am selling you color televisions."[10]

By the 1980s, "Japan's policy toward China [was] schizophrenic."[11] One could say the same about Tokyo's relationship with Moscow. Trade with the Soviets after 1982 declined sharply because of its military buildup, as Japan fell from being Moscow's second to fifth largest trading partner. Total trade value dropped that year from $5.56 billion to $4.2 in 1985. By contrast, the total value of trade with the PRC for the same years rose from $8.9 billion in 1983 to $19.5 billion, demonstrating how political controversy had more potential to damage Japan's relations with the Soviet Union than with China. An increase in political stability under Deng after 1983 attracted more Japanese investment, despite competition from Hong Kong and Taiwan, and resulted in a long-term trade deal early in 1985. Japan also wanted closer ties with Beijing to counter the Soviet military threat and agreed in 1984 to exchange intelligence. But a U.S. consulting firm seemed to understand more clearly the postwar challenge for Japan of contending with the Communists. "The major potential market is Red China," it advised. "The major potential raw material supply is Russian Siberia. The major potential customer is the U.S. All of these are important; all are in conflict with each other; all use their foreign business activities as an arm of foreign policy."[12]

NOTES

1. Paul Langer and Rodger Swearingen, "The Japanese Communist Party," *Pacific Affairs* 23 (December 1950): 351.

2. Quoted in J.A.A. Stockwin, "The Japanese Socialist Party under New Leadership," *Asian Survey* 6 (April 1966): 192.

3. James W. Morely, "Japan's Image of the Soviet Union, 1952–1961," *Pacific Affairs* 35 (Spring 1962): 58.

4. David I. Hitchcock Jr., "Joint Development of Siberia: Decision-Making in Japanese-Soviet Relations," *Asian Survey* 11 (March 1971): 295.

5. Donald C. Hellerman, "Japan's Relations with Communist China," *Asian Survey* 4 (June 1964): 1088.

6. Nobutaka Ike, "Japan, Twenty Years after Surrender," *Asian Survey* 6 (January 1966): 26.

7. Dennis T. Yasutomo, "Sato's China Policy, 1964–1966," *Asian Survey* 17 (June 1977): 530.

8. Douglas H. Mendel Jr., "Japan's Public Views of Taiwan's Future," *Asian Survey* 15 (March 1975): 115.

9. Sadako Ogata, "Japan's Attitude toward China," *Asian Survey* 5 (August 1965): 390.

10. Quoted in Paul J. Bailey, *Postwar Japan: 1945 to Present* (Cambridge, MA: Blackwell Publishers, 1996), 159.

11. Hellerman, "Japan's Relations," 1092.

12. Quoted in Robert S. Ozaki, "Japanese Views of Foreign Capital," *Asian Survey* 11 (November 1971): 1076.

Morishita Yoichi, president of Matsushita Electric Industrial Co., right, speaks to reporters, as Yamauchi Hiroshi, the president of Nintendo Co., listens during a news conference in Tokyo, May 23, 1999. Photo courtesy of AP/Wide World Photos.

Engineers and industry officials observe a new type of high-quality display screen made by Sharp Co., that can be used for television or computers. Photo courtesy of AP/Wide World Photos.

Neon signs light up a street of an entertainment district in the Ginza area of Tokyo. Photo courtesy of AP/Wide World Photos.

Sun beams peek out from thick clouds above the national main gymnasium in Yoyogi Sports Center, near the main Olympic Stadium (1964 Olympics). Photo courtesy of AP/Wide World Photos.

5

Pursuing Partners in Asia

After 1952 Japan pursued swift reentry as a respectable member into the global community as a national priority, because its economic recovery required restoration of its access to raw materials and markets for exports. Defeat in World War II had stripped Japan of its imperial possessions, resulting in major losses in investments as well as in control over mineral and agricultural resources. Making its task more daunting were the bitter memories of Japan's colonial exploitation in Korea and Southeast Asia. Tokyo learned to its surprise during the U.S. occupation that the people of Asia hated Japan. The process of reconciliation was slow and difficult, but eventually Japan established productive partnerships with its former imperial possessions. Tokyo's initial aim was to restore commercial links with Korea and in Southeast Asia, but instead it found more lucrative outlets in the industrialized nations. By the 1970s Japan had rediscovered its former colonies, making them targets of increasing amounts of aid and investment. Tokyo's economic strategy in a "region designed for Japanese domination"[1] was to build confidence in its benign intentions and ability to lead East Asia toward modernization.

ECONOMIC FENCE MENDING

Most nations in East Asia expressed reservations about the decision by the United States in the spring of 1950 to move swiftly toward achieving a peace treaty with Japan that would restore its independence. They also experienced sharp anxiety in reaction to U.S. pressure on Japan during the

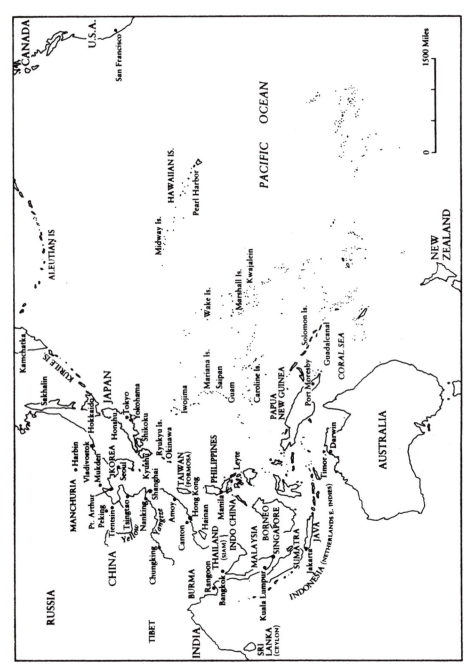

The Asia-Pacific Context

Korean War to rearm as a major priority for strengthening the Japanese-American security alliance. Nevertheless, among victims of Japanese imperialism, only Burma refused to sign the Japanese Peace Treaty, although neither Korea nor China had the chance to act on the matter. Washington's assurances of protection to Japan's neighbors were necessary to achieve this outcome, as the United States signed a security treaty with Australia and New Zealand, the ANZUS Pact of 1951, and similar agreements by 1954 with the Philippines, South Korea, and Taiwan. Washington then took the lead in forming the Southeast Asia Treaty Organization (SEATO) in 1954, ostensibly to deter Communist expansion but also to demonstrate the U.S. commitment to promote stability in the region. Thailand and the Philippines joined SEATO, but Indonesia and Burma followed India's lead of neutrality in the Cold War. Prime Minister Hatoyama saw that Japan would have trouble improving its image in Asia if it did not distance itself from the United States. Therefore, in April 1955, he sent a delegate to the Bandung Conference, where 29 nonaligned states met to mobilize support for neutralism and peaceful coexistence.

Japan's strategy for establishing friendly and productive relations with its former colonial possessions after the U.S. occupation focused on emphasizing its economic weakness while avoiding any sign of aggressive behavior. It acted quickly to satisfy the reparations demands of its Asian neighbors, complying with a provision of the Japanese Peace Treaty. Tokyo negotiated a series of agreements providing consumer goods and industrial equipment—often tied to economic assistance and loan programs—to Burma, Indonesia, Singapore, South Vietnam, and Thailand. Cambodia and Laos accepted "free technical aid" instead of formal reparations. By 1964, Japan had paid over $1 billion in reparations and $490 million in economic assistance to Burma, Indonesia, South Korea, Malaysia, Laos, Cambodia, and South Vietnam. Because economic aid often required the purchase of Japanese manufactured goods, these deals contributed significantly to Japan's economic recovery and later expansion, especially in the steel, shipbuilding, and electronics industries. Tokyo also tried to remake its image in Asia with goodwill visits and agreements for technical advice and training. Southeast Asia soon was Japan's main source of raw materials—especially lumber, iron ore, tin, and copper—restoring a pattern that had its origins in the prewar era. In return, Japan became the main supplier of machinery and transportation equipment to that region.

Prime Minister Kishi wanted to promote greater economic expansion in Japan's former colonies, pursuing a vision for Tokyo to join with Washington in the reconstruction of Asia. Mutual security, he believed, also required close economic cooperation among non-Communist nations in the Pacific.

While working to maintain Japan's alliance with the United States, Kishi initiated independent policies in Asia to promote economic development in nations not aligned with the Soviet Union or the PRC. For example, he advanced a proposal providing for the establishment of an $800 million Southeast Asian Development Fund. Japan would provide technicians and the capital goods bought with U.S. contributions to allow recipient nations to increase the output of raw materials for export. Kishi told officials in Washington that if his proposal was successful, a resumption of trade with Mainland China would be unnecessary. Striving to build cordial relations with former targets of Japanese aggression, he visited nine Southeast Asian nations in 1957, offering greater economic cooperation and a public apology for Japan's previously brutal treatment of its neighbors. Despite a broad popular consensus in support of Kishi's initiatives in Southeast Asia, by 1960 critics were charging that he was practicing an economic diplomacy that was exploitative of the resources of developing nations in Asia.

Prime Minister Ikeda's emphasis on economic development led logically to an elevation of Southeast Asia's importance as a source of raw materials and a market for Japanese manufactured goods. Thus, he tried to build on Kishi's approach of establishing cordial relations with the former targets of Japanese imperialism. In 1961 and 1963 Ikeda visited nations in Southeast Asia to help repair relations Japan had damaged during World War II. He also expanded aid to underdeveloped Asian countries to achieve secure access to natural resoures, labeling his aid program a Japanese Alliance for Progress. During the early 1960s, Tokyo signaled its willingness to share industrial and technological skills to assist new states in Asia in promoting economic development. Contributing to the success of Ikeda's policy was the support of opposition parties for his policies to establish cooperative relations with those nations that had suffered under Japanese imperial rule. From 1958 to 1963, the value of Japanese exports to underdeveloped countries grew by 60 percent to $2.55 billion, and imports received from these nations almost doubled to $2.06 billion. Japan also committed both capital and technical assistance for the development of nickel, timber, and oil in Indonesia; copper and timber in the Philippines; iron ore in Malaysia; and tin in Thailand.

COMPLICATIONS IN KOREA

No Asian nation was more reluctant to reconcile with Japan after World War II than Korea. This was because Koreans had suffered more exploitation for a longer period than any other people who were victims of Japanese imperial rule. After incorporating the Korean peninsula into its empire after

1905, Japan gained ownership of over half the land and 80 percent of Korea's industrial and commercial property. Denying Koreans any self-government, Japan also attempted to eradicate the culture, history, and language of Korea. Korea's postwar leaders reached maturity during the four decades of Japanese occupation, forming attitudes of bitter animosity and deep distrust for Japan. For them, all Japanese were arrogant and untrustworthy in word and deed. Most considered the U.S. occupation reforms cosmetic, bringing no fundamental alteration in Japan's colonialist mentality. Many Japanese confirmed these suspicions, claiming publicly that Japan actually had helped the Koreans, a people unable to rule themselves because they lacked discipline and an ability to work together, and had fulfilled a needed role in Korea's history, bringing beneficial administration and economic development.

Complicating Japan's efforts to reconcile with Korea was the partition of the nation at the end of World War II. In August 1945, officials in Washington proposed dividing the peninsula at the 38th parallel into zones of military occupation, with the Soviet Union accepting the surrender of Japan's forces in the north and the United States in the south. Korea then became a captive of the Cold War, as Washington and Moscow each sponsored creation of a government superficially reflecting its own model for social, economic, and political development. In August 1948, the Republic of Korea (ROK) under President Syngman Rhee formally regained independence, claiming authority over the north despite establishment there in the following month of the Democratic People's Republic of Korea (DPRK) under Communist leader Kim Il Sung. Washington strongly favored reconciliation between Japan and the ROK for both security and economic reasons, especially after the start of the Korean War. But Rhee had spent his entire adult life fighting the Japanese. His hatred for Japan virtually ruled out normalization of relations prior to his resignation in 1960. Other South Koreans feared that restoring relations would invite renewed Japanese economic penetration and exploitation.

A number of disputes on specific issues delayed reconciliation between Japan and the ROK after the U.S. occupation ended in 1952. First, South Korea was critical of how Koreans living in Japan were treated. Roughly 881,000 Koreans had moved to Japan during the years 1905 to 1938. Thereafter, Japan, responding to a labor shortage, forced another 800,000 Koreans to move to Japan to work in mining and war industries. In 1945 SCAP helped 940,000 Koreans return home, and private efforts resulted in the repatriation of another 600,000 people. But economic distress in postwar Korea and an absence of funds motivated approximately 640,00 Koreans to remain in Japan, where they suffered profound social, economic, and political discrimination. The Japanese regarded these Koreans as a threat to ethnic homogeniety. In 1946 SCAP took steps to confirm Japanese citizenship for resident Koreans. But once the Korean War started, Washington deferred permanent action until after the signing of a peace treaty with Japan and the normalization of relations between Japan and Korea. In April 1952, the Yoshida government adopted a policy that allowed Koreans to remain in Japan legally as resident aliens if they could produce a certificate of Korean citizenship within two years. But the law provided for deportation of any Korean not carrying a registration card, thereby allowing the government to invalidate property rights and nullify resident status.

Second, Japan refused to accept the ROK's claim to be the only lawful government on the Korean peninsula. Nor would Tokyo regard all Korean residents in Japan as citizens of the ROK rather than the DPRK. By 1953, in fact, about three-quarters of Koreans living in Japan claimed citizenship in North Korea. Third, Japan and Korea had property and damage claims against each other. Article 4 of the Japanese Peace Treaty gave retroactive approval for the U.S. Military Government's expropriation and disposition of Japanese holdings in Korea, but Tokyo asked for compensation nonetheless. Rhee countered with a demand for Japan to pay $8 billion as compensation for countless gold and art objects taken from Korea, forced labor, and lost Korean investments. Last, there were two major territorial issues. First, in January 1952, the ROK barred foreigners from fishing within 60 miles of Korea's coast, threatening violators of the so-called Rhee Line with seizure and imprisonment. Japanese fishermen who accepted exclusion from their traditional fishing grounds suffered huge financial losses, and those defying the ban were arrested and spent a year in jail. Second, Japan contested the ROK's occupation of Dokto (Takeshima), a barren, rocky, and uninhabited island, claiming it had been a Japanese possession since 1905. South Korea offered contrary evidence and adamantly refused to abandon the territory.

Tokyo and Seoul held preliminary discussions to resolve these issues in October and November 1951. South Korea claimed that the Rhee Line was necessary for its security and conservation of marine life, whereas Japan argued that it violated international law and freedom of the seas. Tokyo demanded the return of imprisoned fishermen, raising the new issue of compensation for Japanese vessels confiscated in Korean waters in 1945. But South Korea defiantly rejected Tokyo's requests, expressing disbelief that Japan, loser in World War II, could be so demanding. Reacting with moral indignation, the ROK pointed to Tokyo's intransigence as proof that the Japanese still were shameless, arrogant, and brazen. Koreans thought Japan needed to atone for its past sins with not only a public apology but submissiveness and concessions in negotiations. As Professor Lee

Hui-sung wrote in 1961 in an open letter to Japanese intellectuals, "Japan must take a positive step toward absolving all the long-drawn aggressive thoughts and actions of the past. . . . [Because] if they had reflected on the thirty-six years of national bondage, the bitter sufferings, and hardship of the 25,000,000 Korean people, they could not begin to utter any accusations against Korea."[2] Criticizing the Japanese as cunning and clever, South Korea suspended the talks in 1953.

A TWO-KOREA POLICY

A mutual desire to support U.S. security policy in Asia led to a reopening of negotiations between Japan and South Korea for a formal peace treaty in the spring of 1958. Talks resulted in the ROK releasing the last imprisoned Japanese fisherman. In May 1960 a new government took power in South Korea, with the new leaders being less emotionally and dogmatically hostile to Japan. But political instability under Rhee's immediate successors delayed progress toward Japanese-Korean normalization because Japan had no confidence in the South Korean government's ability to achieve ratification of a treaty, let alone fulfill terms of the agreement. Pak Chung-hui's seizure of power in a military coup in 1961 altered the situation decisively, meeting Japan's need for stable leadership in the ROK. But many Japanese opposed reconciliation with South Korea. Both the JSP and the JCP lobbied for close relations with North Korea and opposed a treaty with the ROK. Trade and investment in South Korea, leftist politicians complained, would expand its economy and military power, resulting in strengthened U.S. imperialism and a weakened Communist movement in Asia. The JSP also opposed a treaty with Seoul because it would prevent the reunification of Korea while linking Japan with South Korea and Taiwan in an alliance against the PRC. Finally, normalized relations with Japan would help stabilize the repressive government of Pak Chung-hui, who leftists with justification denounced as a fascist military dictator.

During 1964 a series of events aroused security concerns in Japan and accelerated the process toward reconciliation. Among these were the PRC's first nuclear test and U.S. military escalation in Vietnam. That year, Sato Eisaku replaced Ikeda and called for normalizing relations with South Korea as part of his strategy to build more economic growth and closer relations with the United States. During January 1965, Japanese-Korean negotiations began in earnest and progressed steadily. Seoul's formal abolition of the Rhee Line that spring opened the way to a final settlement. Signed in June, the Treaty of Basic Relations between Japan and the Republic of Korea provided for the nullification of prior treaties, mutual exchange of envoys and ambassadors, and establishment of diplomatic and consular relations. Provisions included Japan's commitment to provide the ROK with $200 million in long-term, low interest loans; $300 million in goods and services over 10 years; and $300 million in commercial loans to build South Korea's economy. A key provision provided that those Koreans living in Japan before 1945 and their descendents would receive permanent resident status, as well as a promise of adequate educational opportunities and equal treatment. In 1957 Tokyo had dropped its demand for property compensation, so the treaty was silent on this issue. Both nations accepted a 12-mile limit on fishing rights.

North Korea retaliated against Japan for signing the treaty with its rival, cutting all contacts in 1966, as exports from Japan plummeted to one-fourth of the 1965 level. This ended the DPRK's prior policy of using trade with Japan as leverage for building closer political ties. Pyongyang, in contrast to Seoul, had shown greater hatred for the ROK than Japan, as North Korea's Kim Il Sung after 1948 made the United States a new main target of attacks on imperialism and war. In May 1955, the first official contact occurred to discuss trade, after Kim Il Sung extended fishing rights off North Korea's coast to the Japanese. That October, a joint communiqué committed Tokyo and Pyongyang to promote greater private cooperation on trade, travel, and fishing. But the Hatoyama government then announced that it would "not recognize any personal or material exchanges" with the DPRK. Pyongyang nevertheless maintained for the rest of the decade its "people's diplomacy" and expanded quasi-official contacts. This led to expanded trade, reaching a value for Japan of 70 million yen in exports and 6 million yen in imports by 1959. Japan then approved a repatriation deal with North Korea, ending for "humanitarian reasons" its official policy of not recognizing exchanges. The ROK condemned as "immoral" and "opportunist" Tokyo's decision to allow trade in approved goods, but it could not stop the rise in total value of Japan's trade with North Korea from $9 million in 1962 to $30 million in 1964.

North Korea also wanted Japanese help to industrialize, offering in 1961 to buy a thermoelectric plant and two large freighters from Japan. Tokyo did not approve these deals, fearing that they might alienate both South Korea and the United States. In 1965 Pyongyang inquired about purchasing plants for generating thermal power, producing iron and steel, and refining metal. By that year Tokyo and Pyongyang had extended the repatriation agreement three times, resulting in 93,360 Koreans returning to North Korea to help implement its five-year economic development plan. But Pyongyang warned Japan not to establish diplomatic ties with South Korea before reunification. Responding with predictable hostility to Japan's treaty with South Korea in 1965, the DPRK demanded a separate agreement. Japan's two-Korea policy had problems—for example, leaving uncertain the application of deportation provisions for those Koreans living in Japan who were loyal to North Korea. Tokyo angered Seoul when it rejected asylum for a North Korean boxer who defected to its embassy in Cambodia in December 1966; he was returned to the DPRK. That year, Pyongyang renewed the repatriation deal, persuading more Koreans to return to North Korea with promises of steady jobs, free education, and security—to the embarrassment of South Korea. Koreans who stayed in Japan remained a source of diplomatic discord because they were unskilled, suffering from a low living standard and racial discrimination.

RELUCTANT RECONCILIATION

During the U.S. occupation, compensating targets of previous Japanese military aggression had been an important objective. U.S. planners anticipated that Japan would recapture its old markets in Asia after 1945, although the Cold War caused the United States to restrict Japan's economic contacts with North Korea and China after the Communists took power. Contrary to these expectations, Japanese economic policy during the postwar period focused increasingly on exploiting markets in industrialized countries, while Japan's trade with Asia actually declined. In 1946 Asian states received 64 percent of Japan's exports and provided 53 percent of its imports. By 1969 these levels had declined to 34 percent and 30.4 percent, respectively. Prior to 1965, Tokyo focused on negotiating reparations agreements to rebuild trust with its former colonial possessions. Thereafter, Sato initiated a strategy to provide aid, investment, and advice to expand trade and regional economic development. His efforts contributed to the creation of the Asian and Pacific Council (ASPAC) with Japan as an original member, but South Korea, Taiwan, and the Philippines wanted to form a military alliance in the Pacific. Most nations in Southeast Asia, however, saw this as inviting conflict and delaying prosperity. The Cold War thus provided another reason for the nations of Southeast Asia to be cautious in accepting reconciliation with their former overlord, because Japan was now a close ally of the United States.

Japanese leaders found that regaining a prominent place in postwar Asia would be difficult. In January 1967, U.S. ambassador to Japan Edwin Reischauer identified a key shift in Tokyo's policy in reaction to persistent hostility and fear toward Japan in East Asia. "The Japanese have for the first time since the war," he reported, "begun to look at the problems of defense and their relationships with neighboring countries, not in terms of how Japan should react to American or Communist contentions, but in terms of Japan's own interest and goals."[3] Miki Takeo, serving as Sato's foreign minister from 1966 to 1968, implemented an "Asia-Pacific Concept" aimed at expanding Japan's regional role to coincide with its growing economic power. His plan called for Japan to expand its investment in Asia and serve as a mediator between underdeveloped nations and industrialized countries in the Pacific, notably the United States, Canada, Australia, and New Zealand. In July 1966, the Sato government persuaded the Diet to approve Japan's membership in the Asian Development Bank, joining 31 other countries. Funded initially at $1 billion, the 19 members from Asia contributed roughly 60 percent of that amount. Japan's initial pledge of $200 million was the largest, equaling that of the United States. Many Japanese were upset that the Bank's headquarters would be in Manila rather than Tokyo, but its first president, named to a five-year term, was Takeshi Watanabe, a Japanese expert on international finance.

In 1967 Sato toured Southeast Asia to demonstrate Japan's support for economic integration to promote development and prosperity in the region, visiting Burma, Malaysia, Singapore, Thailand, Indonesia, South Vietnam, Laos, the Philippines, Australia, and New Zealand. Sato believed personal diplomacy not only would publicize Japan's desire for economic leadership but also promote political stability. In Thailand, however, he repeated his firm support for U.S. military operations from that country against Vietnam, reviving fears of a remilitarized Japan in Southeast Asia. Predictably, when Thailand, the Philippines, Malaysia, Indonesia, and Singapore created the Association of Southeast Asian Nations, or ASEAN, on August 9, 1967, they denied membership to Japan. This organization's purpose was to promote political stability and economic development in the region, which the initial members thought would be possible only if ASEAN avoided alignment in the Cold War. Another source of friction was Japan's recognition of the ROC on Taiwan, which many in Southeast Asia viewed as a provocation toward the PRC. A Japanese colony known as Formosa from 1895 to 1945, Taiwan had experienced full integration into the imperial system, facilitating Japanese postwar economic penetration of the island. Under Sato, in an effort to support the U.S. goal of strengthening its allies in Asia, Japan increased its investment in Taiwan, reaching a total value of $200 million in 1966.

Although Sato's support for Taiwan and the U.S. war in Vietnam after 1965 alienated many leaders in Southeast Asia, it won support in the Republic of Korea, contributing to a steady expansion of Japanese economic interests in South Korea. After normalization in 1965, Japanese business and industry engaged in keen competition for investment in the ROK. By

1966 new plant contracts amounted to $800 million in value, and private loans and credit totaled $127 million. That year, Japanese exports to South Korea reached $205 million, second only to that of the United States. When the ROK government refused to approve contracts with companies that had dealings with North Korea, few Japanese firms objected. Japanese trade grew in importance to the point that 40 percent of imports to the ROK in 1969 came from Japan. Economic harmony between Japan and South Korea peaked under Sato, as Tokyo pledged $100 million in loans to South Korea in 1970 and approved $80 million in financing to build the Seoul subway in 1971. South Koreans skillfully exploited Japan's guilt about colonialism to increase aid and trade, although Tokyo would not admit publicly that its previous actions had been immoral or illegal. Yet Japanese trade with the DPRK also continued, as did Tokyo's refusal to recognize all its Korean residents as citizens of the ROK. From 1965 to 1979, Japan nevertheless provided South Korea with $610 million in investments, $1.13 billion in credit, and $2.4 billion in loans.

Meanwhile, the United States had begun to withdraw troops in Vietnam, following President Nixon's announcement in July 1969 that the nations of East Asia no longer should expect protection from U.S. ground forces in the event of war. Japan made plain in its response to this so-called Nixon Doctrine that it had no intention of replacing the United States in defending Asia through collective security. Sato toured Southeast Asia again in 1969, visiting Burma, Thailand, Malaysia, and five other nations. His speeches stressed admiration for nationalism in these countries and a desire for closer economic relations. That year, Southeast Asia was the recipient of 83 percent of Japan's bilateral aid and 79 percent of the total transfer of private capital goods. By the end of the 1960s Japan had become either the first or second trading partner of every nation in the region except Cambodia. In May 1970 Sato attended the Fifth Southeast Asia Conference in Djakarta, Indonesia. This was the first time Japan participated in a regional meeting since World War II. There, Sato promised 1 percent of Japan's GNP, or $4 billion, in aid to Southeast Asia over five years, trying again to fulfill a pledge he had made in 1965. Japan's reason for providing economic aid therefore differed from that of the United States. Whereas Washington's primary concern was to advance its strategic objectives, Tokyo wanted to serve its economic interests.

But awareness among the Japanese was growing that protection of Japan's expansive commercial and economic interests precluded a continuation of passivity. Polls found respondents willing to endorse a more active role in fostering regional peace, but only through the United Nations. Conservatives also disliked Japan's continued role in world affairs as a junior partner to the United States. Sato agreed, becoming the first Japanese prime minister to address the United Nations. He hinted at Japan's desire to join the Security Council and raised the level of his nation's contribution to the International Monetary Fund. In 1969 Japan participated in joint naval exercises with Australia and Malaysia, and a Japanese naval squadron cruised through the Malacca Straits for the first time since World War II. But Tokyo moved cautiously, not wanting to exacerbate lingering fears of Japanese militarism and colonialism. Japan's overriding objective was to guarantee a constant supply of raw materials and to secure export markets to fund imports. Energy needs also motivated rising investments in oil production in the Mideast, Asia, and North America. In 1973 two observers concluded that the "motivation of the Japanese investor is almost always to obtain some degree of lasting control over, or continuing connection with, the foreign operation. For example, loans have been made for the development of nickel mines in Australia and iron ore in Brazil, which will be repaid to Japan in the form of shipments of the metals."[4]

Many Asians, however, resented Japan's tremendous economic success of the 1960s. By 1970 its national wealth dwarfed that of Southeast Asia. For example, Japan's per capita income was 10 times greater and its GNP more than all nations in that region combined. Tokyo recognized the necessity to boost economic development in Southeast Asia and saw ASEAN as a logical partner, providing both counsel and advice after 1970. The Sato government also pressed companies to invest more there to improve infrastructure and communications. Japan concentrated 15.6 percent of its total investment overseas in 1971 in ASEAN, increasing the level to 36.4 percent over the next five years. Japan soon was importing from Southeast Asia 93 percent of its requirements for tin, 90 percent of rubber, and 40 percent of copper, timber, and bauxite. Under Prime Minister Tanaka, Japan sought to expand its economic penetration of the region, normalizing relations in 1973 with a united Vietnam. Tokyo also developed cordial relations with Australia, spurring expanded trade that reached 28 percent of Japan's imports, mostly in wool and mineral ores.

PARTNERS FOR PROSPERITY

Ironically, Japan's use of expanded trade and investment during the early 1970s restored its position both as the major economic power and the main target of resentment in Southeast Asia. When Tanaka traveled to Indonesia, Thailand, Singapore, Malaysia, and the Philippines in 1974, he faced angry demonstrations and accusations of Japanese business arrogance. Protesters criticized wealthy Japanese for being cliquish, aloof, and indifferent to local problems. Moreover, they were angry because Tokyo required the purchase of Japanese goods with its economic aid, preventing these poor countries from paying the lowest prices for imports. Professor of Asian Studies Chalmers Johnson later explained that Tanaka's tour, the so-called Nixon Shocks of U.S. reconciliation with the PRC and dollar devaluation, and the oil crisis after 1973 abruptly ended "collective Japanese amnesia about Asia."[5] These events accelerated a shift in Japanese industrial policy away from building Japan into an industrial workshop that made manufactured goods for export. It was not until U.S. disengagement from Southeast Asia after the Vietnam War, however, that Japan emerged as the dominant trader and investor in the region. In 1977 Japanese overseas investments totaled $22.2 billion, with $5.6 billion (or 25.4 percent) in Southeast Asia. The fact that Japan's prime ministers regularly visited the region after 1979 signaled the rising importance of the region to the Japanese economy.

Investment in Southeast Asia also was part of Japan's efforts for industrial restructuring and integration into the world economy during the late 1970s. It was a way to house-clean the domestic economy, as Japan acted to replace dirty and resource-consuming heavy industries with clean and knowledge-intensive enterprises, reducing pollution at home through investing abroad. Japan built foreign plants to exploit cheap labor to make goods for domestic sales and, after shipment to Japan, reexport abroad. Trading companies, or *sogo shosha*, provided developing nations with credit, technical information, and trade routes. As Japan substituted its previous reliance on exports with manufacturing abroad, it disseminated industrial knowledge with the aim of maximizing production in industrial operations and ventures in extractive industries overseas. This extended to management, as Japan replicated the methods traditionally used to implement industrial policy. Japanese firms, for example, ran subsidiaries like they ran the home company, referring even small decisions to the corporation's headquarters where discussion of proposals resulted in consensus before the announcement of a decision. But Tokyo tried to limit involvement in politics, maintaining an ambiguous and passive approach on these matters until the 1980s.

Japan's policy toward Thailand was typical of its dealings with Southeast Asian nations after the announcement in 1969 of the Nixon Doctrine. Japan's vigorous economic penetration would cause Bangkok to impose a boycott on Japanese goods in October 1972 because Tokyo had been slow in providing aid and investment while denying Thailand a role in development decisions. By 1980 Thailand and Japan had settled jurisdictional disputes, as Bangkok accepted the dominance of Japanese trading companies in decisions related to technology, capital, and management. Friction continued because the executives that Japanese firms sent to lead enterprises in Thailand then returned to Japan after rising in company ranks. Some able and ambitious Thais rose to top corporate posts but often moved between companies as a silent protest against Japan's discriminatory employment system. Nevertheless, by 1983 Japan was providing Thailand with $248 million in loans and grants and had made it the second largest recipient of Official Development Assistance (ODA).

No nation in Southeast Asia had been more economically dependent for a longer period on the United States than the Philippines, especially because of the U.S. military presence on the islands. But Japan's reparations payments were important in offsetting its adverse trade balance, accounting for one-third of all foreign aid to the Philippines from 1952 to 1961. During the 1950s Manila's main source of income was U.S. dollars for military bases and direct aid. By 1960, however, the Philippines was the second largest market for Japan, ranking behind only Hong Kong while outdistancing the United States and Canada. Philippine exports to Japan also were expanding, approaching the total sent to the United States. Japan moved to fill the void that the United States created as it disengaged militarily from Asia after the Vietnam War. By the 1980s Japan ranked second in trade with Philippines and had expanded significantly its ODA funds and investment there, striving to reverse an economic downturn in response to declining U.S. spending.

Although political repression in the Philippines did not hurt Japan's efforts to create a stable economic partnership, it did with South Korea. On August 8, 1973, South Korean agents arrested Kim Dae-jung, a Korean dissident, in Tokyo, returning him to Seoul where he faced execution. Japan protested, but the ROK refused to release Kim, causing Tokyo to terminate ministerial aid talks. After Pak placed Kim under long-term house arrest and the ROK ambassador delivered an apology, Tanaka resumed discussions in December, but Tokyo offered far less financial aid than Seoul had requested. Japanese trade, tourism, and aid to South Korea all fell in 1974, with discord between the two nations climaxing on August 15 when a Korean resident from Japan assassinated the wife of the ROK's president. Angry South Koreans staged demonstrations, and protesters ransacked the Japanese embassy. The ROK arrested two Japanese radicals and sentenced them to 20 years in prison. Pak's release of these radicals helped persuade Miki to reopen talks in September 1975, resulting in Tokyo announcing a commitment to resume aid to the ROK. Opposition leaders criticized Miki for moving closer to Seoul, arguing that his policy served only to delay Korea's peaceful reunification. Then, in 1979, the assassination of Pak ignited a renewed wave of arrests and purges under new military dictator Chun

Du-hwan. His campaign to silence dissent climaxed in a mass killing of protesters at Kwangju in May 1980.

Malaysia, like the Philippines, attracted more attention from Japan after
the war in Vietnam ended because of its resources, the strategic value of the
Straits of Malacca, and the need for stability on the peninsula as protection
for Thailand. To meet rising energy needs in Japan, Tokyo financed a large
project for oil exploration in North Sumatra in 1960. By 1967 Japan was
Malaysia's leading trade partner. But Malaysia was a minor part of Japan's
world trade, following a pattern among ASEAN members. Japanese protectionism was a source of friction because it produced a trade deficit with
Malaysia. Japan, as elsewhere in Southeast Asia, was aggressive during the
1970s in securing investment opportunities, but it also promoted cultural
exchanges to improve its image. In 1985 Japan remained Malaysia's top
trading partner, with oil now the leading import in return for mostly transportation equipment and machinery. But Malaysia still opposed a wider
military role for Japan.

Indonesia was an important postwar source of raw materials for Japan,
providing textiles, forestry products, and fish. But oil soon attracted more
attention. By 1980 Indonesia was Japan's second largest supplier of oil and
received large ODA amounts from Japan. After the war in Vietnam, Japan
promoted joint ventures in Indonesia to transform the nation within its economic sphere of influence. By 1976 Japan had $2.6 billion invested in Indo-
nesia, with five companies controlling almost all of it. These Japanese firms
retained total authority, requiring Indonesian subsidiaries to buy manufactured goods and raw materials from Japan at inflated prices. Japanese investment increased nevertheless from $7 billion in 1980 to $74 billion in
1984, surpassing that of the United States. Japan's Indonesian partners increasingly resented the way in which the Japanese acted unilaterally and
viewed the Indonesians' operations as minor and sideline activities. Indonesia also joined the United States and ASEAN members in criticizing Tokyo for blocking outside investment in Japan and for maintaining
self-serving economic policies. After over a decade of effort, Japan still had
not achieved the creation of genuine partnerships for prosperity in Asia.

ASIA FOR THE ASIANS

After Prime Minister Tanaka's hostile reception in Southeast Asia, Japan understood that expanded investment and trade alone would not make it
the leader of a new Asia for the Asians. In February 1976, ASEAN did not
even invite Japan to its Bali Summit because Tokyo had not fulfilled promises of funding major development projects. Fukuda Takeo, who became

prime minister later that year, worked to mend relations with Southeast Asia, stating in March 1977 Japan's new commitment to foster stability and economic development in the region. Then, in Manila, Fukuda issued a policy statement soon known as the Fukuda Doctrine. It committed Japan to promoting understanding in Southeast Asia; to seeking partnerships on the basis of equality encouraging regional stability and peace; to renouncing military ambition and the production of nuclear weapons; and to doubling aid, expanding investment, and raising Japanese imports from the region over five years. Thereafter, Japan made great strides toward improving relations with Southeast Asia. In 1977, for example, it passed the United States as the leader in providing economic aid to the region. Fukuda also established a loose partnership with ASEAN to influence the future of Indochina. In 1978 annual Japan-ASEAN Foreign Minister Conferences began, providing a way for Tokyo to help in resolving political problems in the region, such as ending the mass murders the Pol Pot regime committed in Cambodia after the Communist Khmer Rouge seized power in the spring of 1975.

Ohira Masayoshi worked to build on the initiatives of Fukuda after becoming prime minister in 1978. He proposed a large aid package, envisioning Japan as an economic engine for development in Southeast Asia. Miyazawa Kiichi, who was Ohira's foreign minister from 1978 to 1979, pressed for more Japanese economic aid and investment along with better business ties in Asia to build regional stability. Many ASEAN members reacted with skepticism to Japan's new activism, suspecting that the United States and Japan sought to upstage and eventually replace ASEAN as dominant forces in Asia. To reassure these Southeast Asian leaders, Ohira's government pledged huge amounts of credit for ASEAN and aid to refugees. But even though Tokyo agreed to fund half of the UN Human Rights Commission's expenses in the region, it would not provide a new home to the "boat people" fleeing the political repression and economic hardship in Indochina after the Vietnam War. One writer's negative assessment was that the Japanese do not "show much concern for the welfare of others in their international economic relations. They do not seem to show much responsibility for other people, unless it will bring them profit."[6] Indeed, Ohira's plans and Fukuda's promises were not fulfilled because of infighting in ASEAN and the Japanese bureaucracy. Worse, a new oil crisis after the revolution in Iran early in 1979 halted implementation.

The Soviet military buildup in Southeast Asia after the Vietnam War partially explains Japan's emphasis on increased aid, especially after Moscow signed a treaty with Vietnam allowing it to use Danang and Camranh Bay in 1978. In response, Ohira issued with President Jimmy Carter a joint

Prime Minister Suzuki Zenko monitors Japan's economic policy in Southeast Asia. *Far Eastern Economic Review*, January 9, 1981.

proclamation calling for a wider role for Japan in the region, creating a study group to develop plans for the establishment of a Pacific Basin Community. Early in 1979, Ohira offered grants and loans to Vietnam to deter it from invading Cambodia, but Hanoi rejected the offer. Japan then terminated aid and imposed sanctions on Vietnam in response to Hanoi's invasion of Cambodia and in compliance with ASEAN's request. In January 1980, reacting to his declining popularity at home, Ohira visited Australia, New Guinea, and New Zealand to build support for his Pacific Basin initiative. He joined with Australia's Prime Minister Simon Fraser in establishing the Pacific Economic Cooperation Conference as a forum for discussing concerns in an unofficial Asia-Pacific Community. No longer building bridges to the region, Japan now was providing consistent support for ASEAN to demonstrate its value as a political partner. But Tokyo continued to focus on economics, maintaining a low profile in political disputes such as the one between Vietnam and Cambodia.

Prime Minister Nakasone's desire to support the Reagan administration's efforts to deter the Soviets in Asia motivated his attempts to strengthen ties with South Korea. In 1983 he visited South Korea and pledged $4 billion in aid, acknowledging publicly Japan's cultural debt to Korea and emphasizing the ROK's importance to security in Asia. His personal diplomacy restored stable and cooperative relations between Japan and South Korea, resulting in Chun Du-hwan becoming the first ROK president to visit Japan in the fall of 1984. He requested a five-year, $10 billion loan while voicing support for Japan to act as a mediator in talks between Seoul and Pyongyang. Later that year, Nakasone approved a $6 billion loan to South Korea but urged the ROK to make greater strides toward democracy. Tokyo also publicly called for the admission of both Koreas to the United Nations and "cross recognition"—the PRC and the Soviet Union recognizing the ROK, with the United States and Japan recognizing the DPRK. But then, in 1986, Nakasone's minister of education angered the governments of both Koreas when he suggested that Korea's rulers had agreed to Japan's annexation of Korea in 1910. Worse, he called the famous 1919 March First Rebellion a "riot." Nakasone fired him and issued an apology. Japan's revival of this old source of friction, however, infuriated South Koreans already upset about the treatment of minorities in Japan and Tokyo's denial of free access to its markets and technology.

In 1972 the ROK criticized Prime Minister Tanaka for adopting a more flexible approach toward North Korea that paralleled his policy of improving relations with the PRC. That year, Pyongyang pressed Tokyo to recognize the DPRK, but Tanaka refused without Seoul's approval. By 1973 Japanese trade with the DPRK nevertheless had grown by 40 percent in one year, and Japanese newsmen began visiting North Korea. However, the discovery of tunnels under the demilitarized zone and Kim Il Sung's increasingly bellicose pronouncements combined with the Communist triumph in South Vietnam to create anxiety in Tokyo. Prime Minister Miki met with President Gerald Ford in August 1975 and issued a communiqué acknowledging the ROK's security as vital for the maintenance of peace on the Korean peninsula, as well as peace and security in Northeast Asia. Miki confirmed that the United States could use its bases for military operations should war resume. Yet after 1976 Japan emerged as the DPRK's leading non-Socialist economic partner. But then in 1983 a North Korean terrorist's bombing in Rangoon that killed ROK officials caused Japan to impose economic sanctions against the DPRK. Two years later, Tokyo lifted trade sanctions and contacted Pyongyang about joint ventures despite its having defaulted on earlier loans. Restoration of amicable relations led to Japan's trade with North Korea reaching a total value of $358 million in 1986.

Under Prime Minister Nakasone, Japan continued to pursue in Southeast Asia a stronger relationship with ASEAN. By 1984 Japan's neighbors in Southeast Asia had responded favorably to new initiatives for cooperation to promote the development of human resources in the region. Japan also expanded its participation in joint military exercises in Southeast Asia and established closer military ties with South Korea and Taiwan. Nakasone revived the Ohira-Carter initiative for the creation of a Pacific Basin Community when he visited New Zealand and Australia in 1985, but he stressed the need to rely primarily on economic means to achieve stability. Meanwhile, he voiced growing concern about the Soviet threat to the shipping lanes from the Mideast and Southeast Asia. By 1985 between 140 and 150 ships went through the Malacca Straits each day, and 44 percent of these vessels were Japanese. Nakasone was successful in persuading Singapore and Indonesia to accept coordination in the jurisdiction of this key waterway. In 1988 Japan contributed $700 million to help create the Overseas Economic Cooperation Fund. Its use of aid for comprehensive security reasons reflected in part Japan's increased willingness to accept a wider political role in world affairs, as well as an awareness of the potential to use its economic power to exert diplomatic influence.

In sum, diplomacy served Japanese economic interests for four decades after the end of World War II, particularly in dealing with its former colonial possessions. This helps explain political scientist Donald C. Hellman's remark that "Japanese foreign policy is like a bamboo thicket: Full and attractive in appearance, resilient in all kinds of weather, but lacking in real substance and crowding out all around it that is reached by its roots."[7] Businessmen were the most influential in developing policy toward Southeast Asia, creating, for example, in November 1983 the Japan-ASEAN Economic Council. By then Japan was the top trade partner for all nations in the region except for Singapore and the Philippines. Its trade total with Southeast Asia reached $140 billion in 1990, almost equal to that with the United States. Japan had used trade and investment to reestablish economic dominance in the region, and its actions were not wholly altruistic. Tokyo realized that promoting peace and stability in the region enhanced Japan's own prosperity. Southeast Asian countries, however, wanted trade, not aid. Yet Japan was unwilling to compromise its own economic security, ignoring calls from ASEAN to open its home market. By 1987 Japan's investment in ASEAN nations also had declined, suggesting a limited commitment to the promotion of economic development. Those who warned that Japan was pursuing plans for a new co-prosperity sphere in Asia were overestimating Tokyo's economic and political power.

NOTES

1. Herman Kahn and Max Singer, "Japan and Pacific Asia in the 1970s," *Asian Survey* 11 (April 1971): 412.

2. Quoted in Chong-sik Lee, "Japanese-Korean Relations in Perspective," *Pacific Affairs* 35 (Winter 1962–1963): 321.

3. Soon Sung Cho, "Japan's Two Koreas Policy and the Problems of Korean Unification," *Asian Survey* 7 (October 1967): 718.

4. Isaiah A. Litvak and Christopher J. Maule, "Japan's Overseas Investments," *Pacific Affairs* 16 (Summer 1973): 260.

5. Chalmers Johnson, "The Patterns of Japanese Relations with China, 1952–1982," *Pacific Affairs* 59 (Fall 1986): 426.

6. Quoted in Mikiso Hane, *Modern Japan: A Historical Survey* (Boulder, CO: Westview Press, 1986): 387.

7. Donald C. Hellman, "Japan and Southeast Asia: Continuity amidst Change," *Asian Survey* 19 (December 1979): 1189.

feat in World War II to reassume an ill-defined position of global leadership at the time of his death. Many people in the United States and other nations, who blamed Hirohito for Japanese military aggression, welcomed his death and opposed any official expressions of respect or condolences. On the day of his funeral in February 1989, however, representatives from 164 nations and 28 world organizations were there, recognizing Japan's international status. Akihito, the deceased emperor's son and successor, not only had avoided the stigma of prewar militarism, but had come to symbolize the "New Japan," especially after marrying Shoda Michiko, the commoner daughter of a flour milling company president, in 1959. He assumed as his reign name Heisei ("Achieving Peace") but did not leave it entirely to the government to achieve this ambitious objective. Akihito, for example, took the lead in practicing "apology diplomacy" (*shazai gaiko*). In April 1989 he personally apologized to visiting Chinese premier Li Peng for Japan's wartime role in China. In May 1990 he expressed his "deepest regret" for the "brutality" of Japanese occupation and colonial rule in Korea during the state visit to Japan of South Korean president No Tae-u.

Japan's economic strength remained, however, the key ingredient in its status as a world power. Under Prime Minister Nakasone the Japanese economy continued to grow, as did the trade surplus. Simultaneously, however, Japan amassed huge debts in bonds to cover yearly government deficits starting after the oil crisis of 1973, with its debt service reaching 20.9 percent of its budget in 1987. Then, on October 20, 1987, the New York Stock Market crashed, sparking a 15 percent drop in Japan's Nikkei stock prices. That same day, Nakasone picked Takeshita Noboru as his successor. Upon election as prime minister, Takeshita declared his dedication to Japan and the cause of "world peace." Similarly vague were his promises to keep Japan out of trouble, reflecting his political reputation as a mediator between factions and a leader without clear ideas. Takeshita had to take steps to reduce a $1 trillion national debt and eliminate barriers to rising consumption. Added pressure came from Washington's demands for access to Japan's rice market. Under Takeshita's leadership, economic growth resumed in 1988, with the GNP increasing by 10 percent, wages rising, bankruptcies reaching a 13-year low, the trade surplus widening, and the Nikkei showing solid recovery. Early in 1989 the Diet passed a $45 billion tax cut measure, causing Takeshita to secure enactment in April of a 3 percent sales tax on goods and services to offset the loss of revenue.

Takeshita made many foreign trips as prime minister, consistently trying to promote Japan's image as a contributor to global economic prosperity and stability. In 1988 he endorsed $50 billion in ODA spending to make Japan the largest provider of economic development assistance in the world.

Under his leadership, Japan provided more financial support to the United Nations while being more assertive at the International Monetary Fund and World Health Organization. Takeshita also dispatched his foreign minister to monitor such activities as elections, troop withdrawals, and ceasefires in Cambodia, the Middle East, and elsewhere around the globe. Nevertheless, he lacked Nakasone's skill as a statesman, as revealed when U.S. president Ronald Reagan called to congratulate him on his election as prime minister and asked, "Mind if I call you Noboru? Just call me Ron." Takeshita politely declined the offer. But after his meeting with Reagan, he supported raising consumption in Japan and spending more money on defense. This won him praise in Washington but revived the fears on the part of some Asian nations about Japanese militarism. Takeshita responded with reassuring words, as well as action in being one of few postwar prime ministers not to visit the Yasukuni Shrine on the anniversary of Japan's surrender in World War II.

Responding to U.S. pressure, Takeshita braved certain opposition from his traditional constituency when he ended import quotas on beef and citrus products. To placate farmers, he devised a program for rural improvement aimed at raising the standard of living and creating jobs. A political science professor sneered that "the only thing he really cares about is politics. You can see him start to get bored when you talk about policy matters."[3] Indeed, Takeshita was a champion fundraiser, collecting over $14 million at a typical cocktail party in June 1987. This helps to explain the Recruit-Cosmos Scandal that brought down his government, as Nakasone, Miyazawa, and other associates accepted cash, stock bargains, and lavish parties in return for waiving codes, bending regulations, and providing preferential treatment in the purchase of a supercomputer. The scandal, one observer wrote, "could not have done a better job in eliminating a particular generation of LDP leaders if they had planted bombs beneath LDP headquarters."[4] Replacing Takeshita in June was Uno Sosuke, his foreign minister, who quickly resigned after a former geisha claimed she had been his mistress for two decades. As bad as Japan's first postwar sex scandal was, a cabinet member's derogatory remark about women was worse. In 1985 a bill had prohibited gender discrimination but included no penalties, other than the wrath of disgusted voters.

In July 1989, the LDP suffered a crushing defeat at the polls that left the party with only 109 of 252 upper house seats, and for the first time in the postwar era the opposition took command of one house in the Diet. Of 148 women candidates, 22 won seats, an increase from 9 in 1980. Meanwhile, the LDP had replaced Uno with former minister of education Kaifu Toshiki, the member of a small faction which most political observers regarded as a stopgap leader. Kaifu faced the continuing pressure to end incentives for individual saving and to reform the tax code. Rising consumption combined with trade liberalization would appease Washington, and tax increases would generate funds to lower the national debt. Still dependent on outside energy, food, and raw materials, Japan feared that a refusal to reform its trade practices would cause critics to close their markets. Steps toward formation of the European Economic Community and adoption of the North American Free Trade Agreement (NAFTA) underscored the need for Japan to work more closely with ASEAN during the 1990s. By then, developing countries already exceeded the United States in the value of exports and imports, showing how critical East Asia was to Japan for markets and investment. Then, in 1991, recession hit Japan, lowering to 1 percent its annual economic growth for the next two years. A decade of failure and frustration had begun.

RELATIONSHIPS IN TRANSITION

Japan was still struggling to clarify a comprehensive security policy when the Cold War ended in 1989. It had begun this process early in the 1970s in response to dramatic changes in world affairs, including the Sino-American rapprochement, the Soviet-American détente, the 1973 oil crisis, and the U.S. withdrawal from Vietnam. New developments in the 1980s only added to Japan's rising sense of insecurity. Prime Minister Nakasone shared with most Japanese the desire to rely on economic power to exert global leadership, but he acted to increase military spending in response to the Soviet military buildup in Asia to the point that Japan had the third largest defense budget in world. The Soviet refusal to discuss the return of the "Northern Territories" only added to Japanese apprehension. In 1985 Soviet premier Mikhail Gorbachev tried to improve relations after coming to power, initiating talks to resolve major differences. This led to an increase in trade and agreements for the economic development of Siberia. After the fall of the Berlin Wall in November 1989, Gorbachev, responding to calls for compromise in the Soviet Union, made it easier for Japanese citizens to obtain visas to visit the Kuriles and reduced the Soviet military presence there. Gorbachev's growing political weakness resulted in a cautious and defensive policy that kept relations with Japan frosty until the Soviet Union collapsed late in 1991.

During the 1990s Japan intensified its efforts at economic penetration of Europe, working to improve a relationship that was a mixture of mutual fear, disdain, and admiration. Western European nations previously had shown only modest interest in developing a closer relationship, because they saw Japan as a surrogate of the United States. Hirohito visited seven European nations in September 1971, but trade increased slowly during the 1970s. In search of new economic opportunities, Japan expanded its contacts in the 1980s. Its trade surplus with Europe rose from $12 billion in 1981 to $23.6 billion in 1988, while investment grew from under $2 billion in 1985 to $14 billion in 1988. Nakasone wanted to expand links with Western Europe in preserving regional security, but there was little joint defense coordination during the 1980s beyond informal ties to NATO and some cooperation on nuclear arms control. Thereafter, Tokyo resumed its previous policy of working through the United States to maintain its security relationship with Western Europe. And the emerging European Economic Community let the United States take the lead in working to remove barriers to Japan's market. Under Nakasone, Japan also showed more interest in improving relations with Israel, toward which Japan had tried to be neutral since 1967. Prime Minister Yitzhak Shamir visited Japan in September 1985, discussing steps to expand the exchange of goods and joint ventures. Total trade in that year reached $630 million.

In 1989 the PRC was Japan's second largest trading partner in Asia, behind only Hong Kong and Macao. Prime Minister Takeshita provided more than $4.2 billion in development aid after negotiating an Investment Protection Treaty in 1988. Japan briefly froze all investment and aid to the PRC in response to the violent suppression of student-led pro-democracy demonstrations in Tiananmen Square in 1989, but then it broke with G-7 members and was the first ODA donor to reestablish bilateral programs. In 1990 the PRC received $617.8 million from Japan in ODA funds, which was 46 percent of the total that year. By 1992 China was Japan's top choice for investment in cars, transportation, and banking as Beijing began to implement economic liberalization policies. The Tiananmen Square Massacre, however, had ended abruptly the shallow Sino-Japanese military coordination, which did not resume until 1998. This was the result of Russian sales of aircraft carriers and MiGs to China, which allowed Beijing to project its influence into the China Sea, leading to tense disputes over the Spratley and Paracel islands. Nevertheless, China simultaneously became the leading recipient of Japan's investment, especially in textiles, electronics, transportation equipment, and oil and gas exploration. Japan built ports, roads, airports, and railways. During the 1990s China's share of Japan's trade with Asia doubled.

Asia became a major economic target for Japan after 1985. Japanese investment there rose to $60 billion in 1992, exceeding that of the United States, and imports from the region grew to 31 percent of Japan's total. Japan also became the world's largest donor of foreign aid by 1989. In contrast to other nations that focused on political and civil infrastructure, Japan concentrated its aid on building an economic foundation for self-sufficiency. With the end of the Cold War, many donors placed conditions on receiving aid to promote democratization, and Japan's foreign ministry was susceptible to *gaiatsu*, or foreign pressure, to follow suit. Despite objections from MITI, the Miyazawa government in June 1992 issued the ODA Charter, which set the following priorities in granting aid: support for conservation, democracy and human rights, limits on military spending, and market-oriented economic practices. This policy "was more rhetorical than real"[5] because coalition governments after 1993 lacked the unity required to control Japan's bureaucracy. Still receiving a disproportionate amount of aid were countries in which Japan had the highest levels of trade and investment. Tokyo rarely punished nations that defied its ODA Charter; for example, it continued sending aid to Cambodia even after a bloody coup took place there in July 1997.

Japan began to expand its participation in the affairs of the United Nations during the 1980s. It played an important political role in key noncombat activities, notably acting as a mediator and resolver of conflicts. But Tokyo was indifferent on the issue of international human rights. It was not until 1982 that Japan joined the UN Commission on Human Rights (UNCHR), waiting two years more before establishing a Human Rights and Refugees Division in the foreign ministry. Fiercely protective of its internal affairs, Japan would not support United Nations resolutions to punish or intervene in nations violating human rights. For example, in Burma, Chairman of the Revolutionary Council Ne Win, whom Japan trained during World War II, eliminated private enterprise with nationalization policies that slowed economic development, yet Burma received two-thirds of all Japanese ODA funds from 1973 until Tokyo halted aid briefly after a coup in 1988 that resulted in the massacre of thousands of civilian demonstrators. Japan broke with the United Nations and ended its boycott of trade and aid to Burma when the new leaders promised free elections and reform. Prime Minister Kaifu added a human rights condition for receipt of ODA funds in 1991 but was silent that year when Indonesia brutally repressed independence advocates on East Timor. Nor did a coup in Thailand cause Tokyo to end ODA help. Indifference on human rights violations damaged Japan's global image and made less likely for success its bid for a permanent seat on the UN Security Council.

By the 1990s, however, Tokyo was more direct and blunt in advancing proposals at G-7 meetings of the industrialized nations while demanding a greater voice in decisions at the Asian Development Bank, World Bank, and International Monetary Fund. And after the Cold War, many Japanese voiced opposition to continued close partnership with the United States, favoring instead a closer relationship with the rest of Asia. In 1992 Tokyo joined in discussions of security issues with ASEAN, but more significant was Japan's role in the Asia-Pacific Economic Cooperation (APEC) forum, established in 1989. By 1992, APEC's members were Japan, China, South Korea, Taiwan, the ASEAN countries (excluding Vietnam), Hong Kong, Australia, Papua New Guinea, New Zealand, Mexico, Chile, Canada, and the United States. Tokyo's low profile in APEC was a prime example of its reactive foreign policy during the 1990s. Japan conceived of APEC as a loose consultative forum in which to seek consensus, raising the issues of energy, the environment, human resources training, and building infrastructure without offering any specific plans. Japan allowed the United States to take the lead in pressing for regionwide trade and investment liberalization, but at the Osaka meeting in 1995 it expressed doubts about devising "a concrete blueprint to realize that 'noble dream'."[6] Japan also refused to support Malaysian president Mohamad Mahathir's proposal in 1990 to create an East Asia Economic Caucus comprised only of Asian states and not subject to U.S. domination. Japan's tentative, cautious, and passive diplomacy in Asia hardly resembled that of a global power.

RESTRAINED INVOLVEMENT

Japan's trade dispute with the United States intensified in the 1990s because the Cold War no longer provided cement to reinforce the alliance. After 1992 consultation and coordination were even more difficult because both governments were weak and fragmented politically. The U.S.-Japanese relationship was complex and competitive, with domestic politics dictating positions on market access, direct investment, monetary policy, indirect investment, technology transfer and security, and military burden sharing. Prime Minister Kaifu worked toward liberalization of trade in 1990, joining the United States in approving the report on the Structural Impediments Initiative, committing Tokyo to implement steps to eliminate barriers to foreign trade and investment in Japan. He even extended provisions to rice imports. Kaifu's higher diplomatic profile early in 1990 also pleased Washington, creating speculation that Japan was moving toward a more active international role after the Cold War. In January, Kaifu visited Europe, pledging nearly $2 billion in aid for Poland and Hungary. During his tour of five South Asian nations in May, he extended to India $645 million in low-interest loans. Kaifu boldly spoke of a new order for the global economy that would tackle the problems of the environment, drugs, terrorism, and population growth. Skeptics saw this as a continuation of Japan's policy of using economic power to achieve political aims as it had done in Asia.

Iraq's invasion of Kuwait in August 1990 ignited a volatile and dynamic debate about whether Japan could continue its inert and inarticulate world role. MITI urged caution, but Kaifu ignored this advice and approved a four-point economic sanctions package on Iraq, even though it owed Japan $4.7 billion and, along with Kuwait, provided 11 percent of Japan's oil. Initially, U.S. president George Bush was "ecstatic at Japanese decisiveness."[7] Kaifu then vacillated for three weeks. In response to Bush's direct appeal, Japan finally pledged $1 billion to finance the military buildup against Iraq. But Japan seemed willing to respond only with economic means, also offering to pay half of U.S. security treaty costs in Japan. After a multilateral force, with UN approval, was deployed in Saudi Arabia and the Persian Gulf, the Bush administration criticized Japan's aid package as inadequate. U.S. politicians with popular support demanded more, arguing that the multilateral force was acting to protect access to oil supplies that were vital to Japan. U.S. ambassador Michael Armacost told the Japanese government that its hopes for a UN Security Council seat were in jeopardy. Congress then threatened to withdraw U.S. troops in five years if Japan refused to pay for all U.S. security treaty costs, causing Kaifu to raise Japan's contribution to $4 billion. After the Gulf War began in January 1991, he then pledged $9 billion, resulting in Japan financing about 20 percent of the cost of operations against Iraq.

Washington was unhappy with Japan's performance throughout the Gulf crisis, complaining about slow payments and delayed support for initiatives, such as the dispatch of Japanese medical personnel. The United States was particularly distressed when Kaifu failed to persuade the Diet to approve use of SDF aircraft to evacuate refugees from the Gulf. The Komeito Party forced the adoption of limitations on spending to nonlethal aid and the imposition of taxes on oil and corporate profits to offset the costs. After the war in April 1991, Kaifu did obtain the Diet's approval to send SDF minesweepers and supply ships to the Middle East to help clear the Persian Gulf of mines. Opposition among many Japanese to involvement in the war was responsible for this reluctant participation. Hostility to Washington's pressure led to what Japanese called *kenbei*, or extreme criticism of United States. It also weakened the base of Kaifu's political support. But it was the onset of the worst recession since 1973 that ended any hope that Kaifu had for reelection. This created a new opportunity for Miyazawa Kiichi, who stated publicly that "our civil servants cannot establish goals for Japan. They look to the Prime Minister's office for decisions, which were not forthcoming."[8] In October the Takeshita faction had deserted Kaifu, but none of its members was willing to replace him. By default, Miyazawa emerged as the favorite to be the next prime minister.

Upon election in November, Miyazawa declared his commitment to seek close coordination with the United States on economic and political policy, but he stated his intention to respond "frankly" to Japan's critics in America. As prime minister, Miyazawa faced daunting challenges, such as finding ways to open Japan's markets to foreign rice without alienating Japan's farmers. He also had to define the nature and extent of Japan's influence in world affairs while addressing the issue of campaign reform. A new challenge was North Korea. South Korea's recent rapprochement with the Soviet Union and the PRC forced Tokyo to seek normalized relations with the DPRK as a means to promote stability in Northeast Asia. In 1990 a Japanese delegation traveled to North Korea with a letter from Kaifu to Kim Il Sung offering an apology for the "agony and damage" of Japanese occupation from 1910 to 1945. In return for a promise of treatment equal to what South Koreans had received in Japan, Pyongyang released Japanese fishermen incarcerated on charges of spying. Japan and the DPRK then opened negotiations for a normalization treaty, but Tokyo did not have enough trade with North Korea to provide the leverage necessary to secure favorable terms. In 1992 Tokyo broke off talks after North Korean agents captured Japanese citizens and took them back to the DPRK.

At the start of the 1990s, the last decade of the century, the Japanese wanted their nation to be proactive rather than reactive in world affairs, but had trouble defining the specifics of the new activism they desired. Moreover, Japan had a small foreign ministry and no intelligence agency. During the Gulf War the government showed that it was unprepared to deal with a global crisis, as Kaifu did not convene the National Security Council or consult the Self-Defense Agency. The nation remained divided on how to participate in UN operations. Worse, Japan resented its image as an international automated teller machine (ATM) that needed a kick-start. Under Miyazawa, trade friction only increased Japanese unhappiness, resulting in "contempt for the United States" (*bubei*), which reflected a new Japanese sense of power in response to persistent U.S. economic weakness. From 1987 to 1992, however, the percentage of those who said they trusted the United States declined only slightly (from 52.3 to 50.7 percent). And few Japanese genuinely disliked the United States. Most thought that relations between the two countries were good, but criticism of the United States was rising. By 1992 Japan confronted a watershed comparable to Commodore Perry's arrival in 1853 and the attack on Pearl Harbor in 1941, as the nation debated its future role in the world. Although some were calling for reconsideration of limitations on defense spending, most wanted Japan to expand economic commitments for stability, especially because the world owed Japan $400 billion.

POLITICAL PARALYSIS

Miyazawa's replacement of Kaifu as prime minister only increased public disillusionment with politics because he had resigned as finance minister in 1988 after implication in the Recruit-Cosmos Scandal. Then came investigation of another close ally for accepting illegal campaign funds from Japan's parcel delivery company that had close ties to organized crime. National outrage placed pressure on Miyazawa to revive bills for political reform. Worse, after modest economic growth in 1991, the GNP declined by 1.5 percent in 1992. Nissan for the first time reported losses, signaling that Japanese industrial dynamism had ended. Many firms, hampered by the high cost of capital at a time of weak demand, found themselves increasingly vulnerable. Lack of consumer and business confidence caused the Nikkei to fall by 1,400 points in the first seven months of 1992, igniting a sharp decline in profits and land prices. Critics of Miyazawa found fault as well with his firm support for close ties with the United States, arguing that he would succumb to U.S. demands on trade. The fact that he was Japan's first prime minister to speak fluent English led to criticism of him for not always conducting negotiations in Japanese.

In January 1992 Miyazawa met with President George Bush in New York, declaring his intention to use "every possible means" to stimulate Japan's economy. Then, during a state visit to Japan, Bush pressed Miyazawa to open the Japanese market to U.S. cars, computers, paper, and glass, believing that closing the American trade deficit of $46 billion with Japan was vital to U.S. economic recovery and Bush's own reelection. Top U.S. automobile executives accompanied Bush, prompting one critic to deride the trip as a "Detroit circus" and the Americans as "crybabies and bullies."[9] Miyazawa resisted Bush's pressure to participate in several joint projects, causing an observer to describe Japan's reaction as a "mix of disappointment, pity, and subtle scorn for an aging and weak role model."[10] Further embarrassment came at a state dinner when Bush, afflicted with the flu, vomited into the lap of the prime minister. But after Bush left, Miyazawa persuaded the Bank of Japan to lower the interest rate again, one of five times during the one-year period after July 1991. Nevertheless, the slowdown in economic growth that began in 1991 persisted, as losses for electronics and computer firms combined with bankruptcies of software companies to cause mass layoffs. Nissan shut down one of its plants near

Tokyo in 1993, the first closure of a Japanese automobile assembly plant in the postwar era.

For Miyazawa, the Diet's refusal to pass the Peacekeeping Operations bill (PKO) typified Japan's hesitant and painful birth as a genuine global power. His vigorous lobbying contributed to the Diet finally approving the PKO on June 15, 1992. It authorized deployment of 2,000 noncombat SDF troops overseas for noncombatant peacekeeping operations under UN auspices for the first time since World War II. The bill's conditions were that Japanese forces, although not participating in any operations with a military component such as monitoring ceasefires, would carry only light arms, maintain neutrality, and fire only in self-defense. Among the SDF's new tasks would be observing ceasefires, patroling buffer zones, inspecting the arms trade, and collecting and disposing of weapons. Japan now had a new way to exert influence in the world beyond its economic power, but the PKO did not constitute a basic shift in Japan's security policy. It was reactive to foreign pressure, and its main purpose was to rehabilitate Japan's world image and enable it to gain acceptance as a credible global power. In September 1992 Miyazawa sent 1,800 troops to Cambodia, to both help keep the peace and monitor elections under UN supervision. In 1993 Japan dispatched 50 SDF personnel to participate in peacekeeping operations in Mozambique, and in 1994 it sent a contingent of air and ground forces to Rwanda. Peacekeeping had no direct commercial benefit, but it did reduce foreign criticism of Japan's "checkbook diplomacy."

Japan thus pursued a slow and deliberate expansion of its world role. It had no intention of transforming its role from peacekeeper to peacemaker. Tokyo's softer response to mounting evidence in 1992 that North Korea was developing nuclear weapons thus created increasing friction with the United States. Although the provocative actions of the desperate renegade Stalinist state created profound fear and anxiety in Japan, the Miyazawa government feared reigniting the Korean War. Only later, in 1994, would Japan agree to make a $1 billion contribution to help finance, with the United States and the ROK, the building of two light water nuclear reactors in North Korea in return for Pyongyang's pledge to end its nuclear weapons program. Tokyo pursued a more activist course in Southeast Asia in July 1991 at an enlarged ASEAN meeting in Kuala Lumpur where Kaifu proposed regular discussions of regional security. During 1992 Miyazawa supported an Australian proposal that the members of APEC hold regular summit meetings to discuss regional economic and security matters. On a visit to Thailand in January 1993, he promised Japan's active participation in talks concerning the longer-term security interests of the Asia-Pacific region. Many Japanese applauded these efforts to clarify for Japan an expanded world role.

Despite rising apprehensions about regional security, Japanese spending on defense had declined 3 percent annually during the 1990s. This sharply reversed the trend of the previous decade, when the annual military budget rose by an average of 6.4 percent. By 1990 Japan's defense industry had grown tremendously, resulting in a 220 percent rise in military production. About 20 firms provided three-fourths of Japan's defense needs, applying civilian technology to military production and exporting much of its new equipment and systems. The United States enthusiastically promoted Japan's military industries in the late 1980s and early 1990s, viewing its development as an answer to the steady decline in U.S. defense spending. Critics charged that courtship would lead to marriage of the U.S. military-industrial complex and the Japanese *keiretsu*. Indeed, President Bush applied heavy pressure on Japan to purchase U.S. military hardware, especially sophisticated weapons systems, as a hedge against recession. But Japan's defense budget was not large enough to have a major impact, even if Tokyo raised it to 3 percent of its GNP. By the early 1990s, the SDF still had limited training and minimal capabilities with a main mission of disaster relief. SDF ground forces ranked number 25 in the world in size behind Ethiopia, Spain, and Thailand. Although Japan's air force was among the world's most modern, its pilots were poorly trained. Japan certainly did not qualify as a global power in terms of military strength.

Miyazawa succeeded in building public support for a broader world role, and Japanese voters reacted positively to his leadership, widening the LDP's majority in the upper house elections in July 1992. But the appreciation of the yen continued, with the exchange rate by the spring of 1995 at 83 yen to the dollar. This made exports more expensive, accelerating the shift of Japanese manufacturers to overseas production and allowing for the first time cheaper imports—especially from South Korea and Taiwan—to compete successfully with Japanese products. Miyazawa was unable to control the economy or his party, as factional rivals linked to corruption openly defied his leadership. In June 1993 the Diet passed a no confidence vote of 255 to 220, forcing Miyazawa to resign and call for new elections. The results led to the LDP losing control of the government for the first time since 1955, as Hosokawa Morihiro emerged as the leader of a seven-party rainbow coalition. Defeat of the LDP provided clues about Japan's future place in the new world order. Because the Socialist Democratic Party, successor to the JSP, sustained major losses, people apparently were not voting for a smaller global role. Rather, the end of the Cold War had created new insecurities for the Japanese people, who wanted fresh and innovative policies in foreign affairs. Rejecting past approaches, concerned voters were electing younger leaders to the Diet. It was recession and scandal, however, that had shattered the LDP, requiring Hosokawa's government to focus at first on domestic affairs.

COALITION GOVERNMENT

Japan entered a new period of political instability and shifting alliances after the end of LDP dominance that made it difficult to address effectively a series of tough issues. The new Hosokawa government, however, promised the passage of major electoral reform, as well as measures for access to open administration, stockholder protection, a cleaner environment, streamlined government, consumer protection, and more jobs for women. Skeptics had doubts that a new style of politics would emerge, because LDP factional bolters belonged to the coalition. Japan experienced in 1993 a 1.5 percent growth rate, but government officials remained gloomy because the economy was still vulnerable and dependent on the U.S. stock market. Hosokawa, late in 1993, managed to build a weak consensus supporting his proposal to open Japan's rice market to foreign competition. The public applauded when he agreed in GATT negotiations to permit rice imports equivalent to between 4 and 8 percent of domestic consumption for six years, after which tariffs would replace import controls. The LDP policy of protecting Japan's rice farmers thus finally had ended, although the government subsidy had been declining gradually throughout the 1980s. This policy change, however, did not have a dramatic impact on domestic rice producers because westernization had caused the amount of rice in Japan's total cereal consumption to fall steadily in postwar years. The United States thus was disappointed with the meager rewards of access to Japan's rice market.

Hosokawa's government also worked to implement a readjustment plan focusing on deregulation, decentralization, and a consumer orientation. This included steps to protect the environment, responding to the public desire for action to improve the quality of living especially in urban areas. Previous laws had been ineffective. Neither the 1967 Basic Law for Pollution Control nor the 1972 National Environmental Preservation Law had specific goals or enforcement provisions. Local and community action had been much more successful in fighting pollution, showing the importance of consumer input, rather than allowing business total control. Responding to public pressure to improve air quality, the Keidanren in May 1991 endorsed a strategy for economic growth along with environmental protection that would combine market mechanisms and government planning not only to make better use of technology but to alter lifestyles and attitudes. This corresponded with its recent commitment to open the Japanese market, working in the 1980s to improve standards and certification systems and then shifting to promote deregulation and inward foreign direct investment in the 1990s. With the Keidanren's help, Hosokawa persuaded the Diet to approve the strongest environmental measure in Japanese history, providing a statement of vision and funding for education and recycling. Thereafter, the government would act vigorously at home and abroad against global warming, ozone depletion, and pollution.

Hosokawa's apparent submission to U.S. pressure in opening Japan's rice market brought harsh criticism, especially from the Socialist Democratic Party (SDP). Hosokawa also committed acts of discourtesy, militancy, and voluability, as well as rejecting tax cuts because of continuing budget deficits. He then clashed with the foreign ministry when his UN ambassador stated in an unapproved speech that Japan still was determined to have a permanent seat on the Security Council. This illustrated the ineffective coordination between the parties in power and the bureaucracy under Japan's coalition governments. During April 1994, Hosokawa resigned amid charges of financial corruption after just nine months in office. Hata Tsutomu became prime minister, but his government was fatally weakened from the outset when the SDP refused to join the coalition. An impending no-confidence vote caused him to resign in June, resulting in a bizarre political realignment. Murayama Tomiichi, a 70-year-old Socialist, won election as prime minister, leading a three-party coalition. Murayama's was the seventh government in six years, resulting in a lack of continuity in Japan's policies at home and abroad. The atmosphere of crisis and confusion under Hosokawa ended under Murayama, who quickly addressed major issues. In November, he gained approval from the Diet for an economic stimulus package that reduced income taxes and raised the consumption tax to 5 percent, to take effect in April 1997.

Under Murayama, Tokyo's trade dispute with Washington continued. In 1995, $66 billion of Japan's $145 billion worldwide trade surplus was with the United States. Washington complained that its exports constituted only 1.5 percent of Japan's market, while Japanese exports commanded 24 percent of the U.S. market. Whereas 60 percent of Japan's trade surplus with the United States was in cars and car parts, only 7 percent of Japanese dealers sold U.S. automobiles. The Clinton administration therefore announced in May 1995 that unless Tokyo agreed to open its own car market to American products, the United States would impose punitive sanctions on Japanese luxury car exports. Despite reaching a compromise, U.S. complaints about Japanese obstructionism on trade continued. Worse, Washington barred Daiwa Bank from operating in the United States on the basis of blatant violations of banking regulations, resulting in a three-year ban to cover stock trading losses. With Japan in recession, the Murayama government had limited ability to satisfy U.S. complaints. At the same time, Japanese economic ties with the United States were becoming less important because Japan's influence in Asia was growing. Its two-way trade with Asia in 1995 exceeded that of the United States, and Asian nations received nearly two-thirds of its total development aid.

Several events in 1995 dampened Japan's commemoration of the 50th anniversary of the end of World War II. The recession continued despite six economic stimulus packages, the latest coming in September 1995. Banks reported $375 billion in nonperforming loans. Optimists pointed to stable and full employment to argue that Japan was merely passing through a phase in restructuring (*kisei kanwa*). But pessimists asserted that the end of LDP dominance made it impossible to rally people behind a program to achieve economic prosperity and political stability. Two disasters in 1995 provided support for this cynical view. During January an earthquake in Kobe killed over 5,000 people and caused over $100 billion in losses. The government became the target of angry criticism for being ill prepared, uncoordinated, slow, and feeble in managing relief operations. Then in March a nerve gas (sarin) attack on the Tokyo subway killed 12 people. Authorities attributed the crime to the followers of Aum Shinrikyo ("Way of Supreme Truth"), one of thousands of "new religions" legally registered in Japan. Police raided the sect's compound near Mount Fuji and found stockpiles of chemicals, equipment to manufacture automatic rifles, and technology for biological warfare. These incidents confirmed the growing belief among the Japanese people that the government was incapable of managing national affairs.

CRISIS AND CONSTERNATION

Japan would pay a huge price for failing to resolve domestic challenges after 1990. Reports of corruption in 1996, for example, "made the whole nation look like a haven for salaried thieves and crooks."[11] There also was no progress on administrative reform. Government debt rose to 90 percent of GNP, and economic growth declined further after a five-year slump. Yet the LDP regained its majority in the Diet's lower house in the fall elections of 1997, while it headed a majority coalition in the upper house with the SDP and the Sakigake, a small LDP splinter party. Hashimoto Ryutaro, who had replaced Murayama as prime minister in January 1996, won easy reelection that September. But results of local elections showed that the

LDP was not as strong and popular as this suggested, because nonregular, nonpartisan voters defeated its candidates. Nor were rank-and-file party members obedient, as many cooperated with Ozawa Ichiro's New Frontier Party. Also, a steady decline in voter turnout continued, especially after opposition leaders staged a childish three-week sit-in to prevent the bailout with public funds of seven bankrupt housing loan (*jusen*) companies. When Nakasone forced Hashimoto to name a politician convicted of bribery to his cabinet, coalition allies howled and his popularity fell by 31 points to 28 percent. Worse, the recession continued, attributed to the rise in the consumption tax to 5 percent and higher health care costs.

But Japan's central problem was an unhealthy banking system. Because banks refused to cancel a growing number of unperforming loans, there was less capital to lend to clients who could invest the funds in more productive ventures. Banks also suffered losses owing to rising business failures resulting from falling stock prices wiping out hidden assets of stock that companies held in other firms. The failure of other loans secured with land occurred as property declined in value. The government refused to divulge the extent of the problem to avoid further depressing already low business and consumer confidence. This also prevented implementation of corrective action. And another $125 billion was at risk in loans to financially unstable Asian clients after Japanese investors exported yen to compensate for declining business at home. Finally, in January 1998, the government announced that Japanese banks held $658 billion in nonperforming loans, constituting roughly 16.3 percent of the gross domestic product (GDP). The figure was undoubtedly higher because the government had compiled the numbers in the summer of 1997. By that time a raft of small banks had failed, and the Long-Term Credit Bank of Japan, the nation's second largest, was nearing a crisis. The government talked about recapitalizing weak banks and, in July 1997, proposed a bridge bank plan but did not implement it. Then news broke that bureaucrats had received lavish entertainment and gifts for tipping off banks of surprise inspections.

"Japan in 1997 was thus in a sad state economically and politically,"[12] an observer concluded. Powerful executives were arrested and indicted for paying off racketeers; these executives were from four of the largest securities firms, two leading city banks, a large department store, and a major food company. By November the weight of mounting debts had driven a leading city bank, Hokkaido Takushoku, and a major securities firm, Yamaichi, into bankruptcy. Soon thereafter, what a U.S. official called "crony capitalism" caused nervous investors to remove $100 billion from Japan's stock market, triggering the collapse of regional economies. Tokyo's response to the spreading financial crisis was a huge disappointment in Asia. Japan at first spawned high hopes, proposing the establishment of an Asian Monetary Fund (AMF) that would have been capitalized at $100 billion from the reserves of Japan, the PRC, Taiwan, and Hong Kong. Governments whose currencies were under attack could have drawn cash from the AMF to counter the speculators. But the United States opposed the idea because it would make it impossible to force reforms. At a joint IMF–World Bank meeting in Hong Kong, Japan, submitting to pressure from the United States, agreed to add other nations outside of Asia and set as a condition for financial help steps for rapid liberalization, deregulation, and privatization. This allowed the United States to use the financial crisis to compel the opening of trade and monetary markets.

Deep pessimism gripped Japan as economic conditions worsened during 1998. In 1997 the GPD shrank by 0.7 percent, and that level more than doubled in 1998. This was the first two-year annual GDP decline since 1945. Public cynicism and apathy reflected a widespread belief that the nation lacked the domestic leadership to overcome shaken confidence. Land prices had fallen for seven straight years, and stock prices were at a twelve-year low. Lower production, consumption, and profits had resulted in a mounting number of bankruptcies, as unemployment reached a postwar record high. To promote recovery, the government had expanded public works spending and lowered interest rates from 0.5 to 0.25 percent. In July the LDP suffered huge losses in upper house elections, losing 17 seats. After Hashimoto resigned, the party named Obuchi Keizo as president, despite his dull personality and platform. Although he was known as a consensus builder, the people did not like Obuchi, who became prime minister with the lowest postwar approval rating of 25 percent. He pushed through the Diet six bills to deal with the banking crisis. Closing weak banks or making them bridge banks, the government provided money for the surviving banks to regain viability. The largest economic stimulus package in Japan's history provided $133 billion in spending and $59 billion in new taxes. Finally, Obuchi implemented a tax rebate of $5.8 billion in the form of coupons to be spent over six months.

Washington criticized Obuchi's plan for not doing enough to stabilize Japan's financial system, stimulate domestic consumption, and raise purchases of imports. An observer noted the irony, remarking that "American pressures on Japan in the 1990s have thus gone from trying to contain its economy to efforts to prevent it from collapsing. Times have changed."[13] The United States also suspected that Japan planned to export its way out of recession while not absorbing goods from Asia that would flood into the U.S. market. By contrast, cooperation on security matters resulted in completion of the U.S.-Japan Defense Cooperation Guidelines that

Hashimoto's government had announced in September 1996, providing for expanded joint military and paramilitary action. Japan would cooperate in meeting emergencies in areas surrounding the home islands with area support in noncombat-related supplies such as food, fuel, and medical assistance. SDF forces would join in search and rescue operations and aid U.S. forces with intelligence gathering, surveillance, and minesweeping. The financial crisis stalled passage of the legislation authorizing the SDF's implementation of its provisions. Then on August 31, 1998, North Korea launched a missile into Japan's airspace, prompting Tokyo to suspend the light water nuclear reactors deal, reject a pending aid request, and end normalization talks. Spurred by what North Korea said was a rocket to put a satellite into orbit, Japan allocated funds for joint research with the United States on a ballistic missile defense system.

By 1999 a $500 billion government bailout had stabilized the banking industry as Japan searched for an alternative to "Japan, Incorporated." A traditional banking system had helped Japan build its economic miracle, eliminating a need for more flexible capital markets. But after 1996 the government had begun deregulating the financial industry, breaking down barriers between banks, brokerages, and insurance companies, and encouraging more competition even from abroad. Mergers, failures, and alliances reduced from 20 to 9 the number of independent banks. Indications of Japan's intention to launch an economic revolution emerged with incentives for people to move a portion of $12 trillion in personal savings out of the old-fashioned bank accounts for reinvestment in stocks, bonds, and mutual funds. In 1999 only 10 percent of Japanese investments were in stocks and bonds, compared to 36 percent in the United States. J. P. Morgan, Morgan Stanley, and Merrill Lynch acted vigorously to enter Japan's stock market. These reforms reinvigorated the Japanese economy as businesses no longer had to rely on banks for capital, and public optimism spurred consumption. There also were new demands on companies to turn a profit, requiring them to be more cost efficient. More important for Obuchi, his reforms had stimulated a fragile economic recovery during early 1999.

Obuchi's decisive action to lift Japan out of its financial crisis prompted a 40-point increase in an approval rating that reached 57 percent in October 1998. Progress on assorted issues in foreign affairs contributed to this rise in popularity. For example, Obuchi presented South Korean president Kim Dae-jung during his visit to Japan in October with a formal written apology expressing deep remorse and heartfelt apology for the tremendous damage and suffering Japan caused Korea under colonial rule. He then announced a new $3 billion loan package for South Korea. But Tokyo could not agree to China's wording of a formal apology when Jiang Zemin made a state visit in

Japan's economic aid to South Korea allows newlyweds President Kim Dae-jung and Prime Minister Obuchi to jump over troubling puddles. *Far Eastern Economic Review*, October 22, 1998.

November. That month, Obuchi signed a joint communiqué in Moscow that committed Japan to achieve a peace treaty by 2000 and promote investment in Russia. He then pledged $30 billion in loans and other arrangements to rebuild the hardest hit economies in East Asia. But early in 1999, Obuchi's popularity began to decline as a result of his manueuvers to increase his and the LDP's political power in the Diet. After visiting Beijing in July and failing to improve relations, Obuchi was shuffling his cabinet in September when an accident at a nuclear plant resulted in two deaths and 47 casualties. Worse, despite government spending totaling $300 billion, the return of economic recession had by November reduced Obuchi's approval rating to 32 percent. Then, after a sumo wrestling match-fixing scandal and a volcano eruption, Obuchi suffered an incapacitating stroke in April 2000. Mori Yoshiro, his successor, had a reputation both for pragmatism and links to corruption.

Japan struggled during the decade after the Cold War ended to replace the core axioms that had guided its foreign policy since 1945. Previously, it had focused on economics to avoid the conflict, suffering, and humiliation of a militarist and imperialist past. Tokyo's reluctance to substitute a proactive for a reactive global role was most evident in the Gulf War, as Japan listened to worldwide ridicule for having suggested that it deserved a permanent seat on the UN Security Council. Events in 1999 indicated that Japan was ready to match its decisiveness in meeting its financial crisis with new assertiveness in world affairs. In March, Tokyo instructed a destroyer to fire live rounds at two suspected North Korean spy ships, forcing their retreat from Japanese territorial waters in the first such action since World War II. In May the Diet approved new defense guidelines for joint SDF military operations with U.S. forces. In July, lawmakers passed a bill to form constitutional "research councils" early in 2000 to provide a forum for discussion of Article 9. Also, Obuchi endorsed legislation granting official status to the national flag and anthem, powerful symbols closely associated with Japan's militarist past. A poll in October 1999 found that 70 percent of respondents were worried about countering threats to national security. But those predicting Japan's transformation into a bona fide world power needed to remember the advice of an Asian adage: "Speaking of next year makes the devil laugh."[14]

NOTES

1. Gary D. Allinson, *Japan's Postwar History* (Ithaca, NY: Cornell University Press, 1997), 166.

2. Hugh Cortazzi, *The Japanese Achievement* (New York: St. Martin's Press, 1990), 251.

3. Quoted in Clyde Haberman, "A Step-by-Step Leader for Japan," *New York Times*, October 20, 1987, p. 3.

4. Hans H. Baerwald, "Japan's House of Councilors Elections: A Mini-Revolution," *Asian Survey* 29 (September 1989): 836.

5. Steven W. Hook and Guang Zhang, "Japan's Aid Policy since the Cold War," *Asian Survey* 38 (November 1988): 1060.

6. Yong Deng, "Japan in APEC: The Problematic Leadership Role," *Asian Survey* 37 (April 1997): 359.

7. Kent E. Calder, "Japan in 1990: Limits to Change," *Asian Survey* 31 (January 1991): 31.

8. Quoted in *New York Times*, September 26, 1991, p. 4.

9. Gregory W. Noble, "Japan in 1992: Just Another Aging Superpower?" *Asian Survey* 33 (January 1993): 9.

10. Gerald J. Cardinale, "Through the Japanese Looking Glass," *Asian Survey* 32 (July 1992): 639.

11. Haruhiro Fukui and Shigeko N. Fukai, "Japan in 1996: Between Hope and Uncertainty," *Asian Survey* 37 (January 1997): 23.

12. Haruhiro Fukui and Shigeko N. Fukai, "Japan in 1997: More Uncertain, Less Hopeful," *Asian Survey* 38 (January 1998): 30.

13. Robert Uriu, "Japan in 1998: Nowhere to Go But Up," *Asian Survey* 39 (January/February 1999): 122.

14. Quoted in Michael Blaker, "Japan 1976: The Year of Lockheed," *Asian Survey* 17 (January 1977): 90.

Biographies: The Personalities Behind Japan's Emergence

Doi Takako (November 30, 1928–   ), Socialist Party leader

In September 1986, Doi Takako became the first woman in Japanese history to lead a major political party when she gained election as chair of the Japan Socialist Party (JSP). She was born in Kobe, and her father was a doctor who had progressive attitudes regarding the role of women in Japanese society. An admirer of U.S. president Abraham Lincoln, Doi later said that she pursued a law degree at Doshisha University in Kyoto because "defending the poor and the deprived as a very idealistic lawyer was very attractive to me." She instead became a lecturer on Japan's Constitution at Doshisha in 1958 and joined the JSP, which had widespread support among Japan's intellectuals. In 1969 a newspaper report that Doi was planning to run for a seat in the Diet altered her career. When she told the deputy mayor of Kobe that the rumor was erroneous, he sarcastically replied, "Wouldn't it be really stupid to run in an election you know you have no chance of winning?" Insulted and infuriated, Doi became a candidate and won a seat in the lower house, winning reelection seven consecutive times thereafter. She immediately earned respect for taking forceful positions on controversial issues related to environmental matters, constitutional law, and foreign affairs.

Doi's willing participation in private party gatherings to discuss strategy led to her appointment as vice chair of the JSP in 1983. Many of her male colleagues bristled as this assertive woman broke traditional gender taboos, and her deep voice brought unflattering remarks about her femininity. But she gained popularity among average Japanese because she shared many interests with common people, including playing pachinko (a game akin to pinball popular among Japanese), rooting for the Hanshin Tigers baseball team, and singing at karaoke bars. Her riceroots popularity placed her in an ideal position to become the JSP's leader after it suffered the worst electoral defeat in decades in the lower house elections during July 1986, winning only 86 of 512 seats. A surge in the JSP's popularity followed, as Doi's so-called Madonna strategy brought a flood of women into the political process for the first time. Doi's success was the result not only of gender politics but also of the continuation of her predecessor's efforts to move the JSP away from adherence to strict Marxist-Leninist ideology. In foreign affairs, for example, she refused to criticize the U.S.-Japan Mutual Security and Cooperation Treaty or call for liquidation of Japan's Self-Defense Forces. In domestic affairs Doi, like a European Social Democrat, favored a market-based economy.

Doi's popularity grew after Prime Minister Takeshita Noboru resigned in June 1989 and his successor did so as well in the face of public protests after he refused to admit a sexual escapade with a geisha. That July, during the upper house election campaign, Doi urged women to voice grievances, demonstrating that, in the words of one journalist, she "knows that women across the country are furious . . . with politicians, furious at the tax, furious at the husbands." Ten of twelve women candidates triumphed, as the JSP won 46 of 126 open seats and the Liberal Democratic Party (LDP) lost control of the upper house in the election. As JSP chair, Doi was the target of blame when the LDP retained control of the lower house in the elections of February 1990. Doi also failed as promised to form a majority coalition in the upper house under JSP leadership. After the JSP's crushing defeat in national elections in April 1991, Doi resigned as party leader. But two years later, Socialist prime minister Hosokawa Morihiro selected her to become speaker of the Diet. In 1996 she joined the Socialist Democratic Party and became its chair. Doi's impact on Japanese postwar politics was dramatic, mobilizing voters to speak out against government corruption and encouraging women to achieve greater equality of opportunity in public affairs. Highly respected for her pragmatic approach to politics, tart-tongued Doi is known as the Iron Butterfly.

Honda Soichiro (November 17, 1906–August 5, 1991), industrialist

The founder of Honda Motors Company in 1948, Honda Soichiro earned a reputation as a rebellious and innovative industrialist who created one of the world's largest motorcycle and automobile companies. He was born in a small village, and his father was a blacksmith and bicycle repairman. For

Honda, seeing his first automobile in 1914 created a lifelong passion for machines and the smell of gasoline. In 1922 he dropped out of school in the tenth grade, leaving behind his impoverished family and heading for Tokyo and a job in a machine shop. At first he provided child care for the owner, but after the Great Kanto Earthquake of 1925 there were many new job opportunities—and he become a master mechanic. Returning home, Honda opened an auto repair shop in 1928, devoting his spare time to womanizing, drinking, and racing cars. A spectacular racing accident in 1935 left him hospitalized for a year, but Honda resumed work repairing cars after recovery. He briefly attended technical school at night but dropped out after deciding that a diploma was "worth less than a movie ticket." During World War II Honda expanded his auto repair shop into a production facility that made all the piston rings and propellers for airplanes that Japan's military could buy—until U.S. bombers destroyed the plant in 1945. Two years later, seeing the need for inexpensive transportation in postwar Japan, Honda went back into business, buying 500 surplus radio generators, attaching them to the rear wheel of bicycles, and then selling his crude motorcycles.

Honda achieved dominance in the global motorcycle industry during the 1950s and then matched this success in auto production. But he remained something of an outsider even in Japan, as his success generated as much resentment at Toyota as it did in Detroit, despite his sagacity. "You have to act as if everyone around you is a guest, a customer," Honda once advised. Also, as one observer noted, he was "sensitive to seemingly trivial psychological matters"; for example, he barred Honda's subsidiaries in the United States from flying the Japanese flag. Rarely in his office, he spent most of his time in the factory, one time solving a body noise problem with chalk on the floor. His workers called Honda "Pop" around the plant but also Kaminari, or "Thunderbolt," for his outbursts of temper. Once he picked up a wrench and hit a worker in the back. "I touched him," Honda admitted later. "In a way, it showed our closeness. And I thought he'd forgive me." Although he retired in 1973, Honda stayed actively involved as the company director, major stockholder, and self-appointed spokesman, lecturing youth groups about self-reliance, hard work, respect for parents, and safe driving. The "supreme advisor" also devoted himself to the Honda Foundation, which he created in 1979. It sponsored seminars on the use of technology, focusing on improvements to prevent accidents and curtail pollution from auto exhaust. In 1989 Honda was admitted to the Automotive Hall of Fame.

Always the maverick, Honda delighted in offering stinging critiques of the way corporate Japan controlled the lives of its workers. He crowed about how he prevailed over the government in demonstrating the superiority of his approach to making automobiles. Honda bristled at the most frequently offered explanation for Japan's industrial success: that its population was able to sublimate individual to group needs. "First, each individual should work for himself—that's important," he emphasized in a 1987 interview. "People will not sacrifice themselves for the company. They come to work at the company to enjoy themselves." To the end, Honda dreamed of new technology. By his own account, he produced 470 new ideas and designs throughout his career; these included Japan's first cast-iron wheel spokes (which replaced wooden ones), automatic machinery for manufacturing piston rings, and the lightweight Super Cub motorcycle. He owned 360 patents. "I think best," Honda once said, "with a wrench in my hands." But it was his independence, technical skills, innovative management philosophies, and flair that carried his name into almost every reach of the globe.

Ikeda Hayato (December 3, 1899–August 13, 1965), LDP prime minister

An economist and tax expert with superior administrative ability, Ikeda Hayato carried out policies as prime minister from 1960 to 1964 that transformed Japan into a global economic power. The son of a prosperous sake brewer, he studied law and economics at Kyoto Imperial University. After graduation in 1925, Ikeda worked in several prefectural offices of the Ministry of Finance until he became bedridden with a rare skin disease (pemphigus) for five years during the 1930s. Acting on his mother's advice, he visited shrines and temples in Buddhist robes in search of a cure, emerging after recovery a vegetarian with a new sense of piety and stoicism. Thereafter, during World War II, Ikeda headed the tax sections in Osaka and in Tokyo before becoming chief of the Tax Bureau in the Ministry of Finance in 1945. During the U.S. occupation he established close ties with Yoshida Shigeru, who appointed him vice minister of finance early in 1947 when Yoshida was prime minister. Then, as finance minister after Yoshida returned as prime minister late in 1948, Ikeda worked closely with Joseph Dodge the following year to implement a U.S. economic austerity plan to halt inflation. When critics complained that people could not afford to buy rice, Ikeda's typically blunt and acerbic reply was "Let them eat barley!" As Yoshida's representative in Washington during talks on the Japanese Peace Treaty, however, he worked to revise the economic policies imposed under the U.S. occupation.

In 1949 Ikeda gained election to his first of five consecutive terms in the lower house of the Diet. But his sharp tongue and arrogant manner while he was a member of Yoshida's cabinet ignited numerous angry disagreements with colleagues. In November 1952 Ikeda was forced to resign after passage in the Diet of a no-confidence vote in response to his reply to attacks on his retrenchment measures that it could not "be helped if small businessmen go broke and hang themselves." Yoshida then sent Ikeda, among his most trusted allies, to Washington to negotiate the U.S.-Japan Mutual Defense Assistance Agreement of 1954; this agreement provided for increases in Japan's defense force, shared the cost of Japan's military development between the two governments, encouraged U.S. capital investment in Japan, and retained the strategic export embargo on the People's Republic of China (PRC). When Yoshida resigned late in 1954, Ikeda retired briefly, returning to serve as minister of finance under both Ishibashi Tanzan and Kishi Nobusuke. Because of his contacts abroad and his close ties with businessmen and bankers, Ikeda was the logical choice as prime minister when Kishi resigned in July 1960. Apologizing profusely for "disgraceful and unworthy stubbornness" in seeking the job, Ikeda set as his primary goal "restoring America's confidence in Japan."

Ikeda adopted a "low posture" to rebuild political harmony at home and abroad after the acrimonious fight over renewal of the U.S.-Japan Security Treaty. His projected ten-year Income Doubling Plan led to tremendous economic growth in Japan, and in other measures he extended Social Security coverage, invested government funds in public utilities and small business, reduced taxes, and revised the election system. In June 1961 Ikeda met with U.S. president John F. Kennedy in Washington, D.C., but he also resumed economic ties with the PRC without making political concessions. His two visits to Southeast Asia helped repair relations that had suffered as a result of Japan's actions during World War II, and his expansion of aid for economic development was also welcomed. To the end, Ikeda was respected and admired, but his stubbornness and inability to tolerate fools lightly limited his popularity. In a half-hour interview during 1960, he stunned a newsman when, after 29 minutes and in the middle of a question, he stood up and said, "The half hour is ended. Good day!" In November 1964, throat cancer forced Ikeda to retire, naming Sato Eisaku as his successor on his deathbed to break a party deadlock. In that year Ikeda presided over the Tokyo Summer Olympics, the crowning event of an administration that restored Japan to international prominence.

Ishizaka Taizo (June 3, 1886–March 5, 1975), business leader

From 1956 to 1968 Ishizaka Taizo served as the second president of Keidanren (Federation of Economic Organizations), acting essentially as

the equivalent of an economic prime minister for Japan's business, industrial, and financial community. He deserves a major share of the credit for
the emergence of Japan as a global economic power. Born in Tokyo,
Ishizaka graduated from Tokyo University with a law degree and then
worked briefly in the Ministry of Communications. He joined the Daiichi
Seimei Insurance Company in 1915, rising through the ranks to become its
president in 1938. Under his direction the firm rose from thirteenth to second place in size among Japanese insurance companies. Then, in 1946, U.S.
occupation authorities purged him along with the chief executive officers of
all other large firms who had links to the military. Ishizaka resurfaced in
1948, reflecting adoption of the "reverse course" in U.S. occupation policy
that sought Japan's rapid economic recovery. He served as head of Tokyo
Shibaura Electric, which later became the giant electronics manufacturer
Toshiba Corporation. Postwar labor strife almost had brought the firm to
bankruptcy, but Ishizaka developed and implemented a tough management
policy that facilitated swift recovery. Toshiba eventually would be known
as the "General Electric of Japan."

In 1956 Ishizaka started to use his influence as president of the Keidanren
to advance his view that Japan needed to become more deeply involved in
global economic affairs; he lobbied in particular for more liberal policies regarding foreign capital investment in Japan. In December 1965 Ishizaka accepted the presidency of Expo '70 to supervise preparations for the World
Exposition in Osaka. Many saw this as an honorary appointment, but his seri-
ousness soon was dramatically apparent. The government had pledged substantial funds for the world's fair, but the finance minister then maneuvered
to reduce the cost. Meeting with Prime Minister Sato Eisaku, Ishizaka was
blunt and direct, stating that "Expo is a national commitment, not just a businessman's undertaking. If the world points the finger of scorn at Japan over
Expo, it is not I who will be put to shame. It is you." Within days of this warn-
ing, he received word that the government would make good on its financial
pledge, committing $163 million to cover construction costs. Thereafter
Ishizaka let others work out the details, ranging from arrangements for ac-
commodations to resolving disputes over architectural styles. "The secret of
his success as an organizer," remarked one subordinate, "is that he is not
afraid to delegate authority."

Expo '70, Ishizaka hoped, would strengthen Japan's confidence in its
own economic power. This would silence those who argued that Japanese
industry still needed protection against both foreign capital and imports.
"Japan is overflowing with youthful vitality," he emphasized. "There is no
need to limit the growth of the Japanese economy. It is endless." In 1968 he
resigned as president of the Keidanren to become president of the Arabian

Oil Company, an easy transition because he already was chairman of the board. A skilled business diplomat, Ishizaka was a strong opponent of government intervention in economic affairs, especially in trade and capital liberalization. He led Japan's business-industrial community in supporting policies conducive to maintaining good relations with the United States. During his long career, Ishizaka held approximately 300 honorary positions in business and public affairs, including vice president of the Japanese Red Cross, president of the Boy Scouts of Japan, and member of the advisory committee to Chase Manhattan Bank.

Kishi Nobusuke (November 23, 1896–August 7, 1987), LDP prime minister

Kishi Nobusuke's determination as prime minister after 1957 to force the Diet to approve renewal of the U.S.-Japan Security Treaty prompted violent public demonstrations of opposition in 1960, damaging Japan's image abroad and forcing him to resign. His father was a sake brewer and minor prefectural official whose surname was Sato, after adoption into the family of his wife. This remains an accepted way for a Japanese family without a male heir to maintain the family name and ancestral line, and for a young man to improve his socioeconomic prospects. Kishi's strong-willed mother, a descendent of politicians who led the Meiji Restoration, often lectured her son never to "forget you are a samurai. Never take second place." In 1917 he enrolled at Tokyo Imperial University, coming under the influence of Uesugi Shinkichi, a leader of a conservative nationalist organization. His opportunities improved after his father's elder brother adopted Kishi upon marriage to his daughter, thus allowing him to retake his family name. Kishi graduated in 1920 with top honors, despite his drinking and womanizing, and entered the Ministry of Agriculture and Commerce, where he became the leader of a skilled group of young bureaucrats who cooperated with the politically ambitious military. In 1926 Kishi headed the Japanese Pavilion at a trade fair in Philadelphia, touring the United States during the following year and studying its steel industry. After returning to Japan, Kishi cultivated ties with leading businessmen at restaurants and on the golf course. His supervisor complained that "Kishi behaves as if he were the Minister instead of me."

In October 1936, Kishi went to Manchuria to serve as deputy head of the Manchukuo government's business section, working with Tojo Hideki, the chief of staff of the Japanese occupation army. After Japan seized northern China, Kishi reorganized industry in the region as part of a five-year plan to make it a strong economic dependency that would contribute to placing Japan on a war footing. Kishi then returned to Japan and held a series of government posts until October 1941, when then Prime Minister Tojo named him head of the Department of Commerce and Industry. In that position Kishi supervised the conversion of peacetime industries into wartime industries and also signed the declaration of war against the United States. After a brief stint in the Diet, he rejoined Tojo's wartime cabinet as state minister and vice minister of munitions, displaying notable skill in mobilizing the economy for the war. Disagreement with Tojo's war-at-all-costs military strategy in 1943 brought demands for Kishi's resignation. He saw Saipan as key to defense of the home islands, urging surrender if the United States seized the island. Tojo, viewing Kishi as incompetent in military matters, forced him out in July 1944, one month after Saipan fell. Shortly thereafter, *Mainichi*, a top newspaper in Japan, published an essay by Kishi criticizing Tojo, providing impetus for the collapse of his government.

U.S. occupation officials arrested Kishi in 1945, holding him in Sugamo Prison for three years as a "Class A" war criminal. Prior to his release, he not only cleaned floors and latrines but read about Western liberalism. "I became convinced" in prison, he recalled, "that Japan must never again be involved in war." In early 1953 he won election to the lower house of the Diet as a member of the Liberal Party. In late 1954 Kishi conspired behind the scenes to form the Democratic Party that ousted Yoshida Shigeru as prime minister, replacing him with Hatoyama Ichiro. Kishi then was a key figure in the merger that created the Liberal Democratic Party, persuading colleagues that only unity on the right would stop the "ceaseless underground efforts of the Communist Party" from resulting in a leftist seizure of power. Kishi failed, however, to gain enough support to pass his constitutional revisions abolishing the antiwar clause and restoring the emperor as head of state. When a stroke forced the resignation of Hatoyama in 1956, Kishi also did not secure a majority of votes as prime minister. Compromise choice Ishibashi Tanzan won election by just seven votes over Kishi in December 1956, after which he appointed Kishi as foreign minister. A bronchial disorder forced Ishibashi's resignation in February 1957. Predictably, Kishi gained election as his replacement.

Kishi's term was stormy. Students, Socialists, and intellectuals saw him as an unreconstructed fascist and a hated symbol of the old era. Criticized as well because of his staunch anti-communism and firm support for close ties with the United States, Kishi ignited bruising battles over efficiency ratings for teachers and a bill to expand police powers. But the political instability under Kishi peaked in the summer of 1960 with massive demonstrations in opposition to the revision of the U.S.-Japan Security Treaty. Denunciations of his heavy-handed and undemocratic behavior in gaining ratification were widespread, forcing him to resign in July. Kishi deserved credit, however, for working to improve Japan's image in Asia, as he visited Southeast Asia in 1957 and offered reparations, economic aid, and an apology for Japan's formerly exploitive and brutal treatment of those nations. Thereafter Kishi remained an influential representative in the Diet and a major leader of those members of the LDP who advocated close ties with South Korea and Taiwan. Clearly a man of authoritarian instincts, he often seemed most interested in reestablishing traditional Japanese values and re-creating the "authentic" nation of his childhood days. Despite claiming to practice "statesmanship of the humble heart," the astute and self-assured Kishi never displayed humility in pursuing the most militant conservative goals.

Miyazawa Kiichi (October 8, 1919–   ), diplomat and LDP prime minister

Bright, witty, and urbane, Miyazawa Kiichi was the first Japanese prime minister who spoke fluent English. More a cosmopolitan statesman than a politician or bureaucrat, he disdained fundraising and had neither the taste nor the aptitude for factional infighting. He was born in Tokyo into a privileged and influential political family; his grandfather was minister of justice, and his father served six terms in the Diet. Educated at Tokyo Imperial University, Miyazawa joined the Ministry of Finance in 1942, a year after his graduation. He rose through the ranks and became the minister's private secretary in 1949. Then he served in the same post in the Ministry of International Trade and Industry (MITI), where he gained expertise in foreign trade policy. In 1953 Miyazawa became the youngest member of the Diet's upper house, serving there until 1965. Joining the Liberal Democratic Party (LDP), he served as vice minister of education under Kishi Nobusuke and was Prime Minister Ikeda Hayato's main advisor on foreign economic policy matters. After winning his father's seat in the lower house in 1967, Miyazawa served three times as director general of the Economic Planning Agency. He was head of MITI under Prime Minister Sato Eisaku, supervising construction of the facilities for the World Exposition at Osaka and representing Japan in negotiations to resolve a serious textile dispute with the United States.

Miyazawa was foreign minister during the oil crisis from 1974 to 1976, sharply criticizing the United States for "dragging its feet on energy" and thus creating budget deficits and inflation. Prime Minister Miki Takeo's resignation in December 1976 brought speculation that Miyazawa might be his successor. Sony president Morita Akio supported Miyazawa as the ideal transitional figure from old to new leadership. But Fukuda Takeo and then

Ohira Masayoshi served as prime minister before Suzuki Zenko added Miyazawa to his government as minister of state in 1982. Two years later Miyazawa subdued a mugger posing as a campaign contributor outside a Tokyo hotel, thereby receiving favorable publicity that aided his bid to replace Nakasone Yasuhiro as prime minister. Miyazawa opposed Nakasone's rearmament program, proposing a "social asset doubling plan" that harked back to Ikeda's Income Doubling Plan, which called for increased spending on public works and decreased emphasis on foreign trade. But Nakasone continued to win reelection, and in 1986 he finally appointed his rival to be finance minister in his third cabinet. Serving concurrently during 1987 as Nakasone's deputy foreign minister, Miyazawa played a key role in tough negotiations with the Reagan administration over currency exchange rates and Japan's trade surplus with the United States. Unable later that year to defeat Takeshita Noborou as prime minister he stayed on as finance minister, but then was discredited for accepting bribes in the Recruit-Cosmos Scandal of 1988.

Kaifu Toshiki's timid leadership during the Gulf War enabled Miyazawa to resurface and gain election as prime minister in November 1991. He made little progress in opening rice markets over objections from farmers, negotiating with the Soviet Union about ownership of the disputed Kurile Islands, addressing the issue of campaign reform, and boosting domestic consumption. His main achievement was securing Diet approval, in June 1992, of the controversial Peacekeeping Operations bill that allowed deployment of Japanese troops abroad for the first time since World War II. Miyazawa's support for an anti-corruption bill in early 1993 revived and intensified discord in the LDP, leading to a no-confidence vote in June and his subsequent resignation. Economic recession was a primary reason for the LDP suffering huge losses in lower house elections in July, resulting in the election of the first non-LDP prime minister since 1955. Even though Miyazawa deserved credit for persuading the nation to assume a wider world role, he failed to control his party. He had contacts with many foreign leaders, who described him as mild-mannered, soft-spoken, and courtly. Yet at times he was aloof, arrogant, and abrasive; his elitism, a critic scoffed, gave "the impression he should be wearing scholars' robes." But even his rivals respected and relied on Miyazawa. In fact, in 1998 Prime Minister Obuchi Keizo named him minister of finance to help end Japan's severe financial crisis.

Mogi Yazuburo (February 13, 1935–   ), food producer

Mogi Yazuburo extended Japan's global economic reach as the leader of an old family business, the Kikkoman Corporation, whose primary product is soy sauce, a traditional Japanese food seasoning. Eight families merged to form the company in 1917, after having made soy sauce in competition with each other in Noda, Japan, for more than three hundred years. This enabled them to pool their capital to improve technology and equipment to exploit an expanding market in Japan. Postwar labor problems solidified the managerial unity, especially after a protracted strike in 1927 and 1928, the third longest in Japan's history. In response to workers protesting against low pay and inadequate working conditions, the Mogi family asked Professor Ueda Teijiro, who was a labor relations expert at Tokyo University of Commerce (now Hitotsubashi University), for advice. Ueda sent two of his top students as advisors; one was Keizaburo, the father of Yazuburo. After helping end the strike, Keizaburo's adoption through marriage into the Mogi family followed in 1929. He rose in the ranks of Noda Shoyu, reaching in 1962 the presidency of what by then had become Kikkoman Corporation. During his subsequent career he revolutionized the production processes and management procedures of soy sauce manufacturing.

During the 1930s just 10 percent of Kikkoman's business was overseas, but it was almost entirely confined to Japanese living in Manchuria, and North China, and Japanese Americans residing in the United States and Hawaii. Also, as late as 1949, Kikkoman produced only nine brand-name products. During the 1950s Mogi Keizaburo was the leading advocate and planner of a strategy of diversification aimed at tapping the American market. He realized that the Japanese home market for soy sauce had peaked, and although he still acted to expand sales in Japan, he focused on a vigorous advertising and marketing campaign in the United States. Safeway stores began carrying Kikkoman soy sauce in 1956, registering over the next decade annual sales increases of nearly 20 percent and for the following decade 10 to 15 percent each year. Active in overseas expansion, Mogi started soy sauce production in the United States during 1973. Avoiding the embargo against Japanese soybeans, Kikkoman opened a soy sauce plant in Walworth, Wisconsin, in 1973. By 1985, international operations accounted for 27 percent of the company's overall business, as it diversified and sold three dozen brand-name food or food-related products (including Del Monte tomato ketchup, Disney brand fruit juices, Ragu spaghetti sauces, and Mann's wines).

Mogi Yazuburo entered high school in Tokyo in 1950. Expected to enter the family business, in 1953 he enrolled at Keio University, where he studied management and business administration. Mogi devoted much effort to learning English because he wanted to study in the United States. In 1958 he enrolled at the Columbia University Business School, where he earned an MBA in 1961 in general management with a minor in marketing and international business. Returning to Japan that fall, he worked in the Noda factory for six months, learning how to make soy sauce and performing a variety of jobs like other new employees. Thereafter, he did clerical work in the Accounting Department. Mogi also served on a committee of young workers that devised and implemented plans for introducing computers at Kikkoman. In 1965, while working in the Corporate Planning Department, he conducted a cost study for the construction of a factory in the United States. His findings resulted in postponing plans to open a plant, but also a decision to form a partnership in 1967 with a California bottling company to cut rising freight costs.

Increased sales in the United States led Kikkoman in 1970 to authorize Mogi to conduct a feasibility study for building a plant abroad. He chose Walworth, Wisconsin, because it was convenient for distribution, close to soybeans and wheat, and a stable farming community. Mogi personally attended the town board meeting and county board public hearing in Wisconsin to dispel local fears of industrial pollution. When it opened in 1973, the Walworth plant employed 100 American workers. Mogi selected the first 12 Japanese biochemists, soy sauce brewers, and production managers to supervise the production process at Walworth, organizing an eight-month English-language program for them before leaving Japan.

Mogi's success in opening Kikkoman's plant in the United States led to his appointment as general manager of the International Department in 1977. Two years later he was appointed to the board of directors and in 1982 was promoted to managing director in charge of International Operations and Accounting and Finance. Before becoming president of Kikkoman, Mogi often spent three to four months each year in the United States helping to manage Kikkoman's international business operations. He authored two general business books and two other works about his personal business experiences. Mogi also served on several government committees studying issues related to overseas investment and international communication. His understanding of how U.S. marketing and distribution practices were businesslike, impersonal, and horizontally organized enabled Mogi to transform Kikkoman into one of Japan's most prosperous international industries.

Morita Akio (January 26, 1921–October 3, 1999), electronics producer

Morita Akio and Ibuka Masaru founded the company that eventually became the Sony Corporation. Morita's supervision of design, finance, marketing, and advertising operations made Sony a familiar symbol of Japan's postwar leadership in technology, quality, and innovation. Born near Nagoya into a family of wealthy sake brewers and soy sauce producers, Morita had a surname that literally means "prosperous rice field." The oldest of three sons, Morita was trained to become the manager of the family business, but his interest from childhood was in electronic physics. A mediocre student, he had to spend a year cramming before being admitted to Osaka Imperial University. Upon graduation with a physics degree in 1944, Morita was commissioned as a lieutenant in the Imperial Japanese Navy. He met Ibuka while working as a technical engineer developing heat-seeking bombs, and the two men established a close friendship over the course of regular collaboration. Following World War II, Morita taught at Tokyo University until a U.S. occupation edict barred former military officers from teaching. He and Ibuka then started a communications equipment business in a boarded-up shell of a bombed-out department store in Tokyo.

In May 1946 Morita used the equivalent of $500 from his family to form with Ibuka an electronic equipment company that manufactured shortwave converters for AM radios. After moving his 50 employees into a former army barracks outside the city in 1947, he made vacuum-tube voltmeters, amplifiers, and communications devices, which he sold to the Japan Post Office and the Japan Broadcasting System. In 1950 his first product targeted at the consumer market was a bulky tape recorder weighing nearly 40 pounds; it failed to attract consumers, but schools bought it for $500. Unable to import recording tape, Morita made his own, beginning a pattern of using foreign technology to make new products. Ibuka made the key breakthrough for the company after reading that Bell Laboratories in the United States had developed transistors for use in hearing aids. Perceiving that there was a consumer market for radios in the United States, Ibuka ("Mr. Inside") proposed buying the right to make transistors in Japan. Morita ("Mr. Outside") visited the United States, and its huge number of radio stations convinced him that prospects for radio sales were limitless. After the Japanese government approved payment in 1955 of $25,000 to Western Electric for the right to manufacture transistors in Japan, Morita's company marketed the first AM transistor radio.

Morita went to the United States in 1956 to discuss with a well-known American company its offer to make a large order if it could put its brand name on the radios. Morita rejected the proposal. "You are stupid," his American counterpart replied, "because our name has been around for fifty years." Morita proved him wrong. In 1958 he renamed his company Sony (from the Latin *sonus*, for "sound"), building it into a giant in global electronics. As president until 1976 and then chairman and chief executive officer, he was an outspoken critic of Japanese management practices. Indeed, he described Japan's work environment as reflecting a rigid corporate family, or "social security organization" with a stagnant caste system. Jobs and promotions were the rewards not of talent but of educational background and seniority. And it was almost impossible to fire anyone. Morita followed custom but incorporated Western modifications more so than his rivals did. Sony workers changed jobs according to ability and need, not an organizational chart. The atmosphere was relaxed, as Morita and Ibuka walked along assembly lines dressed in the same blue smocks that other employees wore. Morita mandated that "mental incentives" and "freedom to experiment" dictate advancement in rank, although seniority did bring automatic promotion.

To assemble its products, Sony hired young women with elementary school educations, paying fairly good wages and providing them with a high school education. There were dormitories for unmarried women employees and company housing and nurseries for those who were married. Morita emphasized that Sony was like a family, but he crushed an effort to organize a union in 1961. He resembled more an industrial salesman than an operating executive after 1983, serving on the U.S.-Japan Advisory Commission and working to ease trade friction. Adamantly insisting that Japan's markets were open to foreign products, Morita lectured Americans to work harder. During his long career he gained a reputation for being vocal, cheerful, open, and frank that he attributed to being too "Americanized." A brilliant marketer, he once ordered the shirt pockets of salesmen to be enlarged to hold Sony radioes. But critics described him as brazen and pushy. In particular, Americans resented his condescending attitude toward solving U.S. economic woes. "We never force you to buy," he remarked in 1985. "You decided to buy because Japanese products are of good quality and because the price was right." Out of place among stiff and formal competitors, his freewheeling style made the Sony Corporation something of an outcast in Japan. But Morita's flexible operating methods and innovative design policies placed Sony in the vanguard of Japan's emergence as a world economic power.

Nagano Shigeo (July 15, 1900–May 6, 1984), industrialist

Nagano Shigeo rose to prominence in the steel industry and served as president of the Japan Chamber of Commerce. His father was head priest at a Buddhist temple on the small island of Kamakari near Hiroshima that his family had owned for centuries. Nagano graduated in 1925 from Tokyo University and became manager of Fuji Iron, a bankrupt steel firm. After revitalizing the company, he became its managing director in 1933. Thereafter Fuji

Iron joined all other steel companies in a merger resulting in the formation of the government-dominated Nippon Steel Company. Nagano initially was director of the Purchasing Department in this huge combine, but he rose to serve as director from 1940 to 1946. In 1941 the Japanese government named him a member of the Iron and Steel Control Council that helped supervise wartime economic mobilization. As a result, U.S. occupation officials briefly purged Nagano after World War II, but he rejoined Nippon Steel as managing director in 1947. As the vice-director of the Japanese government's Economic Stabilization Board, he implemented measures to achieve Japan's swift postwar economic recovery. "We were afraid of food riots and a possible revolution as in Russia," he later confessed. "However, because of American money and supplies, the Japanese survived."

In 1950, passage of the Excessive Economic Power Decentralization Law forced the division of the Nippon Steel Company into (1) Yawata Iron and Steel Works, and (2) Fuji Iron and Steel Works. Nagano became the first president of the latter firm, once again systematically revitalizing a shattered company. He implemented policies to modernize and expand mills, emphasizing the manufacture of finished and semi-finished steel products. His leadership brought a spectacular rise in productivity during the 1950s that met rising demand, mainly from shipbuilders that were Fuji Iron and Steel's largest customers. Nagano's firm also provided steel products for the railway and appliance makers. In 1970 Inayama Yoshihiro, who had become president of Yawata Iron and Steel Works (which after 1945 was Japan's largest steel producer), joined Nagano to arrange a merger of the two companies. The formation of Nippon Steel Corporation ended competition for production facilities and secured a stable supply of steel, resulting in the new company becoming the world's largest producer of steel. Nagano became the first chairman, and Inayama served as president.

Meanwhile, Nagano had established a reputation as an important leader in the Japanese business-industrial community, becoming chairman of the Japan and Tokyo Chambers of Commerce and Industry in 1969. These two organizations, representing five million small and medium-sized companies in Japan, became far more active and influential than their counterparts in the United States, largely as a consequence of Nagano's strong leadership and direction. "Businessmen must always be in the front lines, but small businessmen cannot go abroad," he observed, because "they don't know how things are in Australia and Russia." Already in the late 1950s, Nagano had acted as an unofficial ambassador of Japanese small business in dozens of countries. Then and later, he regularly participated in domestic politics, lobbying strongly for tax exemptions for companies posting small profits and government credit for hard-pressed enterprises. Universally praised as a consensus builder, Nagano escaped criticism from leftist politicians who appreciated his work to improve Japan's postwar economy.

In the 1970s Nagano advocated two major projects that illustrated his world view. One initiative called for the development of natural resources in Soviet Siberia, using Japanese technical skill and money to recover Soviet natural gas, coal, timber, and other resources. "As long as we have to buy these things," he advised, "we should buy from the nearest source at the cheapest price." A second project was to build another Panama Canal near the existing facility, which was, Nagano argued, unable to handle the huge crude oil tankers and other superships then dominating ocean traffic. He was not afraid to support controversial causes, endorsing a ban on the sale of arms by Japanese companies. He also urged voluntary limits on selected Japanese exports, such as cars. After 1962 Nagano served as an advisor to the Ministry of Foreign Affairs. In 1971 he was named vice-president of the Pacific Basin Economic Council. A forceful, determined, and amiable industrialist, Nagano promoted Japan's emergence as a global power.

Nakasone Yasuhiro (March 27, 1918–), LDP prime minister

Nakasone Yasuhiro ranks among Japan's most popular and forceful postwar leaders, serving as prime minister from 1982 to 1987. Unlike most Japanese politicians, he was amiable and outgoing, if not flamboyant, with a straightforward speaking style. Nakasone gained fame at home and abroad because of his vigorous leadership. His father was a wealthy lumber dealer whose status helped Nakasone gain admission to Tokyo University, where he studied political science. Graduating in 1941, he went to work in the Ministry of Home Affairs. During World War II, Nakasone served in the Imperial Navy's paymaster corps at postings in Taiwan and the Dutch East Indies, later leading a crew that built airfields in the Southwest Pacific. In 1945 Nakasone joined the Interior Department as a Tokyo police inspector before entering politics. In 1946 he participated in a political debate with members of the Communist Party, arguing in favor of swift restoration of Japan's sovereignty and rearmament. By then, U.S. occupation officials had identified Nakasone as a nationalist extremist.

Nakasone's supporters formed the Lofty Aspirations Society during the U.S. occupation to organize political campaigns that stressed restoring Japanese independence and fostering Asian democracy. In 1947 he won a seat in the Diet, the first of 15 consecutive terms. Joining the Liberal Democratic Party (LDP) in 1955, the outspoken young Nakasone won admiration for his intelligence, earnestness, and organizational skills. A song he wrote in 1956 declared: "So long as there is this constitution, unconstitutional surrender will continue." After serving in the government of Prime Minister Kishi Nobusuke, Nakasone inherited the leadership of Ichiro Kono's faction upon his political mentor's death in 1965. Thereafter, his support for Prime Minister Sato Eisaku, Ichiro's bitter rival, earned him the nickname "Mr. Weathervane." Nakasone advised in response that "a weathercock stays set but moves his body. That's the essence of politics." From 1970 to 1971, as director general of the Defense Agency, he worked closely with the United States for joint use of its military installations and sharing of nuclear technology for use to power electricity plants. "I am a nationalist," Nakasone stated at that time, "and oppose communism at home, but I am not anti-Soviet, nor am I anti-Peking. Least of all am I a militarist. I believe in peaceful coexistence."

In the Tanaka government Nakasone was the minister of International Trade and Industry until he resigned in 1974 because of the Lockheed Scandal when Tanaka accepted $4.5 million in bribes for persuading Air Nippon to buy planes from Lockheed instead of a rival U.S. company. He then worked to change party rules for the election of the LDP's president, explaining that "one cannot become prime minister simply by wishing." But his reputation as a militarist and dogmatic nationalist bent on overturning a U.S.-imposed system slowed progress toward attaining his ambition. In 1978 Nakasone finished third among four candidates, having campaigned for a more activist world role for Japan, increased spending on defense, and constitutional revision to legalize a stronger military. He then worked in the Suzuki government before winning, with the help of Tanaka, election as LDP president. He assumed office as prime minister in November 1982. Although he denied subservience, doubters said Tanaka was the head of the new government and Nakasone the hat. He soon proposed cutting taxes and interest rates to stimulate a stagnant economy. His measures for administrative reform alienated bureaucrats, and his privatization of state-owned businesses drew criticism from labor leaders. Nakasone sought improved relations with the United States, agreeing to open Japan's market and make a larger contribution to defense in the Pacific. After he persuaded the Diet to raise military spending, public criticism and a $57 billion deficit prevented him from achieving further increases.

Several summit meetings with President Ronald Reagan that the press referred to as the "Yasu and Ronnie Show" brought Nakasone international fame. This reinforced his determination to compromise with Washington on trade and remain hawkishly nationalistic on defense spending. But his refusal to back demands for the removal of those members of the Diet who had been involved in the Lockheed Scandal led to a failed conspiracy to remove him. Then, in April 1985, he delivered an unprecedented television address appealing to the Japanese people to buy more, especially imported goods. This alienated business interests. But his gamble succeeded, as he won approval to waive LDP rules making possible a one-year extension of his term. His popularity plummeted in 1987 after he proposed a sales tax and Washington imposed sanctions for dumping, leading to his resignation that October. Although Nakasone may have been Japan's most cosmopolitan postwar prime minister, his biggest gaffe came in 1986 when he told a group of LDP leaders that in the United States, the education "level is somewhat lower than average because there are many blacks, Puerto Ricans, and Mexicans." Nakasone maintained influence in the Diet until his implication in bribe-taking in the Recruit-Cosmos Scandal forced him to resign from the LDP in 1989. He then devoted his energies to service as chairman and president of the International Institute of Global Peace.

Ogata Sadako (September 16, 1927–   ), human rights activist

In 1991 Ogata Sadako became United Nations High Commissioner for Refugees (UNHCR) and confronted the enormous task of directing efforts to provide food, shelter, and medical care for millions of people worldwide in areas suffering from starvation, disease, and massive displacement as a result of aggressive war or genocidal slaughter. When "the international community makes a mess of a crisis like Bosnia or Rwanda," one newsman explained, "it is Ogata who's left to pick up the pieces—she's the chief surgeon in the world's emergency room." She was born into the prominent Nakamura family, and her grandfather was a foreign minister and her father a career diplomat. When she was a youth, her parents encouraged Ogata to value an education and pursue her intellectual interests, unlike other young women of her generation. After living with her family in the United States, she was in Tokyo in 1945 when U.S. bombing raids destroyed the city. "The war," she later explained, "gave me sympathy for victims." Graduating from the University of the Sacred Heart in Tokyo in 1951, Ogata was one of the first postwar Japanese to pursue graduate study in the United States, earning a master's degree in 1953 from Georgetown University in international relations.

Ogata taught at Sacred Heart and was a researcher at Tokyo University before enrolling in 1956 at the University of California at Berkeley to study political science. Family members by then had named her "the American." Interrupting her studies, she married Tokyo economist and banker Ogata Shijuro in 1961, after which she stayed home and raised two children. Subsequently she earned her doctorate in 1963, choosing an academic career because entering the foreign service, her preferred choice, was virtually impossible for women at that time. After ten years as a lecturer, in 1974 she became an associate professor of international relations at Sophia University in Tokyo, thereafter serving as the first woman in a major administrative position at the institution. Ogata occupied her first diplomatic post as a member of Japan's delegation at the UN General Assembly from 1968 to 1978, becoming head of Tokyo's UN Mission with the rank of ambassador after 1976. UN general secretary Kurt Waldheim appointed Ogata in 1979 as special emissary to investigate conditions for Cambodian refugees trapped on the Thai-Cambodia border. During the 1980s she was Japan's representative on the UN Commission for Human Rights and chair of the executive board of UNICEF.

Simultaneously, Ogata served as dean of the faculty of foreign studies at Sophia University. She set aside her career as a full-time academic to become United Nations High Commissioner for Refugees in 1991 (a position created in 1951 to resettle 1.2 million refugees left homeless after World War II). "No doubt," an observer noted, "the General Assembly was swayed by the opportunity to make an important gesture to Japan, a major donor to the U.N. humanitarian relief budget, and to score a double by electing a woman to one of the U.N. system's highest posts." As UNHCR, by 1993 Ogata was in charge of a staff of more than 5,000 in 115 nations, supervising a budget of $500 million and worldwide relief efforts serving more than 15 million people. She quickly displayed leadership and ferocious dedication when she confronted the displacement of one and a half million Kurds who fled Iraq during and after the Gulf War. Ogata flew to Teheran, persuading the suspicious government of Iran to allow UNHCR workers to set up refugee camps for the Kurds on the Iran-Iraq border. Ogata was the constant target of intense scrutiny during her supervision of a series of vast resettlement projects. Undaunted, she would flash an unreadable half-smile and persevere. "She's a very controlled person," said a subordinate, "but when she sees people not being treated like human beings, she gets angry. And that's what it takes to do this job. You don't get depressed, you get angry."

After 1992, Ogata helped refugees in areas such as the former Yugoslavia and Rwanda, as she spent considerable time struggling to gain increased funding for the UNHCR. Traveling frequently to the 22 nations that made voluntary contributions to her agency, she regularly had to plead for them to make good on promises of financial support. In June 1993, Ogata chided representatives from the United States at her office headquarters for not providing sufficient funds. She was especially harsh in criticizing Japan for its failure to offer shelter and adequate money to help the world's refugees. Ogata won respect and admiration for her unwavering resolve, earning the nickname "Diminutive Giant" after her defense of the Kurds. Her staff also praised Ogata for running the UNHCR with a firm hand, restoring its credibility after years of administrative and financial mismanagement. Ogata's low-key and gracious demeanor made her a prime candidate to replace United Nations Secretary General Boutros Boutros-Ghali, causing some to call her "Sadako Sadako-Ogata." An uncommon postwar Japanese leader, Ogata would say what no one wanted to hear, reflecting the steady shift in the way Japan defined its role as a global power.

Ohira Masayoshi (March 12, 1910–June 12, 1980), LDP prime minister

Ohira Masayoshi gained prominence in postwar Japan first as foreign minister and later as prime minister until his death from a sudden heart attack in 1980. In public he appeared sleepy-eyed, slow, and deliberate, often pausing for a whole minute before finishing a sentence. In private, the well-read and honest Ohira was quick-witted and self-effacing. Born into a poor farming family on the island of Shikoku, after the death of his father he balanced farm chores with studies at Takamatsu Commercial High School. Graduating in 1933, Ohira attended Tokyo Commercial College (now Hitotsubashi University), and majored in economics. He was a good athlete who ran the marathon and was a sumo wrestler; a classmate even recalled how he "frequently carried a rolled-up judo uniform over his shoulder and walked with dragging feet, wearing heavy shoes. Even today I don't think he cares much about what he wears." Joining the Ministry of Finance in 1936, he collected taxes in Inner Mongolia while keeping his distaste for militarist excess to himself. From 1937 to 1945 he served as superintendent of the internal revenue office at Yokohama. In 1949 Ohira served as private secretary for Ikeda Hayato when he was minister of finance. In 1952 Ohira won election to the Diet, retaining his seat for the rest of his life.

Ikeda named Ohira foreign minister following his reelection as prime minister in 1962. Ohira admitted after the appointment that "I am an amateur as far as foreign policy is concerned, and I fully realize the limitations of my ability." He became responsible for implementing a "low posture" foreign policy, causing critics to charge that seeking cooperation with the Japan Socialist Party, instead of ramming unpopular policies through the Diet, resulted in unnecessary concessions. But Ohira believed that achieving domestic political unity and strength was essential before Japan could perform a more active world role. His plan to expand Japanese exports to boost economic growth led him to press for more open markets for Japan's goods in the United States. He also defended Japan's small but expanding trade with the People's Republic of China (PRC), pointing to Japan's guilt over previous aggression in China and "a sense of kinship which goes way back in our historical and cultural relationship." In 1963 Ohira spoke before the United Nations in favor of steps to control nuclear testing beyond the Nuclear Test Ban Treaty. He was a moderate on expanding defense spending, but he thought Japan should assume a greater share of the responsibility for its own military protection.

Under Prime Minister Sato Eisaku, Ohira served as head of the Ministry of International Trade and Industry (MITI) from 1968 to 1972. As foreign minister under Tanaka Kakuei, in 1972 he engineered diplomatic reconciliation with the PRC, although he continued to align on most global issues with the United States. While admiring his skill in diplomacy, colleagues in the LDP respected more his talent as a master political infighter. When Tanaka resigned as prime minister amid charges of corruption in 1974, Ohira stepped aside and endorsed Miki Takeo as the new prime minister, serving as his finance minister. He failed in 1976 to defeat Fukuda Takeo in the contest to replace Miki, but then he reignited a bitter rivalry by criticizing Fukuda's call for renewed militarization. Ohira, with Tanaka's strong financial and political support, worked quietly behind the scenes to build a coalition to replace Fukuda. Just two weeks before the election for prime minister in December 1978, he declared his candidacy, initiating an expensive campaign blitz that featured him stumping the nation with promises to improve rural living conditions. Tanaka's machine played the key role in Ohira scoring an overwhelming victory as party president and then prime minister. The outcome shocked Fukuda, and Ohira claimed the victory "was a surprise to me, too." Critics, however, branded the party election as "polluted" because of widespread vote buying and participation of many not registered as LDP members.

As prime minister, Ohira worked to expand Japan's global role, offering grants and loans to deter Vietnam from invading Cambodia and promising to expand Japan's domestic market for U.S. goods. In July 1979 he hosted the Tokyo summit of industrialized nations. Ohira had less success ending an economic downturn in Japan, but he gained reelection as prime minister after a bruising battle in June 1979. For the next eight months, a barrage of corruption charges against influential LDP members further weakened Ohira because of his inaction on reform. Rising inflation and Ohira's call for more defense spending emboldened Socialists in the Diet on the eve of upper house elections to propose a no-confidence vote. In a dramatic surprise, the measure passed when 69 members of the LDP under Fukuda's leadership abstained. A shocked Ohira, soon hospitalized from exhaustion, dissolved the Diet and called for elections in both houses. His unexpected death 10 days before the elections was largely responsible for the bitterly divided LDP's shocking and stunning victory. Nicknamed "Papa," he did not drink or smoke. Critics portrayed the solemn and brooding Ohira as "a bland, soft-edged, apparently opinionless man of consensus." Admirers applauded his skill in politics as a tactician and his refusal to promise what he could not deliver.

Sato Eisaku (March 27, 1901–June 3, 1975), LDP prime minister

Holding office from 1964 to 1972, Sato Eisaku served longer than any other postwar prime minister and presided over the most sustained period of economic growth in Japan's history after World War II. His father was a rice wine brewer and briefly a prefectural government official. He gave up his surname, Kishi, after adoption into his wife's family at the time of their marriage. Sato's mother was descended from Choshu *samurai*; his uncle, Matsuoka Yosuke, was Japan's militant foreign minister from 1940 to 1941; and his older brother, Kishi Nobusuke, was prime minister from 1957 to 1960. After earning his degree in German law at Tokyo Imperial University in 1924, Sato, hoping to travel abroad, went to work for Nippon Yusen Kaisha, Japan's largest steamship company. Thereafter he entered government service, working for 13 years in obscurity in the Ministry of Railways as an engineer, fireman, and stationmaster, building a reputation for efficiency and firmness. Sato served two tours in China, where he provided advice on railroad construction. By 1941 he had risen in the Ministry of Railways to chief of the Bureau of Controls, and then he served as head of the Automobile Bureau in the Transportation Ministry.

When World War II ended, Sato was head of the national railway system. Because his brother was in jail as a war criminal, U.S. occupation officials blocked Prime Minister Yoshida Shigeru from appointing Sato chief cabinet secretary. But Socialist prime minister Katayama Tetsu named him deputy minister of transportation in 1947, a post in which he displayed remarkable skill in resolving strikes that often disrupted railroad transportation. He then served as chief of the cabinet secretariat when Yoshida returned as prime minister in October 1948, and he gained election to the Diet in the following year. Although Sato emerged as one of Yoshida's closest advisors, the government in 1954 issued arrest warrants against him (as minister of construction at the time) for allegedly taking $56,000 in bribes from a shipbuilding association to ease anti-trust action. Yoshida forced the minister of justice to withdraw the warrants, arguing that Sato's participation was vital for the effective operation of the Diet. Indicted later on a lesser charge, he was acquitted as part of a general amnesty celebrating Japan's admission to the United Nations in 1956. Sato joined Yoshida in shunning the Liberal Democratic Party (LDP) after its creation in 1955, staying out of public life for the next two years.

Early in 1957 Sato joined the LDP when his brother Kishi became the party's president; thereafter Sato served in the Kishi government. Ikeda Hayato, a high school friend of Sato's, defeated Sato in 1960 by ten votes to become prime minister but named his rival minister of International Trade and Industry. Sato then served in various jobs under Ikeda, helping to supervise government preparations for Japan's hosting of the 1964 Olympic Games. With strong business and bureaucracy support, Sato became prime minister later that year when cancer forced Ikeda to resign. Sato then promoted a wider international role for Japan commensurate with its status as a global economic power, signing a treaty with South Korea in 1965 and visiting Southeast Asia to expand political and economic measures for development with nations in that area. An advocate of close ties with the United States, he firmly supported the U.S. war in Vietnam. This generated criticism of Sato, as did corruption in the LDP when three cabinet members resigned after taking bribes. Responding to a series of angry student demonstrations against the war in Vietnam, he endorsed a bill allowing the minister of education to take control of any university where protests lasted more than nine months. Further boosting his popularity, in 1969 Sato signed a communiqué with U.S. president Richard Nixon that led to the restoration of Japan's control over Okinawa in 1972 and more economic cooperation between the two nations.

Leftist protests against Sato persisted during his time in office because of his close ties to the LDP's pro-Taiwan faction. Hoping to silence these critics, Sato publicly enunciated the Three Non-Nuclear Principles (the non-manufacture, non-possession, and non-introduction into Japan of nuclear weapons). But public dissatisfaction grew in response to strained relations with the United States because of disputes over textile exports, revaluation of the yen, and the sudden announcement of Nixon's forthcoming visit to China. Inflation, pollution, and a money crisis added to mounting pressure, forcing Sato to resign in July 1972. Sato was neither flamboyant nor personable; a critic even ridiculed him as an unimaginative plodder who would tap his way across a stone bridge to ensure it was safe. But Sato was a competent administrator, shrewd backroom politician, and master builder of consensus. In 1969 he survived public embarrassment when his wife said in an interview that her husband repeatedly beat her early in their marriage, adding that in his political campaigns "before he opened his mouth, his hand came out." In 1974 Sato won the Nobel Peace Prize, detractors attributing this to a businessman having waged a costly publicity campaign on his behalf. Critics viewed the award as an example of black humor because it recognized him as "the main exponent of a reconciliation policy that contributed to a stabilization of conditions in the Pacific area." Reflecting his popular image as a dark and shadowy figure, Sato earned the nickname "Black Belly," which is a Japanese epithet for schemer.

Tanaka Kakuei (May 4, 1918–December 16, 1993), LDP prime minister

Tanaka Kakuei was the youngest prime minister of postwar Japan at the time of his election in July 1972, and he resigned amid charges of corruption two years later. However, for the next two decades this "shadow shogun" ruled the LDP with an iron-fisted grip. Nicknamed "the computerized bulldozer," he had a background that was entirely different from that of his predecessors. A self-made businessman with a technical school education, not a university degree, he cultivated an image as a "man of the masses." His father was a farmer and horse and cattle dealer who went bankrupt, forcing his family into poverty. Diptheria left Tanaka in frail health as a child, and he struggled to overcome a speech impediment, but it was impoverishment that forced him to take a job in 1933 as a construction laborer. Moving to Tokyo, he then worked as a clerk and apprentice to a building contractor, a reporter for an insurance business journal, and a salesman with a mercantile firm. After graduating from high school in 1936, Tanaka abandoned plans to attend the Imperial Naval Academy and instead started a small building construction contracting firm. Three years later, he was drafted and sent to Manchuria. After surviving a serious case of pneumonia, Tanaka was discharged in 1941 and resumed his construction business. In 1943 he founded the Tanaka Civil Engineering Company and secured lucrative wartime contracts. He also bought strategically located land in war-torn Tokyo at a fraction of its actual value.

After World War II, Tanaka's firm was one of the biggest construction companies in Japan. Despite making large contributions to the Progressive Party, he failed to win election to the Diet until 1947 but then retained his seat in 10 consecutive elections thereafter. Tanaka served in the cabinet of Prime Minister Yoshida Shigeru in 1948, but he resigned after being accused of accepting bribes from coal mining firms. After acquittal, he established close ties with Sato Eisaku's faction. Meanwhile he expanded his wealth and economic power, leading several companies and serving widely as a consultant. Tanaka was one of the first members of the Liberal Democratic Party formed (LDP) in 1955, which advocated business interests through the pursuit of policies favoring economic growth and close ties with the United States. Accepting big contributions from business organizations, Tanaka's effectiveness as a lobbyist for their interests grew with his political power. After serving in the Kishi government, he was finance minister under both Ikeda Hayato and Sato Eisaku. Responsible for granting television broadcasting licenses in the former post, Tanaka attended numerous international economic conferences in the latter. Forced to resign amid criticism for questionable land speculation deals in 1965, he returned to this post in late 1968 and remained in it until 1971.

Tanaka's skill as a political campaigner and fundraiser made him very popular. Folksy and irreverent, he often mimicked his critics with vicious impersonations. Unlike most LDP leaders, Tanaka supported government regulation of the national economy and a grandiose social welfare system. In 1967 he outlined a "plan for remodeling the Japanese archipelago," and in 1972 he elaborated on it in a best-selling book that proposed solutions to such problems as urban congestion, rural depopulation, and pollution of the environment through a grand infrastructure decentralization scheme involving the construction of new industrial towns in rural areas linked with a national network of modern highways and railroads. Reacting to popular demands for more dynamic leadership, in 1972 the LDP elected Tanaka over Sato's designated choice, Foreign Minister Fukuda Takeo. Tanaka worked for better relations with the United States, but his biggest legacy was reconciliation with the PRC. His redevelopment plan spurred rising land prices in targeted areas, as the government bought open land and approved funds to finance construction, with money pouring into Tanaka's home province of Niigata. Businesses that benefited from these projects then made large contributions to the campaigns of new politicians aligned with Tanaka. But by 1973 Japan suffered from rising inflation, and stories of the prime minister's mistresses and financial schemes received confirmation in a series of exposés printed in a leading magazine. Tanaka's combative and obnoxious public defense left him unable to govern and forced him to step down in December 1974.

A little over a year after his resignation as prime minister, Tanaka was charged with accepting 500 million yen ($4.5 million) in bribes from the Lockheed Company. These payments were in return for Tanaka persuading Air Nippon to cancel a contract with U.S. defense producer McDonnell-Douglas and instead buy the Lockheed L-1011. The incident, which became known as the Lockheed Scandal, spurred a wave of suicides and the fall of Miki Takeo as prime minister. Tanaka was arrested but released after interrogation. No formal charges were brought against him for seven years, during which time he acted as a behind-the-scenes manipulator of politics and government policies with his political lieutenants implementing his instructions. Finally indicted and found guilty in 1983 in the Lockheed Scandal, Tanaka was sentenced to four years in prison, but he filed a series of appeals. In 1985 he suffered a stroke that left him frail and debilitated with slurred speech. Diabetes further weakened his condition, completely removing him from politics. The Supreme Court rejected his appeal in 1987, but more appeals kept the unrepentant Tanaka out of jail until his death from pneumonia. A legendary figure in postwar Japanese history, Tanaka was adept at building political power on an alliance between the iron triangle of party, bureaucracy, and business. He was a master at pork-barrel politics, securing the passage of countless pet projects benefiting his political allies and his own home district. Known for his gruff and gravelly voice, he often repeated the maxim that "Politics equals power, power equals numbers, and numbers come from money."

Tange Kenzo (September 4, 1913–   ), architect

Tange Kenzo occupies a distinguished place among modern architects and city planners. During Japan's postwar era of unprecedented economic growth, he designed major office towers, cultural centers, sports facilities, and government buildings. His creative style blended Japan's architectural traditions with innovative modernist designs. Showing that functionalism did not require rigid geometric style, Tange developed designs that maintained coherence with the Information Age. As a youth, he lived in Hankow and Shanghai, China, where his father was a manager for Sumitomo Bank. After abandoning an early interest in astronomy, Tange pursued interests in literature and the arts. His chance encounter with several design drawings of the French modernist architect Le Corbusier inspired him to follow a career that combined his interest in science and art. "Right then and there," Tange recalled, "I decided to be an architect." But an unimpressive high school record forced him to enroll in the film school division of Nihon University in 1933. Spending much of his free time talking about European novels and philosophy in bars and cafés, he gained admission to Tokyo University's architecture program on his third attempt. Though his admiration for Le Corbusier deepened, Tange retained his modernist love for clean lines and his distaste for extraneous ornamentation. His graduation design won an award in 1938 and earned him a job with one of Japan's top architects.

During World War II, Tange returned to Tokyo University for graduate study, focusing on traditional Japanese architecture and urban planning in ancient Greece and Rome. His reputation grew as a result of winning three major design competitions with proposals that blended ancient shrine elements with modernist forms. In 1946 Tange accepted an appointment as a professor of architecture at Tokyo University. Thereafter he organized the Tanken Team of talented students from several universities who would help rebuild war-torn Japan. For the next 30 years he was both teacher and head of an independent architectural design and urban planning studio. In 1959 Tange earned a doctoral degree at Tokyo University, writing a dissertation on "The Structure of Tokyo City." By then he had designed the Ehime Convention Center in Matsuyama, introducing his bold new concept of a low curving shell of concrete and plastic covering an open circular space with 133 ceiling lights. His first notable postwar project was central to the reconstruction of Hiroshima after its destruction by the atomic bomb. Completed in 1956 and typically Corbusian, the museum, library, and auditorium were a series of reinforced rectangular concrete structures on piers. The Peace Memorial was more evocative, repeating Tange's "shell structure" covering a concrete vault containing a stone block bearing the names of the dead.

A series of other public commissions during the 1950s enabled Tange to experiment with new designs while retaining traditional features of recessed pillars and open peripheral spaces. But he soon concluded that functionalist theory failed to unify and order the multiple functions of a typical office or prepare it for future changes. Introducing a new approach known as "typification of functions," Tange ensured that a building's uses dictated its design while maintaining coherence in spatial structure. His innovative ideas dominated his *Plan for Tokyo 1960*, a visionary $50 billion proposal that Tange presented at the World Design Conference in that year. His concept for a "civic axis" called for a narrow bridge of landfill across Tokyo Bay supporting a vast complex of office towers along with rapid transit and communications facilities. He envisioned this as the model for future urban design, but it was a target of ridicule at the time. Tange then designed the two Yoyogi National Gymnasia for the 1964 Tokyo Olympics. He achieved a practical and spiritual effect in creating what an observer has called playful siblings rather than identical twins. The main gymnasium, viewed from above, resembles ying-yang symbols out of alignment. The use of steel cables to suspend the roofs eliminated the need for internal supports and provided for vast interior space. Regarded as Tange's masterworks, these gymnasia won the Pritziker Award as "among the most beautiful buildings of the twentieth century."

Tange, now at the front rank of world architects, built many structures thereafter that enhanced his reputation, notably the Cathedral of St. Mary and the Yamanashi Press and Broadcasting Center in the Ginza district, both in Tokyo. But his urban planning schemes aroused controversy because he believed cities should grow along straight lines rather than develop into a sprawling hodgepodge. Forming a new design company named Urtec, he secured city development projects in Japan and Skopje, Yugoslavia. Tange's firm designed a large-scale office complex outside Bologna, Italy, in 1975 and then undertook massive government projects for oil-producing nations in the Mideast, Africa, and Asia. Thereafter, Tange focused on designing skyscrapers, and his Overseas Union Bank and the City Telecommunications Centre in Singapore was at that time the world's tallest building. By then his creative leadership was guiding a staff of over 90 young architects and urbanists who revered him as a father figure. A soft-spoken man, he had the ability to disguise decisions as suggestions. "Tradition," Tange preached, "must be like a catalyst that disappears once its task is done." Wealthy and media conscious, he wrote numerous articles for professional journals and collaborated on books about traditional Japanese architecture. In March 1987 he declared that "I'll only retire when I die." Tange's large body of work has enhanced Japan's image as a global power.

Yoshida Shigeru (September 22, 1878–October 20, 1967), prime minister

A career diplomat who retired permanently from diplomatic service in 1938, Yoshida Shigeru reemerged from relative obscurity after 1945 to become arguably the most famous and important leader in postwar Japan. He was prime minister of Japan between May 1946 and December 1954 (except for 16 months), a period of time coinciding with the U.S. occupation. Serving simultaneously as foreign minister, Yoshida developed a close and cooperative relationship with U.S. occupation commander General Douglas MacArthur, implementing his reform program. Known for his conservatism, arrogance, and inflexibility, critics dubbed him "One Man Yoshida." Born in Yokohama, he was adopted by Yoshida Kenzo, a prosperous Kyoto silk merchant and family friend; but he then squandered the fortune he inherited in 1887 on extravagant living. Yoshida graduated from Tokyo Imperial University in 1906 and entered the diplomatic service. His marriage to the daughter of Makino Nobuaki, a close advisor to the emperor, gave him access to powerful politicians, businessmen, and statesmen. His early postings were at Tientsin and Mukden, where Japan had acquired railroad and mining privileges as a result of the Russo-Japanese War. Yoshida would gained experience and contacts in the West while serving in London and Rome from 1908 to 1912. He then returned to Manchuria for four years.

Yoshida's appointment to Japan's embassy in Washington was withdrawn in 1916 when it was learned that he had initiated a small protest against Tokyo's issuance in 1915 of the 21 Demands against China that called for acceptance of a virtual Japanese protectorate over that country. After some insignificant assignments, he became first secretary at Japan's embassy in Britain in 1920, emerging as a critic of the treaties signed at Washington in 1922. He then worked at Tientsin and in Manchuria as consul and advocated an "assertive" policy to control Chinese nationalism. Although Yoshida became identified with the clique in the foreign ministry that was lobbying for friendly relations with Britain and the United States, his interests were oriented mainly toward extending Japanese influence in Asia. This reflected his belief that Japan could not prosper without dominating a close relationship with China. Nevertheless, Yoshida joined a group of powerful Japanese in opposing the ambitions of extreme militarists to control the government in the 1930s. This prevented him, after postings in Sweden and in Italy, from becoming foreign minister. He also declined an appointment as ambassador to the United States and briefly retired in 1935. However, Prime Minister Hirota Koki persuaded him to become ambassador in London after a failed Army attempt to seize power in February 1936.

Yoshida returned home in March 1939 and lobbied against Japan signing the Tripartite Pact with Nazi Germany and fascist Italy to form the Axis alliance. He kept contacts with Western diplomats, sending U.S. ambassador to Japan Joseph C. Grew a letter of apology for the attack on Pearl Harbor. In forced retirement after 1941, the exiled Yoshida worked quietly to oust General Tojo Hideki's wartime government, fearing that defeat would bring a Communist victory in Japan. Just four months prior to Japan's surrender, Yoshida was imprisoned for helping draft, in February 1945, the Konoe Memorial, which urged steps toward an advantageous peace. When Yoshida was released in August 1945, General Douglas MacArthur approved his appointment as Japan's first postwar foreign minister because of his well-known opposition to militarism and aggression. Among the few prominent unpurged politicians, he retained that post when Shidehara Kijuro became prime minister in October 1945. He soon emerged as a vocal defender of the old civilian elites and a blunt critic of constitutional revision or structural renovation. He helped arrange the symbolically significant meeting between the emperor and MacArthur on September 27, 1945, that some believe solidified MacArthur's support for preserving the monarchy. Thereafter, Yoshida served as prime minister helping to implement U.S. occupation policies to extend the political purge and enact reforms—notably constitutional revision, land reform, and basic labor laws.

Primary Documents of Japan's Emergence

BLUEPRINT FOR POSTWAR JAPAN

During World War II, U.S. officials devoted much time to planning for the reconstruction of a defeated Japan. The result was a policy directive, of which excerpts appear here, that the State, War, and Navy departments jointly prepared and President Harry S. Truman approved on September 6, 1945. General Douglas MacArthur, the Supreme Commander of the Allied Powers (SCAP), received the substance of the document on August 29 with instructions to use it as a guide for action in administration of the U.S. occupation of Japan.

Document 1
UNITED STATES INITIAL POST-SURRENDER POLICY
FOR JAPAN, AUGUST 29, 1945

The ultimate objectives of the United States in regard to Japan, to which policies in the initial period must conform, are:

(a) To insure that Japan will not again become a menace to the United States or to the peace and security of the world.

(b) To bring about the eventual establishment of a peaceful and responsible government which will respect the rights of other states and will support the objectives of the United States as reflected in the ideals and principles of the Charter of the United Nations. The United States desires that this government should conform as closely as may be to principles of democratic self-government but it is not the responsibility of the Allied Powers to impose upon Japan any form of government not supported by the freely expressed will of the people.

These objectives will be achieved by the following principal means:

(a) Japan's sovereignty will be limited to the islands of Honshu, Hokkaido, Kyushu, Shikoku and such minor outlying islands as may be determined, in accordance with the Cairo Declaration and other agreements to which the United States is or may be a party.

(b) Japan will be completely disarmed and demilitarized. The authority of the militarists and the influence of militarism will be totally eliminated from her political, economic, and social life. Institutions expressive of the spirit of militarism and aggression will be vigorously suppressed.

(c) The Japanese people shall be encouraged to develop a desire for individual liberties and respect for fundamental human rights, particularly the freedoms of religion, assembly, speech, and the press. They shall also be encouraged to form democratic and representative organizations.

(d) The Japanese people shall be afforded opportunity to develop for themselves an economy which will permit the peacetime requirements of the population to be met. . . .

PART III—POLITICAL

1. Disarmament and Demilitarization

Disarmament and demilitarization are the primary tasks of the military occupation and shall be carried out promptly and with determination. Every effort shall be made to bring home to the Japanese people the part played by the military and naval leaders, and those who collaborated with them in bringing about the existing and future distress of the people.

Japan is not to have an army, navy, air force, secret police organization, or any civil aviation. Japan's ground, air and naval forces shall be disarmed and disbanded and the Japanese Imperial General Headquarters, the General Staff and all secret police organizations shall be dissolved. Military and naval materiel, military and naval vessels and military and naval installations, and military, naval and civilian aircraft shall be surrendered and shall be disposed of as required by the Supreme Commander.

High officials of the Japanese Imperial General Headquarters, and General Staff, other high military and naval officials of the Japanese Government, leaders of ultra-nationalist and militarist organizations and other important exponents of militarism and aggression will be taken into custody and held for future disposition. Persons who have been active exponents of militarism and militant nationalism will be removed and excluded from public office and from any other position of public or substantial private responsibility. Ultra-nationalistic or militaristic social, political, professional and commercial societies and institutions will be dissolved and prohibited.

Militarism and ultra-nationalism, in doctrine and practice, including paramilitary training, shall be eliminated from the educational system. Former career military and naval officers, both commissioned and noncommissioned, and all other exponents of militarism and ultra-nationalism shall be excluded from supervisory and teaching positions.

PART IV—ECONOMIC

1. Economic Demilitarization

The existing economic basis of Japanese military strength must be destroyed and not be permitted to revive. Therefore, a program will be enforced containing the following elements, among others: the immediate cessation and future prohibition of production of all goods designed for the equipment, maintenance, or use of any military force or establishment; the imposition of a ban upon any specialized facilities for the production or repair of implements of war, including naval vessels and all forms of aircraft; the institution of a system of inspection and control over selected elements in Japanese economic activity to prevent concealed or disguised military preparation; the elimination in Japan of those selected industries or branches of production whose chief value to Japan is in preparing for war; the prohibition of specialized research and instruction directed to the development of war-making power; and the limitation of the size and character of Japan's heavy industries to its future peaceful requirements, and restriction of Japanese merchant shipping to the extent required to accomplish the objectives of demilitarization.

The eventual disposition of those existing production facilities within Japan which are to be eliminated in accord with this program, as between conversion to other uses, transfer abroad, and scrapping will be determined after inventory. Pending decision, facilities readily convertible for civilian production should not be destroyed, except in emergency situations. . . .

4. Reparations and Restitution

Reparations

Reparations for Japanese aggression shall be made:

(a) Through the transfer—as may be determined by the appropriate Allied authorities—of Japanese property located outside of the territories to be retained by Japan.

(b) Through the transfer of such goods or existing capital equipment and facilities as are not necessary for a peaceful Japanese economy or the supplying of the occupying forces. Exports other than those directed to be shipped on reparation account or as restitution may be made only to those recipients who agree to provide necessary imports in exchange or agree to pay for such exports in foreign exchange. No form of reparation shall be exacted which will interfere with or prejudice the program for Japan's demilitarization.

Restitution

Full and prompt restitution will be required of all identifiable looted property.

Source: Supreme Commander of the Allied Powers, *Political Reorientation of Japan: September 1945 to September 1948* (Washington, DC: U.S. Government Printing Office, 1949), 423–26.

JAPAN'S "MACARTHUR CONSTITUTION" OF 1947

SCAP's Government Section at first allowed Japanese leaders to develop a draft to replace the Meiji Constitution of 1889 but were dissatisfied with the results. Brigadier General Courtney Whitney and Charles L. Kades swiftly wrote a new constitution for Japan that combined elements of the U.S. and British systems. It became effective on May 3, 1947, and remained in place without significant change thereafter. Appearing here are excerpts of the document, excluding Chapters IV through XIII (which describe, respectively, the Diet, Cabinet, Judiciary, Finance, and Local Self-Government).

Document 2
THE CONSTITUTION OF JAPAN, NOVEMBER 3, 1946

We, the Japanese people, acting through our duly elected representatives in the National Diet, determined that we shall secure for ourselves and our posterity the fruits of peaceful cooperation with all nations and the blessings of liberty throughout this land, and resolved that never again shall we be visited with the horrors of war through the action of government, do proclaim that sovereign power resides with the people and do firmly establish this Constitution. Government is a sacred trust of the people, the authority for which is derived from the people, the powers of which are exercised by the representatives of the people, and the benefits of which are enjoyed by the people. This is a universal principle of mankind upon which this Constitution is founded. We reject and revoke all constitutions, laws, ordinances, and rescripts in conflict herewith.

We, the Japanese people, desire peace for all time and are deeply conscious of the high ideals controlling human relationship, and we have determined to preserve our security and existence, trusting in the justice and faith of the peace-loving peoples of the world. We desire to occupy an honored place in an international society striving for the preservation of peace, and the banishment of tyranny and slavery, oppression and intolerance for all time from the earth. We recognize that all peoples of the world have the right to live in peace, free from fear and want.

We believe that no nation is responsible to itself alone, but that laws of political morality are universal; and that obedience to such laws is incumbent upon all nations who would sustain their own sovereignty and justify their sovereign relationship with other nations.

We, the Japanese people, pledge our national honor to accomplish these high ideals and purposes with all our resources.

CHAPTER I. THE EMPEROR

Article 1. The Emperor shall be the symbol of the State and of the unity of the people, deriving his position from the will of the people with whom resides sovereign power. . . .

Article 4. The Emperor shall perform only such acts in matters of state as are provided for in this Constitution and he shall not have powers related to government. The Emperor may delegate the performance of his acts in matters of state as may be provided by law. . . .

CHAPTER II. RENUNCIATION OF WAR

Article 9. Aspiring sincerely to an international peace based on justice and order, the Japanese people forever renounce war as a sovereign right of the nation and the threat or use of force as means of settling international disputes.

In order to accomplish the aim of the preceding paragraph, land, sea, and air forces, as well as other war potential, will never be maintained. The right of belligerency of the state will not be recognized. . . .

CHAPTER III. RIGHTS AND DUTIES OF THE PEOPLE

Article 13. All of the people shall be respected as individuals. Their right to life, liberty, and the pursuit of happiness shall, to the extent that it does not interfere with the public welfare, be the supreme consideration in legislation and in other governmental affairs.

Article 14. All of the people are equal under the law and there shall be no discrimination in political, economic or social relations because of race, creed, sex, social status or family origin. . . .

Article 19. Freedom of thought and conscience shall not be violated.

Article 20. Freedom of religion is guaranteed to all. No religious organization shall receive any privileges from the State, nor exercise any political authority.

No person shall be compelled to take part in any religious act, celebration, rite or practice.

The State and its organs shall refrain from religious education or any other religious activity.

Article 21. Freedom of assembly and association as well as speech, press and all other forms of expression are guaranteed.

No censorship shall be maintained, nor shall the secrecy of any means of communication be violated. . . .

Article 24. Marriage shall be based only on the mutual consent of both sexes and it shall be maintained through mutual cooperation with the equal rights of husband and wife as a basis.

With regard to choice of spouse, property rights, inheritance, choice of domicile, divorce and other matters pertaining to marriage and the family, laws shall be enacted from the standpoint of individual dignity and the essential equality of the sexes. . . .

Article 26. All people shall have the right to receive an equal education correspondent to their ability, as provided by law.

All people shall be obligated to have all boys and girls under their protection receive ordinary education as provided for by law. Such compulsory education shall be free. . . .

Article 34. No person shall be arrested or detained without being at once informed of the charges against him or without the immediate privilege of counsel; nor shall he be detained without adequate cause; and upon demand of any person such cause must be immediately shown in open court in his presence and the presence of his counsel. . . .

CHAPTER IX. AMENDMENTS

Article 96. Amendments to this Constitution shall be initiated by the Diet, through a concurring vote of two-thirds or more of all the members of each House and shall thereupon be submitted to the people for ratification which shall require the affirmative vote of a majority of all votes cast thereon, at a special referendum or at such election as the Diet shall specify.

Amendments when so ratified shall immediately be promulgated by the Emperor in the name of the people, as an integral part of this Constitution.

CHAPTER X. SUPREME LAW

Article 97. The fundamental human rights by this Constitution guaranteed to the people of Japan are fruits of the age-old struggle of man to be free; they have survived the many exacting tests for durability and are conferred upon this and future generations in trust, to be held for all time inviolate.

Article 98. This Constitution shall be the supreme law of the nation and no law, ordinance, imperial rescript or other act of government, or part thereof, contrary to the provisions hereof, shall have legal force or validity.

The treaties concluded by Japan and established laws of nations shall be faithfully observed. . . .

CHAPTER XI. SUPPLEMENTARY PROVISIONS

Article 100. This Constitution shall be enforced as from the day when the period of six months will have elapsed counting from the day of its promulgation.

Source: Supreme Commander of the Allied Powers, *Political Reorientation of Japan: September 1945 to September 1948* (Washington, DC: U.S. Government Printing Office, 1949), 671–77.

RESTORATION OF JAPAN'S INDEPENDENCE

Japan's postwar leaders cooperated with the United States in the implementation of reforms during the U.S. occupation after 1945, hoping to regain national sovereignty at an early date. However, it was the threat of Soviet expansion in Asia that ultimately caused the Truman administration to move toward the restoration of Japan's independence. In September 1951 at the San Francisco Conference, 48 nations signed the Japanese Peace Treaty. Neither the Soviet Union nor China participated, but this did not prevent Japan from regaining its sovereignty under the treaty in April 1952. Excerpts of the document appear here. Excluded are Article 3, extending U.S. rights over Okinawa, the Bonins, and other islands; Chapter IV, Articles 7 to 13, containing political and economic clauses; Chapter V, Articles 14 to 21, dealing with claims and property; Chapter VI, Article 22, providing for the settlement of disputes through referral to the International Court of Justice; and Chapter VII, Articles 24, 25, and 27, covering ratifications and rights.

Document 3
MULTILATERAL TREATY OF PEACE WITH JAPAN, SEPTEMBER 8, 1951

Whereas the Allied Powers and Japan are resolved that henceforth their relations shall be those of nations which, as sovereign equals, cooperate in friendly association to promote their common welfare and to maintain international peace and security, and are therefore desirous of concluding a

Treaty of Peace which will settle questions still outstanding as a result of the existence of a state of war between them;

Whereas Japan for its part declares its intention to apply for membership in the United Nations and in all circumstances to conform to the principles of the Charter of the United Nations; to strive to realize the objectives of the Universal Declaration of Human Rights; to seek to create within Japan conditions of stability and well-being as defined in Articles 55 and 56 of the Charter of the United Nations and already initiated by post-surrender Japanese legislation; and in public and private trade and commerce to conform to internationally accepted fair practices;

Whereas the Allied Powers welcome the intentions of Japan set out in the foregoing paragraph;

The Allied Powers and Japan have therefore determined to conclude the present Treaty of Peace, and have . . . agreed on the following provisions:

CHAPTER I
PEACE

Article 1

(a) The state of war between Japan and each of the Allied Powers is terminated from the date on which the present Treaty comes into force between Japan and the Allied Power concerned as provided for in Article 23.

(b) The Allied Powers recognize the full sovereignty of the Japanese people over Japan and its territorial waters.

CHAPTER II
TERRITORY

Article 2

(a) Japan, recognizing the independence of Korea, renounces all right, title and claim to Korea, including the islands of Quelpart, Port Hamilton and Dagelet.

(b) Japan renounces all right, title and claim to Formosa and the Pescadores.

(c) Japan renounces all right, title and claim to the Kurile Islands, and to that portion of Sakhalin and the islands adjacent to it over which Japan acquired sovereignty as a consequence of the Treaty of Portsmouth of September 5, 1905.

(d) Japan renounces all right, title and claim in connection with the League of Nations Mandate System, and accepts the action of the United Nations Security Council of April 2, 1947, extending the trusteeship system to the Pacific Islands formerly under mandate to Japan. . . .

Article 4

... (b) Japan recognizes the validity of dispositions of property of Japan and Japanese nationals made by or pursuant to directives of the United States government in any of the areas referred to in Articles 2 and 3.

CHAPTER III
SECURITY

Article 5

(a) Japan accepts the obligations set forth in Article 2 of the Charter of the United Nations, and in particular the obligations

(i) to settle its international disputes by peaceful means in such a manner that international peace and security, and justice, are not endangered;

(ii) to refrain in its international relations from the threat or use of force against the territorial integrity or political independence of any State or in any other manner inconsistent with the Purposes of the United Nations;

(iii) to give the United Nations every assistance in any action it takes in accordance with the Charter and to refrain from giving assistance to any State against which the United Nations may take preventive or enforcement action.

(iv) The Allied Powers confirm that they will be guided by the principles of Article 2 of the Charter of the United Nations in their relations with Japan.

(v) The Allied Powers for their part recognize that Japan as a sovereign nation possesses the inherent right of individual or collective self-defense referred to in Article 51 of the Charter of the United Nations and that Japan may voluntarily enter into collective security arrangements.

Article 6

(a) All occupation forces of the Allied Powers shall be withdrawn from Japan as soon as possible after the coming into force of the present Treaty, and in any case not later than 90 days thereafter. Nothing in this provision shall, however, prevent the stationing or retention of foreign armed forces in Japanese territory under or in consequence of any bilateral or multilateral agreements which have been or may be made between one or more of the Allied Powers, on the one hand, and Japan on the other. . . .

(c) All Japanese property for which compensation has not already been paid, which was supplied for the use of the occupation forces and which remains in the possession of those forces at the time of the coming into force of the present Treaty, shall be returned to the Japanese Government within the same 90 days unless other arrangements are made by mutual agreement. . . .

FINAL CLAUSES

Article 23

(a) The present Treaty shall be ratified by the States which sign it, including Japan, and will come into force for all the States which have then ratified it, when instruments of ratification have been deposited by Japan and by a majority, including the United States of America as the principal occupying Power, of the following States, namely Australia, Canada, Ceylon, France, Indonesia, the Kingdom of the Netherlands, New Zealand, Pakistan, the Republic of the Philippines, the United Kingdom of Great Britain and Northern Ireland, and the United States of America. The present Treaty shall come into force for each State which subsequently ratifies it, on the date of the deposit of its instrument of ratification.

(b) If the Treaty has not come into force within nine months after the date of the deposit of Japan's ratification, any State which has ratified it may bring the Treaty into force between itself and Japan by a notification to that effect given to the Governments of Japan and the United States of America not later than three years after the date of deposit of Japan's ratification. . . .

Article 26

Japan will be prepared to conclude with any State which signed or adhered to the United Nations Declaration of January 1, 1942, and which is at war with Japan, or with any State which previously formed a part of the territory of a State named in Article 23, which is not a signatory of the present Treaty, a bilateral Treaty of Peace on the same or substantially the same terms as are provided for in the present Treaty, but this obligation on the part of Japan will expire three years after the first coming into force of the present Treaty. Should Japan make a peace settlement or war claims settlement with any State granting that State greater advantages than those provided by the present Treaty, those same advantages shall be extended to the parties to the present Treaty. . . .

Source: U.S. Department of State, *U.S. Treaties and Other International Agreements*, Vol. 3, Part 3 (Washington, DC: U.S. Government Printing Office, 1952), 3171–91.

JAPAN'S ALLIANCE WITH THE UNITED STATES

Early in 1950, in an effort to speed the restoration of Japanese independence, Prime Minister Yoshida Shigeru informed the Truman adminstration of Japan's willingness to align with the United States against the Soviet Union in the Cold War. On the same day that Japan and the United States adopted the Japanese Peace Treaty, a security agreement was signed providing rights for U.S. military bases in Japan.

The pact would be the source of intense criticism in Japan thereafter, climaxing in violent demonstrations against renewal during May and June 1960.

Document 4
U.S.-JAPAN SECURITY TREATY, SEPTEMBER 8, 1951

Japan has this day signed a Treaty of Peace with the Allied Powers. On the coming into force of that Treaty, Japan will not have the effective means to exercise its inherent right of self-defense because it has been disarmed.

There is danger to Japan in this situation because irresponsible militarism has not yet been driven from the world. Therefore Japan desires a Security Treaty with the United States of America to come into force simultaneously with the Treaty of Peace between the United States of America and Japan.

The Treaty of Peace recognizes that Japan as a sovereign nation has the right to enter into collective security arrangements, and further, the Charter of the United Nations recognizes that all nations possess an inherent right of individual and collective self-defense.

In exercise of these rights, Japan desires, as a provisional arrangement for its defense, that the United States of America should maintain armed forces of its own in and about Japan so as to deter armed attack upon Japan.

The United States of America, in the interest of peace and security, is presently willing to maintain certain of its armed forces in and about Japan, in the expectation, however, that Japan will itself increasingly assume responsibility for its own defense against direct and indirect aggression, always avoiding any armament which could be an offensive threat or serve other than to promote peace and security in accordance with the purposes and principles of the United Nations Charter.

Accordingly, the two countries have agreed as follows:

ARTICLE I

Japan grants, and the United States of America accepts, the right, upon the coming into force of the Treaty of Peace and of this Treaty, to dispose United States land, air and sea forces in and about Japan. Such forces may be utilized to contribute to the maintenance of international peace and security in the Far East and to the security of Japan against armed attack from without, including assistance given at the express request of the Japanese Government to put down large-scale internal riots and disturbances in Japan, caused through instigation or intervention by an outside power or powers.

ARTICLE II

During the exercise of the right referred to in Article I, Japan will not grant, without the prior consent of the United States of America, any bases or any rights, powers or authority whatsoever, in or relating to bases or the right of ground, air or naval forces to any third power.

ARTICLE III

The conditions which shall govern the disposition of armed forces of the United States of America in and about Japan shall be determined by administrative agreements between the two Governments.

ARTICLE IV

This Treaty shall expire whenever in the opinion of the Governments of the United States of America and Japan there shall have come into force such United Nations arrangements or such alternative individual or collective security dispositions as will satisfactorily provide for the maintenance by the United Nations or otherwise of international peace and security in the Japan Area. . . .

Source: U.S. Department of State, *U.S. Treaties and Other International Agreements*, Vol. 3, Part 3 (Washington, DC: U.S. Government Printing Office, 1952), 3331–32.

CHINESE CHECKER

Another concession that Japan had to make to regain its independence was the choosing of sides in the Chinese Civil War. In the "Yoshida Letter" presented here, Prime Minister Yoshida Shigeru informed the U.S. government of Japan's intention to recognize Chiang Kai-shek's Guomindang government (which had fled to Taiwan late in 1949) rather than the People's Republic of China under Communist leader Mao Zedong even though it had control over the mainland. This decision, a result of Japan's dependent Cold War alliance with the United States, led to two decades of contentiousness in domestic politics and relations with both Chinas.

Document 5
LETTER FROM YOSHIDA SHIGERU TO JOHN FOSTER DULLES, DECEMBER 24, 1951

DEAR AMBASSADOR DULLES:

While the Japanese Peace Treaty and the U.S.-Japan Security Treaty were being debated in the House of Representatives and the House of Councillors of the Diet, a number of questions were put and statements made relative to Japan's future policy toward China. Some of the statements, separated from their context and background, gave rise to misapprehensions which I should like to clear up.

The Japanese Government desires ultimately to have a full measure of political peace and commercial intercourse with China which is Japan's close neighbor.

At the present time it is, we hope, possible to develop that kind of relationship with the National Government of the Republic of China, which has the seat, voice and vote of China in the United Nations, which exercises actual governmental authority over certain territory, and which maintains diplomatic relations with most of the members of the United Nations. To that end my Government on November 17, 1951, established a Japanese Government Overseas Agency in Formosa, with the consent of the National Government of China. This is the highest form of relationship with other countries which is now permitted to Japan, pending the coming into force of the multilateral Treaty of Peace. The Japanese Government Overseas Agency in Formosa is important in its personnel, reflecting the importance which my government attaches to relations with the National Government of the Republic of China. My government is prepared as soon as legally possible to conclude with the National Government of China, if that government so desires, a Treaty which will reestablish normal relations between the two Governments in conformity with the principles set out in the multilateral Treaty of Peace. The terms of such bilateral treaty shall, in respect of the Republic of China, be applicable to all territories which are now, or which may hereafter be, under the control of the National Government of the Republic of China. We will promptly explore this subject with the National Government of China.

As regards the Chinese Communist regime, that regime stands actually condemned by the United Nations of being an aggressor and in consequence, the United Nations has recommended certain measures against that regime, in which Japan is now concurring and expects to continue to concur when the multilateral Treaty of Peace comes into force pursuant to the provisions of Article 5 (a) (iii), whereby Japan has undertaken "to give the United Nations every assistance in any action it takes in accordance with the Charter, and to refrain from giving assistance to any State against which the United Nations may take preventive or enforcement action." Furthermore, the Sino-Soviet Treaty of Friendship, Alliance and Mutual Assistance concluded in Moscow in 1950 is virtually a military alliance aimed against Japan. In fact there are many reasons to believe that the Communist regime in China is backing the Japan Communist Party in its program of seeking violently to overthrow the constitutional system and the present Government of Japan. In view of these considerations, I can assure you that the Japanese Government has no intention to conclude a bilateral Treaty with the Communist regime of China.

Source: U.S. Department of State, *Foreign Relations of the United States, 1951,* Vol. 6: *Japan* (Washington, DC: U.S. Government Printing Office, 1977), 1466–67.

NORMALIZATION OF RELATIONS WITH THE SOVIET UNION

After Soviet leader Joseph Stalin died in 1953, his successors sought a relaxation of relations with the United States and it allies, including Japan. It was not until Hatoyama Ichiro became prime minister late in 1954 that Tokyo responded favorably to Moscow's overtures, opening the way to negotiations resulting in an agreement for normalization of relations. Although the Soviet Union fulfilled its promise under the accord to support Japan's petition for membership in the United Nations, leading to admission in 1956, major differences continued to prevent genuine friendship between Japan and the Soviet Union.

Document 6
SOVIET-JAPANESE JOINT DECLARATION,
OCTOBER 19, 1956

In the course of the negotiations, which were held in an atmosphere of mutual understanding and co-operation, a full and frank exchange of views concerning relations between the Union of Soviet Socialist Republics and Japan took place. The Union of Soviet Socialist Republics and Japan were fully agreed that the restoration of diplomatic relations between them would contribute to the development of mutual understanding and co-operation between the two States in the interests of peace and security in the Far East.

As a result of these negotiations between the Delegations of the Union of Soviet Socialist Republics and Japan, agreement was reached on the following:

1. The state of war between the Union of Soviet Socialist Republics and Japan shall cease on the date on which this Declaration enters into force and peace, friendship and good-neighbourly relations between them shall be restored.

2. Diplomatic and consular relations shall be restored between the Union of Soviet Socialist Republics and Japan. For this purpose, it is intended that

the two States shall proceed forthwith to exchange diplomatic representatives with the rank of Ambassador and that the question of the establishment of consulates in the territories of the USSR and Japan respectively shall be settled through the diplomatic channels.

3. The Union of Soviet Socialist Republics and Japan affirm that in their relations with each other they will be guided by the principles of the United Nations Charter, in particular the following principles set forth in Article 2 of the said Charter:

(a) To settle their international disputes by peaceful means in such a manner that international peace and security, and justice, are not endangered;

(b) To refrain in their international relations from the threat or use of force against the territorial integrity or political independence of any State, or in any other manner inconsistent with the Purposes of the United Nations.

The USSR and Japan affirm that, in accordance with Article 51 of the United Nations Charter, each of the two States has the inherent right of individual or collective self-defence.

The USSR and Japan reciprocally undertake not to intervene directly or indirectly in each other's domestic affairs for any economic, political or ideological reasons.

4. The Union of Soviet Socialist Republics will support Japan's application for membership in the United Nations.

5. On the entry into force of this Joint Declaration, all Japanese citizens convicted in the Union of Soviet Socialist Republics shall be released and repatriated to Japan.

With regard to those Japanese whose fate is unknown, the USSR, at the request of Japan, will continue its efforts to discover what has happened to them.

6. The Union of Soviet Socialist Republics renounces all reparations claims against Japan.

The USSR and Japan agree to renounce all claims by either State, its institutions or citizens, against the other State, its institutions or citizens, which have arisen as a result of the war since 9 August 1945.

7. The Union of Soviet Socialist Republics and Japan agree that they will enter into negotiations as soon as may be possible for the conclusion of treaties or agreements with a view to putting their trade, navigation and other commercial relations on a firm and friendly basis.

8. The Convention on deep-sea fishing in the north-western sector of the Pacific Ocean between the Union of Soviet Socialist Republics and Japan and the Agreement between the Union of Soviet Socialist Republics and Japan on co-operation in the rescue of persons in distress at sea, both signed at

Moscow on 14 May 1956, shall come into effect simultaneously with this Joint Declaration.

Having regard to the interest of both the USSR and Japan in the conservation and rational use of the natural fishery resources and other biological resources of the sea, the USSR and Japan shall, in a spirit of co-operation, take measures to conserve and develop fishery resources, and to regulate and restrict deep-sea fishing.

9. The Union of Soviet Socialist Republics and Japan agree to continue, after the restoration of normal diplomatic relations between the Union of Soviet Socialist Republics and Japan, negotiations for the conclusion of a Peace Treaty.

In this connexion, the Union of Soviet Socialist Republics, desiring to meet the wishes of Japan and taking into consideration the interests of the Japanese State, agrees to transfer to Japan the Habomai Islands and the island of Shikotan, the actual transfer of these islands to Japan to take place after the conclusion of a Peace Treaty between the Union of Soviet Socialist Republics and Japan.

Source: U.S. Department of State, *American Foreign Policy Current Documents* (Washington, DC: U.S. Government Printing Office, 1959), 819–21.

A STRATEGY FOR ECONOMIC DOMINANCE

Prime Minister Ikeda Hayato's Income Doubling Plan received approval from his Cabinet on December 27, 1960. Although it had to be revised substantially within the first two years because initial calculations on the rates of consumption and private investment were too conservative, the document's optimistic outlook set the tone for Japan's growth-oriented economy of the 1960s. Japan became an advanced industrial nation, producing products that were shipped to every corner of the world. Implementation of Ikeda's Income Doubling Plan played a key role in accelerating Japan's emergence as a global economic power.

Document 7

IKEDA HAYATO'S PLAN TO DOUBLE INDIVIDUAL INCOME, DECEMBER 27, 1960

1. OBJECTIVES OF THIS PLAN

The plan to double the individual income must have as its objectives doubling of the gross national product [GNP], attainment of full employment through expansion in employment opportunities, and raising the living standard of our people. We must adjust differentials in living standard and income existing between farming and nonfarming sectors, between large enterprises and small and medium-sized enterprises, between different regions of the country, and between different income groups. We must work toward a balanced development in our national economy and life patterns.

2. TARGETS TO BE ATTAINED

The plan's goal is to reach 26 trillion yen in GNP (at the fiscal year 1958 price) within the next ten years. To reach this goal, and in view of the fact that there are several factors highly favorable to economic growth existing during the first part of this plan, including the rapid development of technological changes and an abundant supply of skilled labor forces, we plan to attain an annual rate of growth of GNP at 9 percent for the coming three years. It is hoped that we shall be able to raise our GNP of 13.6 trillion yen (13 trillion yen in FY 1958 price) in FY 1960 to 17.6 trillion yen (FY 1960 price) in FY 1963 with application of appropriate policies and cooperation from the private sector.

3. POINTS TO BE CONSIDERED IN IMPLEMENTING THE PLAN AND DIRECTIONS TO BE FOLLOWED

The plan contained in the report of the Economic Council will be respected. However, in its implementation we must act flexibly and pay due consideration to the economic growth actually occurring and other related conditions. Any action we undertake must be consistent with the objectives described above. To do so, we shall pay special attention to the implementation of the following:

(a) Promotion of Modernization in Agriculture

To secure a balanced development in our national economy, we shall enact a Fundamental Law of Agriculture as a means of promoting modernization in agriculture. The proposed law shall serve as the basis of our new agricultural policies on issues ranging from agricultural production, income and structure, to various other measures.

Concurrent with this, we shall actively secure investment for infrastructure required for agricultural production, and moneys required for promoting modernization in agriculture.

Enhancement of coastal fishing shall be undertaken in a similar manner.

(b) Modernization of Medium and Small Enterprises

To enhance productivity in medium and small enterprises, to relax the ills associated with our economy's dual structure, and to promote vigorously various measures required to attain these objectives, we shall secure an adequate and just supply of funds for modernization of medium and small enterprises.

(c) Accelerated Development of Less Developed Regions

To accelerate development of those less developed regions (including southern Kyushu, western Kyushu, Sanin region, and southern Shikoku) and to adjust difference in income levels, we shall establish without delay a plan for comprehensive multi-purpose development of the land. This will enable us to develop these regions' resources. Special consideration will be given to tax incentives, financing and rates of assistance permitted for public sector investment. We shall study legislation necessary to implement these measures. We shall see to it that industries appropriate to these regions will be located there. In this manner the welfare of the inhabitants in these regions may be advanced and the regions' less developed status may be rectified.

(d) Promotion of Appropriate Locations for Industries and Reexamination of Regional Distribution of Public Sector Projects

It is certainly important to respect the use of sound economic reasons in selecting industrial locations, if we are to maintain for a long period of time our country's high rate of growth, to strengthen international competitiveness, and to heighten the utility of our social capital investment. This must not be carried out in a manner that will promote greater differentials between regions.

While respecting rationality in making economic decisions and at the same time preventing spread of differentials between regions, we must adjust flexibly the amount of moneys invested or loaned for public works in different regions according to the special conditions existing in these regions. In this manner we shall be able to enhance the utility of public works projects consistent with economic development which at the same time contribute toward minimizing differentials between regions.

(e) Active Cooperation with the Development of World Economy

Raising productivity means strengthening our export competitiveness. Bearing in mind that an important key to the success of this plan is in the expansion of our exports and an increase in revenues in foreign currencies, we must promote a viable export strategy accompanied by other measures increasing nontrade revenues such as tourism and maritime transportation. We shall actively seek cooperation with other countries in promoting economic development in less-developed countries and raise their income levels.

Source: Asahi Shimbunsha, ed., *Shiryo Meiji Hyakunen* (A documentary history for the Meiji centennial) (Tokyo: Asahi Shimbunsha, 1966), 561–62.

FROM COLONIAL POSSESSION TO ECONOMIC PARTNER

Korea was among those nations most reluctant to reconcile with Japan after World War II because it had suffered almost a half-century of ruthless exploitation under Japanese colonial rule. After the partitioning of Korea in 1945, Japan's relations were strained with both North and South Korea. But Prime Minister Sato Eisaku, after assuming office late in 1964, saw improved relations with South Korea as a way to expand further on Japan's economic growth in the 1960s. He moved rapidly to break deadlocked negotiations, completing the normalization treaty that appears here. It became effective after mutual ratification in December 1965, opening a new era mutually beneficial of economic cooperation.

Document 8
TREATY OF BASIC RELATIONS BETWEEN THE REPUBLIC OF KOREA AND JAPAN, JUNE 22, 1965

The Republic of Korea and Japan,

Considering the historical background of relationship between their peoples and their mutual desire for good neighborliness and for the normalization of their relations on the basis of the principle of mutual respect for sovereignty;

Recognizing the importance of their close cooperation in conformity with the principles of the Charter of the United Nations to the promotion of their mutual welfare and common interests and to the maintenance of international peace and security; and

Recalling the relevant provisions of the Treaty of Peace with Japan signed at city of San Francisco on September 8, 1951, and the resolution, 195 (III), adopted by the United Nations General Assembly on December 12, 1948;

Have resolved to conclude the present Treaty on Basic Relations and . . . have agreed upon the following articles:

ARTICLE I

Diplomatic and consular relations shall be established between the High Contracting Parties. The High Contracting Parties shall exchange diplomatic envoys with the Ambassadorial rank without delay.

The High Contracting Parties will also establish consulates at locations to be agreed upon by the two Governments.

ARTICLE II

It is confirmed that all treaties or agreements concluded between the Empire of Korea and the Empire of Japan on or before August 22, 1910, are already null and void.

ARTICLE III

It is confirmed that the Government of the Republic of Korea is the only lawful Government in Korea as specified in the Resolution 195 (III) of the United Nations General Assembly.

ARTICLE IV

(a) The High Contracting Parties will be guided by the principles of the Charter of the United Nations in their mutual relations.

(b) The High Contracting Parties will cooperate in conformity with the Principles of the Charter of the United Nations in promoting their mutual welfare and common interests.

ARTICLE V

The High Contracting Parties will enter into negotiations at the earliest practicable date for the conclusion of treaties or agreements to place their trading, maritime and other commercial relations on a stable and friendly basis.

ARTICLE VI

The High Contracting Parties will enter into negotiations at the earliest practicable date for the conclusion of an agreement relating to civil air transport.

ARTICLE VII

The present Treaty shall be ratified. The instruments of ratification shall be exchanged at Seoul as soon as possible. The present Treaty shall enter into force as from the date on which the instruments of ratification are exchanged.

Source: U.S. Department of State, *American Foreign Policy Current Documents, 1965* (Washington, DC: U.S. Government Printing Office, 1968), 787–88.

JAPAN'S "NUCLEAR ALLERGY"

Japan is the only nation in history to sustain an atomic attack. This resulted in the Japanese people opposing nuclear testing and the arms race. Transforming these views into policy, Prime Minister Sato Eisaku first outlined his Three Non-Nuclear Principles in response to a ques-

tion from a Diet leader in the Japan Socialist Party during budget hearings on December 11, 1967. But on January 19, 1968, a U.S. nuclear-
powered aircraft carrier stopped at Sasebo naval base, causing public
concerns about nuclear issues to intensify. Sato thus reiterated the
Three Non-Nuclear Principles on January 27, 1968 in his administration
policy address and again three days later in his response, appearing
here, to a question from Liberal Democratic Party leader Masayoshi
Ohira. Sato's statement provided a definitive explanation of Japan's nuclear policy for its people and the world community.

Document 9
JAPAN'S THREE NON-NUCLEAR PRINCIPLES

I think it is very important for Japanese people to have a correct knowledge of nuclear energy. Therefore, although Mr. Ohira has already described in detail, I would like to explain Japan's nuclear policy so that the
Japanese people are able to understand.

As you well know, there are four major pillars to support our nuclear policy. The first one is the Three Non-Nuclear Principles: Do not develop nuclear weapons, do not permit the presence of nuclear weapons in Japanese
territory, and do not possess nuclear weapons. (There is jeering. You are a
liar!) No, I am not a liar. This policy has been well established.

Secondly, the Japanese, who have had sad and disastrous experiences
caused by nuclear weapons, really hope for the total abandonment and elimination of nuclear weapons. However, since it is impossible for our hope to
become immediately real, we will make efforts to reduce nuclear armament. This is the reason why we have been expressing our opinions on the
international regulation and control on nuclear weapons. We must be patient and persistent in our efforts.

Thirdly, following the spirit of the Japanese Constitution, we will maintain self-defense force against non-nuclear invasion but against nuclear invasion we will depend on the U.S. force which is capable of stopping
nuclear invasion. This is in accordance to the Japan-U.S. Security Treaty.

Fourthly, we will make a full effort toward the peaceful utilization of nuclear energy which is the most important national policy. By doing so, we
will contribute to the progress of science and technology in the world, will
enjoy practical benefits of the progress, will make the Japanese people more
confident, will escalate Japan's dignity and will establish strongly our
stance for world peace.

As Mr. Ohira has emphasized, we have to make ambitious efforts for the
peaceful utilization of nuclear energy. The purposes of the fundamental

laws on nuclear power are: by promoting research, development and utilization of nuclear power, to secure future energy resources, to contribute to the progress of science and technology and the prosperity of industry, and to contribute to the welfare of human society and the improvement of a standard of living for the people.

Japan started the research and development efforts of nuclear energy ten years ago, and is now ranked sixth in the world in the number of nuclear reactors. . . . However, Japan is still at the initial stage of nuclear energy utilization. In the near future, nuclear energy will replace petroleum and coal as the energy sources for heating and transportation. Nuclear energy is now being used in many different areas including medicine, agriculture, construction, transportation, etc. Although it is our natural right to receive the benefits from nuclear energy development, the Japanese people have to, at the same time, have a better understanding of nuclear energy.

As I stated loudly before, the most important thing is to distinguish between nuclear weapons and the peaceful utilization of nuclear energy. We have to clearly distinguish them and express this explicitly with our attitudes. Recently in Japan, people are confused about our attitudes toward the above two. While the majority of the world has been making efforts for the peaceful utilization of nuclear energy as the national problem, Japan has been treating the utilization of nuclear energy as a problem only for a limited number of scientists. This is the reason why the Japanese people are confused about the utilization of nuclear energy. Of course, we, the politicians, have to honestly reflect our responsibilities, and from now on, I will courageously make the effort for the Japanese people to understand the peaceful utilization of nuclear energy.

As you have pointed out, there are unsophisticated feelings of a so-called "nuclear allergy" among the Japanese people. The disturbance and confusion occurred when the nuclear-powered aircraft carrier *Enterprise* came to Sasebo were caused by these feelings [*sic*]. However, as far as the basic policies on nuclear problems are concerned, there are almost perfect agreements among the ruling and opposing parties except for the Japan-U.S. Security Treaty, and I think these agreements are very meaningful. As you know, all the parties excluding the Communist party have agreed upon the Nuclear Non-Proliferation Treaty which will soon be an agenda in the United Nations General Assembly. Thus, I think it is the national consensus that Japan should use the nation's intelligence on the peaceful utilization of nuclear energy. . . .

As the prime minister, I am determined to accomplish the basic responsibility of maintaining the national security, and strongly hope for every body of the country to have the independent mind of a Japanese.

Source: Kanpo (Government report), 3rd issue, January 30, 1968, pp. 11–12. Translated by Henmi Teizi.

A PARTNERSHIP IN TRANSITION

U.S. president Richard M. Nixon and Japanese prime minister Sato Eisaku met in Washington, D.C., on November 19, 20, and 21, 1969, at a critical moment in world affairs. The United States had decided to reduce not only its military role in the Vietnam War but also its security commitments in Asia. Moreover, the U.S. economy was beginning to experience declining productivity and rising inflation. Sato, a strong supporter of Japan's alliance with the United States and the U.S. war in Vietnam, joined in issuing this statement, which identified new challenges in a now more equal U.S.-Japan partnership.

Document 10
SATO-NIXON COMMUNIQUÉ OF NOVEMBER 21, 1969

. . . 3. The President and the Prime Minister exchanged frank views on the current international situation, with particular attention to developments in the Far East. The President, while emphasizing that the countries in the area were expected to make their own efforts for the stability of the area, gave assurance that the United States would continue to contribute to the maintenance of international peace and security in the Far East by honoring its defense treaty obligations in the area. The Prime Minister, appreciating the determination of the United States, stressed that it was important for the peace and security of the Far Fast that the United States should be in a position to carry out fully its obligations referred to by the President. He further expressed his recognition that, in the light of the present situation, the presence of United States forces in the Far East constituted a mainstay for the stability of the area.

4. The President and the Prime Minister specifically noted the continuing tension over the Korean peninsula. The Prime Minister deeply appreciated the peacekeeping efforts of the United Nations in the area and stated that the security of the Republic of Korea was essential to Japan's own security. The President and the Prime Minister shared the hope that Communist China would adopt a more cooperative and constructive attitude in its external relations. The President referred to the treaty obligations of his country to the Republic of China which the United States would uphold. The Prime Minister said that the maintenance of peace and security in the Taiwan area was also a most important factor for the security of Japan. The President de-

scribed the earnest efforts made by the United States for a peaceful and just settlement of the Viet-Nam problem. The President and the Prime Minister expressed the strong hope that the war in Viet-Nam would be concluded before return of the administrative rights over Okinawa to Japan. In this connection, they agreed that, should peace in Viet-Nam not have been realized by the time reversion of Okinawa is scheduled to take place, the two governments would fully consult with each other in the light of the situation at that time so that reversion would be accomplished without affecting the United States efforts to assure the South Vietnamese people the opportunity to determine their own political future without outside interference. The Prime Minister stated that Japan was exploring what role she could play in bringing about stability in the Indochina area.

5. In light of the current situation and the prospects in the Far East, the President and the Prime Minister agreed that they highly valued the role played by the Treaty of Mutual Cooperation and Security in maintaining the peace and security of the Far East including Japan, and they affirmed the intention of the two governments firmly to maintain the Treaty on the basis of mutual trust and common evaluation of the international situation. They further agreed that the two governments should maintain close contact with each other on matters affecting the peace and security of the Far East including Japan, and on the implementation of the Treaty of Mutual Cooperation and Security.

6. The Prime Minister emphasized his view that the time had come to respond to the strong desire of the people of Japan, of both the mainland and Okinawa, to have the administrative rights over Okinawa returned to Japan on the basis of the friendly relations between the United States and Japan and thereby to restore Okinawa to its normal status. The President expressed appreciation of the Prime Minister's view. The President and the Prime Minister also recognized the vital role played by United States forces in Okinawa in the present situation in the Far East. As a result of their discussion it was agreed that the mutual security interests of the United States and Japan could be accommodated within arrangements for the return of the administrative rights over Okinawa to Japan. They therefore agreed that the two governments would immediately enter into consultations regarding specific arrangements for accomplishing the early reversion of Okinawa without detriment to the security of the Far East including Japan. They further agreed to expedite the consultations with a view to accomplishing the reversion during 1972 subject to the conclusion of these specific arrangements with the necessary legislative support. In this connection, the Prime Minister made clear the intention of his government, following reversion, to assume gradually the responsiblility for the immediate defense of Oki-

nawa as part of Japan's defense efforts for her own territories. The President and the Prime Minister agreed also that the United States would retain under the terms of the Treaty of Mutual Cooperation and Security such military facilities and areas in Okinawa as required in the mutual security of both countries.

7. The President and the Prime Minister agreed that, upon return of the adminstrative rights, the Treaty of Mutual Cooperation and Security and its related arrangements would apply to Okinawa without modification thereof. In this connection, the Prime Minister affirmed the recognition of his government that the security of Japan could not be adequately maintained without international peace and security in the Far East and, therefore, the security of countries in the Far East was a matter of serious concern for Japan. The Prime Minister was of the view that in the light of such recognition on the part of the Japanese Government the return of the administrative rights over Okinawa in the manner agreed above should not hinder the effective discharge of the international obligations assumed by the United States for the defense of countries in the Far East including Japan. The President replied that he shared the Prime Minister's view.

8. The Prime Minister described in detail the particular sentiment of the Japanese people against nuclear weapons and the policy of the Japanese Government reflecting such sentiment. The President expressed his deep understanding and assured the Prime Minister that, without prejudice to the position of the United States Government with respect to the prior consultation system under the Treaty of Mutual Cooperation and Security, the reversion of Okinawa would be carried out in a manner consistent with the policy of the Japanese Government as described by the Prime Minister. . . .

11. The President and the Prime Minister expressed their conviction that a mutually satisfactory solution of the question of the return of the administrative rights over Okinawa to Japan, which is the last of the major issues between the two countries arising from the Second World War, would further strengthen United States–Japan relations which are based on friendship and mutual trust and would make a major contribution to the peace and security of the Far East.

12. In their discussion of economic matters, the President and the Prime Minister noted the marked growth in economic relations between the two countries. They also acknowledged that leading positions which their countries occupy in the world economy impose important responsibilities on each for the maintenance and strengthening of the international trade and monetary system, especially in the light of the current large imbalances in trade and payments. In this regard, the President stressed his determination to bring inflation in the United States under control. He also reaffirmed the

commitment of the United States to the principle of promoting freer trade. The Prime Minister indicated the intention of the Japanese Government to accelerate rapidly the reduction of Japan's trade and capital restrictions. Specifically, he stated the intention of the Japanese Government to remove Japan's residual import quota restrictions over a broad range of products by the end of 1971 and to make maximum efforts to accelerate the liberalization of the remaining items. He added that the Japanese Government intends to make periodic reviews of its liberalization program with a view to implementing trade liberalization at a more accelerated pace than hitherto. The President and the Prime Minister agreed that their respective actions would further solidify the foundation of overall U.S.-Japan relations.

13. The President and the Prime Minister agreed that attention to the economic needs of the developing countries was essential to the development of international peace and stability. The Prime Minister stated the intention of the Japanese Government to expand and improve its aid programs in Asia commensurate with the economic growth of Japan. The President welcomed this statement and confirmed that the United States would continue to contribute to the economic development of Asia. The President and Prime Minister recognized that there would be major requirements for the post-war rehabilitation of Viet-Nam and elsewhere in Southeast Asia. The Prime Minister stated the intention of the Japanese Government to make a substantial contribution to this end.

14. The Prime Minister congratulated the President on the successful moon landing of *Apollo XII*, and expressed the hope for a safe journey back to earth for the astronauts. The President and the Prime Minister agreed that the exploration of space offers great opportunities for expanding cooperation in peaceful scientific projects among all nations. In this connection, the Prime Minister noted with pleasure that the United States and Japan last summer had concluded an agreement on space cooperation. The President and the Prime Minister agreed that implementation of this unique program is of importance to both countries.

15. The President and the Prime Minister discussed prospects for the promotion of arms control and the slowing down of the arms race. The President outlined his Government's efforts to initiate the strategic arms limitations talks with the Soviet Union that have recently started in Helsinki. The Prime Minister expressed his Government's strong hopes for the success of these talks. The Prime Minister pointed out his country's strong and traditional interest in effective disarmament measures with a view to achievement of general and complete disarmament under strict and effective international control.

Source: U.S. Department of State, *Bulletin* 61 (December 15, 1969): 555–58.

RESTORING RELATIONS WITH CHINA

In July 1971 President Richard Nixon announced his intention to visit the People's Republic of China with the goal of normalizing relations. This came as a shock to Japan, but it allowed Tokyo to seize this long-awaited opportunity to follow suit. At the invitation of Chinese Premier Zhou Enlai, Prime Minister Tanaka Kakuei visited Beijing from September 25 to 30, 1972, resulting in the signing of a communiqué (presented here) restoring normal diplomatic relations. Japan then withdrew recognition of the Guomindang government on Taiwan and opened negotiations for the signing a treaty of peace and friendship with China in 1978.

Document 11
SINO-JAPANESE JOINT STATEMENT OF SEPTEMBER 29, 1972

Premier Chou En-lai and Foreign Minister Chi Peng-fei had an earnest and frank exchange of views with Prime Minister Tanaka Kakuei and Foreign Minister Ohira Masayoshi, all along in a friendly atmosphere, on various matters between the two countries and other matters of interest to both sides, with the normalization of relations between China and Japan as the focal point, and the two sides agreed to follow the joint statement of the two Governments:

China and Japan are neighboring countries separated only by a strip of water, and there was a long history of traditional friendship between them. The two peoples ardently wish to end the abnormal state of affairs that has hitherto existed between the two countries. The termination of the state of war and the normalization of relations between China and Japan—the realization of such wishes of the two peoples—will open a new page in the annals of relations between the two countries.

The Japanese side is keenly aware of Japan's responsibility for causing enormous damages in the past to the Chinese people through war and deeply reproaches itself. The Japanese side reaffirms its position that in seeking to realize the normalization of relations between Japan and China, it proceeds from the stand of fully understanding the three principles for the restoration of diplomatic relations put forward by the Government of the People's Republic of China. The Chinese side expresses its welcome for this.

Although the social systems of China and Japan are different, the two countries should and can establish peaceful and friendly relations. The normalization of relations and the development of good-neighborly and friendly relations between the two countries are in the interests of the two peoples, and will also contribute to the relaxation of tension in Asia and the safeguarding of world peace.

(1) The abnormal state of affairs which has hitherto existed between the People's Republic of China and Japan is declared terminated on the date of publication of this statement.

(2) The Government of Japan recognizes the Government of the People's Republic of China as the sole legal Government of China.

(3) The Government of the People's Republic of China reaffirms that Taiwan is an inalienable part of the territory of the People's Republic of China. The Government of Japan fully understands and respects this stand of the Government of China and adheres to its stand of complying with Article 8 of the Potsdam Proclamation.

(4) The Government of Japan and the Government of the People's Republic of China decided upon the establishment of diplomatic relations as from September 29, 1972. The two Governments have decided to adopt all necessary measures for the establishment and the performance of functions of embassies in each other's capitals in accordance with international law and practice and exchange ambassadors as speedily as possible.

(5) The Government of the People's Republic of China declares that in the interest of the friendship between the peoples of China and Japan, it renounces its demand for war indemnities from Japan.

(6) The Government of Japan and the Government of the People's Republic of China agree to establish durable relations of peace and friendship between the two countries on the basis of the principles of mutual respect for sovereignty and territorial integrity, mutual nonaggression, noninterference in each other's internal affairs, equality and mutual benefit and peaceful coexistence.

In keeping with the foregoing principles and the principles of the United Nations Charter the governments of the two countries affirm that in their mutual relations, all disputes shall be settled by peaceful means without resorting to the use or threat of force.

(7) The normalization of relations between China and Japan is not directed against third countries. Neither of the two countries should seek hegemony in the Asia-Pacific region and each country is opposed to efforts by any other country or group of countries to establish such hegemony.

(8) To consolidate and develop the peaceful and friendly relations between the two countries, the Government of Japan and the Government of

the People's Republic of China agree to hold negotiations aimed at the conclusion of a treaty of peace and friendship.

(9) In order to further develop the relations between the two countries and broaden the exchange of visits, the Government of Japan and the Government of the People's Republic of China agree to hold negotiations aimed at the conclusion of trade navigation, aviation, fishery, etc., in accordance with the needs and taking into consideration the existing nongovernmental agreements.

Source: Kajima Peace Institute, ed., *Nihon Gaiko Shuyo Bunsho/Nenpyo* (Basic documents on Japanese foreign relations), Vol. 3 (Tokyo: Hara-shobo, 1985), 593–94. Translated by Henmi Teizo

U.S.-JAPAN ECONOMIC AND FINANCIAL FRICTION

During the 1960s the United States began to complain about inexpensive Japanese exports flooding the American market. Adding to Washington's unhappiness in the 1970s were barriers to Japanese consumption of foreign imports. This led to U.S. efforts to press Japan into accepting a series of economic agreements to rectify these grievances. Prime Minister Nakasone Yasuhiro in particular tried to placate Washington, resulting in trade and financial agreements such as the one presented here between U.S. secretary of the Treasury Donald Regan and Japanese finance minister Takeshita Noburo.

Document 12
U.S.-JAPAN JOINT ANNOUNCEMENT OF
NOVEMBER 10, 1983

Secretary Regan and Finance Minister Takeshita have had a number of candid and cordial exchanges of views in recent weeks on a variety of issues of mutual interest. They have agreed that both countries:

1. Will pursue appropriate monetary and fiscal policies that will promote sustained real economic growth with low inflation, reduced interest rates, and higher productive investment.

2. Will cooperate closely in dealing with LDC [Less Developed Country] debt problems in order to promote effective adjustment on the part of debtor countries and the flow of financing necessary to support those adjustment efforts.

3. Consistent with the understandings reached at Williamsburg with the other summit countries regarding exchange rate policy, will consult more

closely on exchange market developments and undertake coordinated intervention to counter disorderly market conditions.

In addition, both Ministers agreed that open, liberal capital markets and the free movement of capital are important to the operation of an effectively functioning international monetary system.

Minister Takeshita stated that the Japanese Ministry of Finance will assure the prompt and thorough implementation, following due procedures, of the measures listed in the "Comprehensive Economic Measures" of October 21, 1983, which would further liberalize Japan's capital markets, internationalize the yen, and allow the yen to more fully reflect its underlying strength. In particular, the Ministry of Finance announced its decisions to:

—Eliminate the real demand rule in forward exchange transactions, effective April 1, 1984.

—Submit a bill in the next ordinary Diet session starting from December 1993, to reform the designated company system, after consultation with agencies concerned.

—Submit a bill in the next ordinary Diet session to enable issuance of foreign currency denominated national bonds abroad.

—Expedite the study concerning establishment of a yen-denominated bankers' acceptance market.

In addition, the Japanese Ministry of Finance announced that it will:

—Seek to lower the minimum denomination of CDs to yen 300 million from its current level of yen 500 million, effective January 1, 1984.

—Seek to enlarge further the ceiling on each bank's CD issues, effective April 1, 1984.

—Ease guidelines on the issue of Euro-yen bonds by residents, effective April 1, 1984,

—In this connection, the withholding tax on interest earnings on Euro-yen bonds held by non-residents will be reviewed, having due regard to maintaining proper taxation including the withholding tax system.

Minister Takeshita also confirmed his policy stance on the occasion of announcing the "Comprehensive Economic Measures" that "we, as one of the major industrial nations, will continue to take positive steps towards the internationalization of the yen and the liberalization of our financial and capital markets."

In reply to questions by Secretary Regan, Minister Takeshita stated that there are no discriminatory restrictions under Japanese laws on the acquisition of Japanese banks by foreign banks. He stated that the banking laws governing acquisitions by foreign banks are identical with those governing acquisitions by domestic banks.

Secretary Regan welcomed the announcement of these measures, indicating that they represented significant progress by the government of Japan in its efforts to liberalize its capital markets and internationalize the yen, and would make an important contribution to the functioning of foreign exchange markets and the world trade and financial system.

In addition, Secretary Regan announced that the U.S. Treasury will:

—Fully take into account the concerns of the Japanese authorities in its review of the issues related to unitary taxation.

—Welcome the issuance of Japanese Government guaranteed bonds in the U.S. market, with or without a currency swap.

—Pursue as quickly as possible a reduction of the U.S. budget deficit through additional measures to reduce government spending.

—Strive for early passage of the legislation enabling the United States to consent to the increase in its IMF [International Monetary Fund] quota,

—Attempt to agree with other IDA [International Development Association] donors on the next replenishment as soon as possible.

Minister Takeshita and Secretary Regan agreed that further progress on these matters is desirable. To that end, they agreed that the Japanese Ministry of Finance and the U.S. Treasury Department would establish a joint ad hoc group of financial authorities on yen/dollar exchange rate issues. The purpose of the group would be to:

—Monitor U.S. and Japanese progress in implementing the agreed upon measures, and to develop and implement additional steps, such as increasing the use of yen in denominating Japanese exports.

—Strengthen mutual understanding and to establish a common recognition of the current state of the yen/dollar rate and its determinants.

This ad hoc group would be co-chaired by Finance Minister Takeshita and Treasury Secretary Regan, with a working group at the Under Secretary level. The working group will meet by February 1984, and submit a report to the Chairmen by Spring 1984. Minister Takeshita and Secretary Regan agreed to continue to be in close contact on these and other economic and financial issues.

Source: U.S. Department of State, *American Foreign Policy Current Documents 1983* (Washington, DC: U.S. Government Printing Office, 1985), 1035–36.

ILLUSIONS OF JAPANESE INVINCIBILITY

Japan came to resent U.S. pressure to change its economic policies. It also resented harsh criticism from American political and business leaders, which was labeled "Japan-bashing." The Americans, many Japanese concluded, were unwilling to accept blame for their own economic problems, which reflected the decline of the United States as the dominant world power. Ishihara Shintaro, a right-wing politician in the ruling Liberal Democratic Party, called on the Japanese people to end the nation's dependence on the United States and assume instead a rightful role as world leader. He made these statements in his book *The Japan That Can Say No* (1989), key excerpts of which appear here.

Document 13
THE JAPAN THAT CAN SAY NO: JAPAN WILL BE FIRST AMONG EQUALS

The handshake between George Bush and Mikhail Gorbachev opening the Malta summit signaled the end of the Cold War, the titanic clash between communism and democracy. . . . Nations that fail to adjust lose control of their own destinies.

Buffeted by events, ties between countries ebb and alter. There is no permanent bilateral status quo. . . . The Japan-U.S. relations will also change in the future. Although the two countries have been very close since World War II, it has not always been marked by full mutual understanding. . . . The United States has not sufficiently appreciated Japan and even taken us all that seriously, because since 1945, we have been under Uncle Sam's thumb. Today, Americans may feel that Japan is getting out of hand. My own view is that Japan should not immediately disassociate itself from the U.S. security system. For our sake and that of the whole Pacific region, the special Tokyo-Washington relationship must be preserved. A breakup could destroy the budding new developments in that region. Japan should play an expanded role in the post–Cold War world order. Effective use of our economic power—technology, management skills, and financial resources—at our own initiative can be the key to stable progress.

The economic dimension of the next era is already unfolding. That communism, a political doctrine no longer meaningful or functional, has remained powerful until recently is an irony of history. Prolonged obsession with ideology was a cultural lag between technology and the human beings who created it. To Japanese, as a pragmatic people inclined toward craftsmanship rather than metaphysics, the end of ideology is good news.

History shows that technology creates civilization and determines the scale and level of its economic and industrial development. Eastern Europe and the Soviet Union want state-of-the-art technology and financial aid to make them productive. What country can provide them? Only Japan. But we cannot meet this challenge alone. It must be a joint undertaking with our partner, the United States.

JAPAN'S WORLD ROLE

In its opinions about Japan, Washington is divided into the so-called Cherry Blossom Club and the Japan-bashers, with the former in the departments of State and Defense and the latter headquartered on Capitol Hill. The U.S. military and foreign service are well aware that Japan's high technology and mass-production system are indispensable in America's global strategy and consider the torrent of congressional attacks unwise. Still the Cherry Blossoms and the Japan-bashers agree on one thing: they do not want Japan to become more powerful than it is now. . . .

The message is clear: We must think and act for ourselves and stop being a dutiful underling who leaves all the hard decisions up to the boss. . . . Some scholars say that in peacetime relations between nations do not change overnight. Nevertheless, in a period of great historical upheaval like the present, there are seminal events that alter our perceptions of the world. To the careful observer, history provides valid principles for a nation's course of action and approach. The echoes of the past reverberate for a while, but it is only the past, after all. Our task is to define the elusive future, to hear those faint portentous sounds of tomorrow. We look back at history to see ahead.

As the tempestuous twentieth century draws to a close, I would like to add a postscript to modernism. Caucasians deserve much credit in the creation of modern civilization, but they were not the only agents of change. Historian Arnold J. Toynbee concluded that we had simply imitated the West. Regrettably, some Japanese agree with the British scholar's interpretation and are delighted at this "high praise." This sad lot does not understand history. What to superficial observers seems like the instantaneous aping of Western ways was actually the fruition of innumerable cultural advances over the course of many centuries.

The modernization that started in Japan in the late nineteenth century was built upon the highly sophisticated culture of the Tokugawa period (1603–1847), which in turn evolved from the Azuchi-Momoyama culture of the late sixteenth century that was so admired by Spanish and Portuguese priests and merchants. Ashikaga Yoshimasa's (1436–1490) aesthetic splendor graced the fifteenth century and so on back a millennium. How preposterous to assert that somehow modern Japan sprang full-blown from Western seeds! China dates from antiquity but lacks cultural continuity and consistency because of dynastic upheaval and foreign rule. In contrast, Japan's superior cultural ethos enabled us to modernize successfully. Toynbee, whether intentionally, unconsciously, or from ignorance, said nothing about this historical heritage.

At any rate, Japanese must understand that today the nation is riding the crest of a great historic wave and, with the United States, will shape the next age. I disagree with the oft-stated view that the twenty-first century will be a pentapolar world—the United States, Japan, Europe, the Soviet Union, and China. The United States will probably pull itself together and continue to be a leader. Eastern Europe and the Soviet Union, however, will ultimately be part of the global network of Japanese technology.

The United States wants to provide massive aid to Eastern Europe, such as the Marshall Plan that stimulated Western Europe's recovery after World War II. Many Americans trace their ethnic heritage to the Old World, and to keep the upper hand with Moscow, Washington should try to establish hegemony over the former Iron Curtain countries.

Mired in debt, however, the United States lacks the financial wherewithal to be the principal aid donor and will be unable to revive its economy and mount such an initiative until early in the twenty-first century. First there must be a massive federal program to improve the school system and retain the labor force. The investment in human resource development will not pay off for at least fifteen years. . . .

In the coming decades, Europe will be dominated by a reunited Germany. The Soviet Union and China will be less dynamic than at present, whereas the Pacific region and Southeast Asia will be more. The Japan-U.S. team must be a constructive influence in this new configuration.

A PARTNERSHIP FOR THE WORLD

Japan's foreign policy is obviously inadequate for a world in flux. . . . With . . . the shift from military confrontation to economic competition, Japan needs a national strategy for global trade relations.

The conflicts among nations will be increasingly economic in nature. With the Cold War over, friction on trade and investment will inevitably intensify. Over the next few years, Japan-bashing in the United States will become even more virulent. Although I see the bilateral relationship as the dominant force in the next century, before we reach that level of cooperation, U.S. policy toward Japan will approximate the stance against the Soviet Union at the height of the Cold War.

First, Americans will argue that Japan is different and therefore a threat. Next, a "collective security system" will be created to block Japan's economic expansion. Then protectionist measures and sanctions against Japanese products will follow one after the other. An alliance is already being formed against Japan. Finally, there will be a witch hunt directed at everything Japanese. We must be prepared for stormy days ahead.

If we try to bend with the wind, making concessions and patchwork compromises as usual, the tempest will abate for a while, only to recur with even greater force. We must not flinch in the face of pressure. The only way to withstand foreign demands is to hold our ground courageously. No more temporizing. When justified, we must keep saying no and be undaunted by the reaction, however furious. A prolonged standoff forces both sides to find areas of agreement. That is the best way to resolve disputes, not unilateral concessions by Japan, which leave the other party unaware of how we really feel. Our lack of assertiveness in the past has led to disparaging epithets like "the faceless people."

Our "yes, yes" style of diplomacy limits freedom of action and confuses the public. Asakai Koichiro, former ambassador to the United States, . . . has decried our concession-prone foreign policy and continued deference to the United States. For example, suppose a Soviet foreign minister said, "We will return the four northern islands. You abrogate the Japan-U.S. security treaty. The Soviet Union is no threat to Japan." A certain segment of the public would welcome the Soviet proposal. How would politicians respond to Moscow and approach Washington? A misstep might cause a political upheaval in Japan, according to Asakai, and he wondered whether the government had the gumption to make the first move.

Source: Shintaro Ishihara, *The Japan That Can Say No: Why Japan Will Be First among Equals,* trans. Frank Baldwin (New York: Simon & Schuster, 1989), 103–17.

FIVE PRINCIPLES FOR A WIDER WORLD ROLE

Japan refused to make a military contribution to help liberate Kuwait after Iraq's invasion of that country in August 1990. Japan then was reluctant to provide substantial monetary support, prompting criticism from the United States and its European allies. To counter criticism of "checkbook diplomacy," the Diet passed the UN Peacekeeping Operations bill in June 1992 after a long debate, allowing for the deployment of Japanese troops overseas for the first time since World War II. The Japan Defense Agency presented a brief but formal list of guidelines for Japan's role.

Document 14
BASIC GUIDELINES FOR JAPAN'S PARTICIPATION IN
PEACEKEEPING FORCES

I. Agreement on cease-fire shall have been reached among the parties to the conflict.

II. The parties to the conflict, including the territorial state(s), shall have given their consent to deployment of peacekeeping force and Japan's participation in the force

III. The peacekeeping force shall strictly maintain impartiality, not favoring any party to the conflict.

IV. Should any of the above guideline requirements cease to be satisfied, the Government of Japan may withdraw its contingent.

V. Use of weapons shall be limited to the minimum necessary to protect the personnel's lives, etc.

Source: Japan Defense Agency, *Defense of Japan* (Tokyo: Japan Defense Agency, 1992).

TOWARD ECONOMIC LIBERALIZATION

Economic confidence in Japan ended with the East Asia financial crisis that began in the summer of 1997. With its banking system teetering on the brink of collapse, Japan struggled to regain global economic dominance. In August 1998, Obuchi Keizo became prime minister, and he soon devised a plan to revive the economy with the advice of former prime minister Miyazawa Kiichi, whom he appointed as finance minister. Miyazawa served as honorary chairman of the U.S.-Japan 21st Century Committee. His contribution to its conference report, appearing here, describes the new direction the Obuchi government was pursuing to achieve economic reform.

Document 15
"JAPAN IS TWENTY YEARS BEHIND"

The collapse of the former Soviet economy at the beginning of the 1990s was taken to signify the failure of central economic planning and the triumph of capitalist market economics. The fall of the Berlin Wall should not, however, be seen merely as a symbol of the defeat of socialist ideology. It is also a sign of the larger movement of global civilization from centralized to decentralized economic and social systems.

The end of the Cold War thus has also led to the defeat of centralized systems of bureaucratic control, one of which is Japan's system of bureaucracy-led cooperative administration. Today, with the nation plagued by economic stagnation, political indecision, lack of individuality and creativity, and a host of other problems, many Japanese have become acutely aware of the defects of the Japanese-style system of social and economic management and of the need for radical reform.

In a worldwide trend, radical administrative and fiscal reform from centralized to decentralized systems, is coming to be seen as the most effective way to break out of such an economic and social impasse and bring renewed vitality. An important means of decentralizing administrative and fiscal systems is the complete abolition of restrictive regulations.

THE NECESSITY FOR REFORM

The first task for Japan, which is 20 years behind the global trend toward liberalization, is to reform its economic structure and the social structure which supports it. There will be time to deal with the pain of reform after major surgery is completed, as in the U.S. If Japan fears pain when it has barely made a start, it can make no progress.

. . . In Japan, as indicated by the expression "the 1941 structure" the bureaucratic regulatory structure was formed under the slogan of catching up with and overtaking the U.S. and the major European nations. Each industry, administered under an "escorted convoy" system, grew as a harmonious whole; incomes also rose equally across the board, and stable employment was assured. During the phase of economic development, regulation had a rationale which was valid up to a point. . . .

As income levels have risen with economic development, consumer needs have grown more diverse, personalized and sophisticated. But it is difficult to respond flexibly to this new diversity while encumbered by regulations dating from an era when uniformity and equality were the goal. A mature society has different values, a different sense of what is right: namely, freedom of choice, as befits the new diversity of consumer tastes. To provide this, suppliers must be able to compete among themselves. It follows that the bureaucratic administration which protects suppliers, and the collusive arrangements it has fostered, is no longer good for society.

Japan is characterized by the fact that this structure of conformism and collusion has been sustained under a system of control headed by the bureaucracy. This can be traced to the bureaucratic culture, a national mentality which, since the Meiji Period, has exalted Japanese bureaucrats, regarding them as brilliant and entrusting the fortunes of the nation to their care. In any case, it is clear that Japan developed its bureaucracy-dominated social and economic system by assigning authority to the bureaucracy, and that the public has accepted this system.

Another source of pressure for economic reform in Japan is the increasingly borderless nature of the global economy. Globalization today refers to the accelerating movement not only of goods and services but also of money, production systems, technology and information across national boundaries. In other words, far more countries and products are now involved in international transfers than in the past. Under these conditions, competition arises among economic systems (including laws and taxation), and unattractive systems are selected out.

In the 1990s, the economic performance of the Anglo-Saxon countries, with the U.S. in the lead, has been remarkable. The U.S. and Britain, in particular, took the great steps to deregulate their economics in the 1970s and have also made striking progress in fiscal reconstruction. New Zealand and Canada have also been successful in restructuring their public finances. In Europe, although the movement toward structural economic reform has been relatively slow, national governments seeking to qualify for the single European currency are pressing ahead with fiscal reconstruction, and there is also a growing trend toward privatization. It should be noted that even Sweden, which was one of the more conservative countries in Europe, has carried out radical regulatory reforms. Japan has thus been left behind.

If Japan is to survive in an era of mega-competition with the dynamic middle-income economics of Asia and the developed nations of Europe and North America, whose structural reforms have increased their efficiency, it must achieve a scale and speed of reform that will make up for 20 years' delay.

THE IDEAL SOCIETY:
FREE CHOICE AND EQUAL OPPORTUNITY

In a society which places importance on democracy and liberal market economics, there are as many ideal societies as there are individuals to make choices. One could say that the particular shape a society takes is the result of those choices. Neither bureaucrats nor politicians can draw a blueprint of the ideal society in advance.

The key points, therefore, are to recognize individual freedom of choice and establish the principle of individual responsibility for outcomes. In terms of the economic system, free consumer choice and free competition among suppliers, according to clear rules, must be promoted by discarding the policy of protecting suppliers under bureaucratic guidance and instead entrusting economic and social activity to market mechanisms.

From the same viewpoint, greater emphasis must be placed on equality of opportunity.

Traditionally, Japan's ethical code has not permitted such freedom. We must now make Japan a society where winners are honored, losers are encouraged to try again, and nonconformists and persons with different abilities can thrive.

Source: Kiichi Miyazawa, "Japan Is Twenty Years Behind," *New Perspectives Quarterly* 15 (Winter 1998): 24–26.

Glossary of Selected Terms

amakudari: "Descent from heaven"; the process whereby government bureaucrats on retirement are employed by private business

Ampo: People's Council for Preventing Revision of the Security Treaty (Ampo joyaku kaitei shoshi kokumin kaigi), formed in 1959 to protest the proposed revision of the U.S.-Japan Security Treaty of 1951

Anpo: Abbreviation for Nichibei Anpo Joyaku (the U.S.-Japan Security Treaty of 1951), used with reference to the protest against the renewal of the treaty in 1960

Article 9: Provision of the 1947 Constitution that seemed to prevent rearmament, prohibiting Japan from maintaining "land, sea, and air forces, as well as other war potential" for all time. Conservatives, with American support, succeeded in interpreting the article to mean renouncing war only to settle international disputes, while allowing for the creation and maintenance of armed forces for Japan's self-defense.

Beheiren: Citizens' Federation for Peace in Vietnam

"black mist": Political corruption

bubei: "Contempt for the United States"

burakumin: Originally, people with no caste or status because of their occupations as, for example, butchers or tanners. Despite formal emancipation, these "hamlet people" continued to suffer discrimination in postwar Japan.

Diet: Bicameral legislative assembly. Under Japan's 1947 Constitution, the lower House of Representatives at first had 466 members from 124 districts with three to five representatives from each elected for four-year terms. The Upper House of Councillors had 250 members elected at the prefectural level and nationwide for six-year terms. A reform bill of January 1994, which became effective in 1995, reduced membership in the lower house from 511 to 500, and abolished the multiple representative district system. It provided for 300 representatives from single seat constituencies and 200 according to each party's proportional share of the vote in 11 regional blocks. Voters would cast two ballots, one for an individual and another for a political party.

Dodge Plan: Implemented in 1949, this was the first step the United States took toward promoting Japan's economic recovery after World War II. Under the direction of Detroit banker Joseph M. Dodge, this comprehensive stabilization program was successful in promoting financial discipline by means of imposing wage and price controls, balancing the budget, ending inflationary loans, restraining government intervention in the private sector with subsidies, and ensuring the allocation of raw materials for export production; the program resulted in the curbing of inflation, the expansion of domestic consumption, and the restoring of private control over foreign trade.

Domei: All-Japan General Federation of Labor, formed in 1946 in a merger of anti-Communist trade unions that supported the right wing of the Japan Socialist Party, as well as later the Democratic Socialist Party

Fukuda Doctrine: Prime Minister Fukuda Takeo issued this statement in Manila in 1977, committing Japan to build understanding in Southeast Asia; to pursue partnerships on the basis of equality contributing to regional stability and peace; to renounce military ambition and the production of nuclear weapons; and to double aid, expand investment, and raise levels of Japanese imports from the region over five years.

gaiatsu: "Foreign pressure"

Guomindang: Political party in China that Sun Yat-sen formed in 1912. It helped topple the last dynasty that year, but it failed to gain control over a new republic that was fragmented when Sun Yat-sen died in 1925. Chiang Kai-shek, his successor, revived Chinese nationalism and united China in 1928, although the Communists eventually replaced his Nationalist government in 1949, forcing the party to flee to Taiwan.

gyosei kaikaku: "Administrative reform"; Nakasone Yasuhiro's government used this term to describe his policies for privatization, reduction in public spending, and the widening of Japan's international ties.

hanbatsu: Factionalism

hanbei: Anti-Americanism

Heisei: Era name for the reign of the present emperor, Akihito, from his accession in 1989; previous era names were Showa, Taisho, and Meiji.

Japan, Inc.: Label attributing Japan's emergence after World War II as a world economic power to a triad of leadership comprised of the Liberal Democratic Party, government bureaucracy, and big business

Jiminto: Liberal Democratic Party, formed in 1955, that as the largest political party in Japan selected the prime minister until 1993

jishu gaiko: Independent diplomacy

Keidanren: Federation of Economic Organizations, the body that advances the interests of business and private enterprise in Japan

keiretsu: Label for conglomerates of economic interest emerging after 1945. These "enterprise groups" usually centered around a particular bank, with interlocking directorates and mutual shareholding tying them together. A trading company often served a coordinating function.

kenbei: Dislike of the United States

kikan: Private militarist organizations

Kikkyoso: Japan Teachers Union

kisei kanwa: Restructuring

kogai: Environmental pollution

kokutai: "National polity"; conservative nationalists used this term to build patriotism and loyalty to the government in Japan before 1945.

Komeito: Clean Government Party, the political wing of the religious movement known as Soka Gakkai

Lockheed Scandal: In February 1976, the U.S. Senate held hearings on allegations that the Lockheed Corporation had paid bribes to officials in Japan's government for favorable treatment in airplane procurement. As a result, just more than a year after he resigned as prime minister, Tanaka Kakuei was charged with accepting $500 million yen ($4.5 million) from Lockheed. These payments were compensation for Tanaka persuading Air Nippon to cancel a contract with U.S. defense producer McDonnell-Douglas and instead buy the Lockheed L-1011. Soon referred to as the Lockheed Scandal, the incident spurred a wave of suicides and the fall of Miki Takeo as prime minister. Tanaka was arrested but released after interrogation. Finally indicted and found guilty in 1983, he was sentenced to four years in prison, but he filed a succession of appeals. The Supreme Court rejected his appeal in 1987, but more appeals kept the unrepentant Tanaka out of jail until his death in 1993.

Maekwa Report: Prime Minister Nakasone Yasuhiro named a study group to examine trade and agricultural policy, with Maekwa Haruo, former governor of the Bank of Japan, as chair. In 1986 the group issued this report, which proposed tax reductions and greater public works expenditures to increase domestic consumption. This would boost economic expansion, creating more jobs and generating increased tax revenue.

Meiji Restoration: This term refers to the time when the great southern feudal domains of Satsuma and Choshu seized the Imperial Palace in Kyoto on January 3, 1868 and announced the formal return of governmental power from the Tokugawa Shogunate to the emperor. The term also describes more broadly the series of political, social, and economic changes that the *genro*, or "elder statesman" who restored the emperor to power, implemented thereafter, thus transforming Japan into a modern, industrialized, and militarized power by the early twentieth century. Meiji was chosen as the name for the era to indicate that Mutsuhito, the young emperor, would institute "enlightened rule."

minshushugi: democracy

Nihon Sekigun: Japanese Red Army, formed in 1972

Nihon Shinto: Japan New Party, formed in 1992

Nikkeiren: Japan Federation of Employers' Associations

Nixon Shocks: During July 1971, after providing Tokyo just hours of advance notice, President Richard Nixon announced his intention to normalize relations with the People's Republic of China. In August 1971, again without giving the Japanese government advance notice, Nixon announced that the United States would allow the value of the dollar to float on world currency markets, making American goods more competitive in world trade at the expense of Japan. The two announcements came to be known as the Nixon shocks.

Nokyo: Leading postwar agricultural cooperative organization

"Northern Territories": Located north of Hokkaido, Japan's most northern main island, these territories include the islands of Etorofu, Kunashiri, Shikotan, and the Habomais; the Soviet Union seized them at the end of World War II along with the rest of the Kurile Islands and has refused to return them to Japan.

Rengo: National Federation of Private Sector Trade Unions, formed in 1987; also active as a political party

reverse course: Refers to change in U.S. occupation policy after 1947 to achieve economic recovery in Japan and transform it into a close anti-Communist ally of the United States

Sakigake: Harbinger Party, formed in 1994

sarariman: White-collar, salaried employee

seikei bunri: A reference to the Japanese foreign policy approach toward Communist China and North Korea after World War II that emphasized the separation of politics and economics

Sekigunha: United Red Army, created in 1969

Shakaito: Japan Socialist Party

shazai gaiko: Refers to the "apology diplomacy" that Japan followed after the death of Emperor Hirohito in 1989

shiken jigoku: The "examination hell" of Japan's education system

shinbun: Newspaper

shingikai: Committees comprised of representatives from major economic interest groups to advise bureaucrats, resolve differences, and build consensus for reports that often provided the basis for legislation approved in the Diet, acting thereafter to ensure compliance

Shinseito: Renewal Party, formed in 1993

Shinshinto: New Frontier Party, formed in 1994

Shintoism: Ancient Japanese religion, literally the "Way of the Gods," derived from the worship of natural objects and forces ranging from mountains and streams to the wind and rain. It evolved into an imprecise collection of cults and ideas, although ritual purity was its central concept. The emperor was thought to be the direct descendant of the god of the sun, and extreme nationalists used this belief to build patriotic devotion and loyalty to the government after 1968.

shushin: Moral education

soga shosha: The leading trading companies

Sohyo: General Council of Trade Unions, formed in 1950; a supporter of the left wing of the JSP in postwar Japan.

Soka Gakkai: "Value-Adding Study Society," a religious movement that derives its beliefs from the Nichiren sect of Buddhism

Sorengo: Federation of Small and Medium Enterprises, created in 1961

tei shisei: A reference to Japan's "low posture" in foreign policy during the decades following World War II

Three Non-Nuclear Principles: Prime Minister Sato Eisaku first enunciated this policy on December 11, 1967. The U.S.-Japan Mutual Security and Cooperation Treaty, a revision of the 1951 agreement, provided that the United States would not bring any nuclear weapons onto Japanese territory without prior consultation. This became a critical issue during the Vietnam War when Japan and Okinawa became important bases for U.S. military operations. To ease public concern, Sato announced the "Three Non-Nuclear Principles" which declared that Japan would never possess, manufacture, or allow the introduction in Japan of nuclear weapons. Japan's Diet formally endorsed these principles in December 1973.

yakuza: A label for large criminal organizations comprised of "gangsters" in postwar Japan

Yasukuni Shrine: This Shinto shrine, located in Tokyo, is dedicated to the spirits of approximately 2.4 million people who have died in Japan's civil and foreign wars since 1853. Emperor Meiji in 1869 established a "Shrine for Inviting the Spirits" (*Shokonsha*) to venerate with a variety of memorials all those who had died in the campaigns to reestablish his imperial rule the prior year. Renamed in 1879 *Yasukuni Jinja* ("Shrine for Establishing Peace in the Empire"), the military used it before World War II to promote patriotic and nationalistic sentiments. Under the Constitution of 1947, however, Japan's government had to terminate all support for the Yasukini Shrine, which became a private religious organization. Leftists, Buddhists, Christians, and intellectuals prevented efforts to restore state support thereafter, denouncing prime ministers and government officials who made "private visits" to the shrine.

Yoshida Doctrine: This term describes the basis of Japan's foreign policy from April 1952 when the nation regained its sovereignty and continuing for the most part until the Cold War ended late in 1989. Prime Minister Yoshida Shigeru both devised and first implemented this approach, providing for Japan to maintain a position as a fully dependent partner of the United States in world affairs. When Yoshida resigned in 1954, a consensus was firmly in place not only supporting reliance on the United States for military protection, but also following Washington's lead on foreign policy issues such as adversarial relations with the Soviet Union, recognition of the People's Republic of China, and the Vietnam War.

Yoshida School: Bureaucrats and politicians closely allied with Yoshida Shigeru during and immediately after U.S. occupation. These men dominated leadership posts in government after 1952 and were proponents of economic growth.

zaibatsu: Term meaning literally "financial clique" used as a label for the largest and most influential industrial concerns during the interwar era, especially Mitsubishi, Mitsui, Sumitomo, and Yasuda.

zaikai: The financial community, or financial circles

zeiken dorobo: "tax thieves," a term used in reference to the military

Zengakuren: All-Japan Federation of Student Self-Government Associations. The group adopted militant stands and often staged violent demonstrations in the years after 1945 under the influence of the Japan Communist Party.

Zenro Kaigi: All-Japan Labor Congress, mainly comprised of militant white-collar workers with links to the Communist Party

Annotated Bibliography

Allen, George Cyril. *The Japanese Economy.* New York: St. Martin's Press, 1981. This book provides an overview of major developments before 1945 and then surveys the recovery and expansion of Japan's economy after World War II. It examines at length Japan's financial system and monetary policy, agriculture, manufacturing industry, industrial relations system, and foreign trade and investment, with emphasis on the contribution of Japan's social and political institutions to the nation's phenomenal economic success.

Allinson, Gary D. *Japan's Postwar History.* Ithaca, NY: Cornell University Press, 1997. An interpretive history of Japan beginning in the 1930s, the book emphasizes the nation's transformation into an industrial and urban state. The author integrates social and cultural forces into political, economic, and diplomatic developments in this concise study.

Apter, David E. *Against the State: Politics and Social Protest in Japan.* Cambridge, MA: Harvard University Press, 1984. This is a study of the huge protest movement against government construction of the Narita International Airport, Chiba Prefecture. After describing the origins of the movement, the author traces developments during the late 1960s and throughout the 1970s, providing the perspectives of farmers, militants, politicians, and government officials.

Baerwald, Hans H. *Japan's Parliament: An Introduction.* New York: Cambridge University Press, 1974. This is a succinct study of Japan's bicameral legislature, tracing its prewar origins and postwar evolution as well as describing its internal organization and rules. The author also discusses the political parties, with emphasis on how factionalism dictated the postwar electoral system, and the controversies and periodic turmoil that have characterized its proceedings.

———. *Party Politics in Japan*. Boston: Allen and Unwin, 1986. This study provides an introduction for the general reader, describing the structure and operation of the party system after 1955. The author discusses the national Diet's operations and its internal governance, the strategies of the parties, rivalries among factions within the Liberal Democratic Party, and the changing relationship between the governing and opposition parties.

Bailey, Paul J. *Postwar Japan: 1945 to Present*. Cambridge, MA: Blackwell Publishers, 1996. This concise book is the best one-volume survey of Japan's history since World War II. Bailey provides detailed coverage of important political, social, economic, and diplomatic developments in Japan during the last half of the twentieth century. Well-written and coherently organized, it references the most recent studies and uses assorted anecdotal information to support perceptive insights.

Barnhart, Michael. *Japan and the World since 1968*. New York: St. Martin's Press, 1995. Barnhart provides a concise survey of Japan's international relations after it opened its borders to the West. In this interpretive study, the author relies extensively on primary sources to offer interpretations of Japanese foreign affairs in the context of internal political developments and the pattern of economic growth.

Beasley, W. G. *The Rise of Modern Japan: Political, Economic, and Social Change since 1850*. New York: St. Martin's Press, 1995. An excellent survey, this textbook provides a comprehensive look at Japan's recent history. Organized chronologically, it achieves the purpose described in its subtitle.

Borden, William S. *The Pacific Alliance: United States Foreign Economic Policy and Japanese Trade Recovery, 1947–1955*. Madison: University of Wisconsin Press, 1984. This book offers an assessment of the economic foundation for a U.S. policy toward Japan after 1945 that identified this former enemy as central to U.S. postwar strategic plans in Asia. It shows how several key decisions of U.S. policymakers regarding Southeast Asia were closely tied to a perception of that region as a market for Japanese exports and source of vital raw materials.

Brinton, Mary C. *Women and the Economic Miracle: Gender and Work in Postwar Japan*. Berkeley: University of California Press, 1993. This sociological study assesses the work experience of women in three cities. Rejecting a Marxist-feminist analysis that stresses the universally patriarchal character of capitalism, Brinton instead elaborates a theory of "human capital development" subject to institutional constraints to explain how Japanese women became increasingly disadvantaged in education and employment during the 1980s.

Buckley, Roger. *Occupation Diplomacy: Britain, the United States and Japan, 1945–1952.* New York: Cambridge University Press, 1982. This study examines British involvement in the Allied occupation of Japan, challenging the conventional view that the occupation was an exclusively American affair. The book describes not only the role of Great Britain, but also that of the Commonwealth countries, especially Australia.

Burks, Ardath. *Japan: Portrait of a Post Industrial Power.* Boulder, CO: Westview, 1981. Embracing the notion of "Japan, Incorporated," this compact study covers the origins before World War II and the development thereafter of Japan's postwar politico-economic system, portraying it as a giant conglomerate.

Cohen, Stephen D. *Uneasy Partnership: Competition and Conflict in U.S.-Japanese Trade Relations.* Cambridge, MA: Ballinger, 1985. This balanced examination of the evolution of U.S.-Japan trade relations seeks to explain the reasons behind the economic discord in the relationship during the 1980s. According to Cohen, the economic rivalry originated in the 1960s when Japan aggressively expanded its worldwide export markets whereas the United States remained economically complacent. The study concludes with a series of recommendations to improve the relationship.

Cortazzi, Hugh. *The Japanese Achievement.* New York: St. Martin's Press, 1990. An insider's survey of Japan's history from the perspective of a British diplomat, the book provides an introductory, chronological guide to the development of Japan from its early history with special emphasis on international affairs.

Cusumano, Michael A. *The Japanese Automobile Industry: Technology and Management at Nissan and Toyota.* Cambridge, MA: Harvard University Press, 1985. In this comprehensive study of two of Japan's leading auto manufacturers from the 1930s to the 1980s, Cusumano describes the different methods these two rivals used to acquire and improve sophisticated foreign technology, as well as their adaptation of modern manufacturing techniques to traditional Japanese production methods and the development of new products and new systems of management and organization. Other issues receiving attention are the character of postwar management-labor relations, Japanese government policy, and the impact of such events as the Korean War.

Destler, M., Haruhiro Fukui, and Hideo Sato. *The Textile Wrangle: Conflict in Japanese-American Relations.* Ithaca, NY: Cornell University Press, 1979. This study shows how the internal politics of both the United States and Japan worked to prevent the easy resolution of economic disputes. In this case, the Nixon administration's attempt to persuade Japan's government to enforce comprehensive controls over the export of synthetic and wool textile products to the U.S. market resulted in a major political crisis that damaged relations between the two nations.

Dower, John W. *Embracing Defeat: Japan in the Wake of World War II.* New York: W. W. Norton, 1999. This well-written work describes how Japan and the United States became inextricably intertwined as a result of the U.S. occupation after World War II. Portraying American policy as ambiguous, arrogant, and bungling, and criticizing censorship and the War Crimes Trials, Dower provides graphic and moving descriptions of life in Japan before economic conditions improved after 1949.

———. *Empire and Aftermath: Yoshida Shigeru and the Japanese Experience, 1878–1954.* Cambridge, MA: Harvard University Press, 1988. This authoritative biography traces in detail the life of a career diplomat who became arguably Japan's most important leader after 1945. The first part covers Yoshida's career before the end of World War II, and a concluding section surveys the reconsolidation and recentralization of conservative power during the "Yoshida era" when he was prime minister and implemented U.S. occupation policies.

Emmerson, John K., and Harrison M. Holland. *The Eagle and the Rising Sun: America and Japan in the Twentieth Century.* Reading, MA: Addison-Wesley, 1988. The authors, two former U.S. foreign service officers in Japan, provide an assessment of the U.S.-Japan relationship focusing particularly on controversies regarding trade and defense. They also examine Japanese relations with the Soviet Union, the People's Republic of China, and the Republic of Korea; and they discuss Japan's plans to expand its role in international affairs.

Fairbank, John K., Edwin O. Reischauer, and Albert M. Craig. *East Asia: Tradition and Transformation.* Boston: Houghton Mifflin, 1989. This is the best textbook covering the history of East Asia, concentrating on China and to a lesser extent on Japan, Korea, and Vietnam. The book presents detailed information and analysis of politics, society, culture, thought, economics, and diplomacy.

Finn, Richard B. *Winners in Peace: MacArthur, Yoshida, and Postwar Japan.* Berkeley: University of California Press, 1992. A U.S. naval officer and, later, foreign service officer who participated in the U.S. occupation, Finn provides a carefully researched and thoughtful study covering well-known topics chronologically. He stresses how the Japanese cooperated with the Americans in a benevolent venture to create a self-sufficient and stable Japan while deemphasizing security concerns in U.S. policy.

Friedman, David. *The Misunderstood Miracle: Industrial Development and Political Change in Japan.* Ithaca, NY: Cornell University Press, 1988. This analysis of the reasons for Japan's spectacular postwar growth in industry focuses on the evolution of machine tool production from the 1930s to the early 1980s with emphasis on government action to regulate production and direct firms toward high-profit markets. The author also examines the emergence of small-scale flexible manufacturing firms capable of introducing extensive product changes more rapidly and easily than their larger competitors.

Gibney, Frank. *Miracle by Design: The Real Reasons behind Japan's Economic Success.* New York: Times Books, 1982. A journalist, businessman, and scholar, Gibney explores the reasons for Japan's miraculous recovery from the defeat and destruction of World War II and for its tremendous economic growth thereafter. He attributes this to Japan's ability to combine traditional values and the Confucian work ethic with capitalist business knowledge acquired from the United States, as well as the intense pursuit of quality control.

Giffard, Sidney. *Japan among the Powers, 1890–1990.* New Haven, CT: Yale University Press, 1994. A former British ambassador in Tokyo, Giffard provides a succinct, balanced, informative, and readable summary of Japanese involvement in world affairs after the Meiji Restoration. Emphasizing the continuities in national institutions and orientations, he explains how Japan implemented pragmatic policies after 1945 to become not just a great power in Asia but an Asian great power. He also shows how changes in the balance of power, as well as domestic factors, impacted Japan's perceptions of its options.

Hane, Mikiso. *Modern Japan: A Historical Survey.* Boulder, CO: Westview, 1986. Arranged chronologically and providing detailed information, this book may be the best one-volume survey of the politics, society, culture, diplomacy, and economy of Japan since the Meiji Restoration.

Hein, Laura. *Fueling Growth: The Energy Revolution and Economic Policy in Postwar Japan.* Cambridge, MA: Harvard University Press, 1990. Hein's stimulating study focuses on the centrality of energy in Japan's industrial economy to explain Japan's changing economic policies from 1945 to 1960. The author offers a detailed and provocative analysis of the shift from coal and hydroelectric power to oil that was a consequence of a political process involving the various conflicting interests and activities of labor, the state, business, and U.S. occupation officials. Changes in the economy were the result of competition among these groups and ad hoc postwar government planning.

Hellmann, Donald C. *Japanese Foreign Policy and Domestic Politics: The Peace Agreement with the Soviet Union.* Berkeley: University of California Press, 1969. This book presents a comprehensive examination of the interrelationship between the Japanese foreign policy process and domestic politics. After describing the process, the author discusses the impact of the Liberal Democratic Party, public opinion, "articulate-opinion" (senior diplomats, businessmen, policy and issue groups, and the press), business interest groups, and both the Ministry of Foreign Affairs and the Diet.

Holland, Harrison M. *Managing Defense: Japan Dilemma.* Lanham, MD: University Press of America, 1998. Harrison examines the role of Japanese bureaucrats and politicians in decision making on national defense policy. Focusing on Japan's defense charter and the Defense Agency's annual review of defense policy, he explains how conflicting domestic and foreign pressures have steered the defense budget down a middle course between those favoring expansion and those opposed to resurgent militarism, to the annoyance of the United States.

Jensen, Marius B. *Japan and China: From War to Peace, 1894–1972.* Chicago: Rand McNally, 1975. Twelve interpretive essays discussing the evolution of Sino-Japanese relations provide a solid introduction to relations between China and Japan in the twentieth century. Jansen's detailed bibliographical essay is valuable as a guide for further reading.

Johnson, Chalmers. *MITI and the Japanese Miracle: The Growth of Industrial Policy.* Stanford, CA: Stanford University Press, 1982. This highly acclaimed book is the authoritative institutional study of the origins, structure, and activities of the Ministry of International Trade and Industry (MITI). For Johnson, MITI played the central role in the growth and evolution of Japan's industrial policy to 1975, directing the collaboration between the state and private business and industry toward the goal of rapid economic development. MITI made Japan a "developmental" state, in contrast to the American "regulatory" state.

Kawai, Kazuo. *Japan's American Interlude.* Chicago: University of Chicago Press, 1960. This balanced assessment of U.S. military occupation and political control of Japan after 1945 emphasizes the significant impact of a number of American reforms. Kawai, editor-in-chief of the *Nippon Times*, Japan's leading English-language daily newspaper at that time, describes the surprisingly subservient attitude of the Japanese people toward the occupation and rapid democratization within Japanese society.

Kondo, Dorrine. *Crafting Selves: Power, Gender, and Discourses of Identity in a Japanese Workplace.* Chicago: University of Chicago Press, 1990. Using feminist and poststructuralist theories, this vividly written study relies on the author's extended fieldwork as a part-time worker in a small confectionary factory in Japan. Kondo exposes the existence of unequal divisions of class and gender in what outsiders have admired as the idealized "family company." Although the employer rarely showed beneficence and loyalty to workers, the female's identity derived from her job to admire, mother, and sexually attract the male artisans.

Kono, Toyohiro. *Strategy and Structure of Japanese Enterprises.* Armonk, NY: M. E. Sharpe, 1994. This study analyzes the product-market strategy, organizational structure, and strategic decision making of 102 large manufacturing companies, including Toyota Motor, Hitachi, Matsushita Electric, and Canon. Making frequent comparisons with top American and British corporations, Kono stresses as a reason for success the innovative, competition-oriented, and centralized nature of strategic management practices in the Japanese firms.

LaFeber, Walter. *The Clash: A History of U.S.-Japan Relations*. New York: W. W. Norton, 1997. This award-winning survey of 150 years of U.S.-Japanese relations emphasizes the contradictions and hypocrisy in the partnership. Reflecting the book's theme, LaFeber quotes a British diplomat in Tokyo in the early 1960s: "The Japanese can neither love the Americans nor endure being loved by them."

Lee, Chae-jin. *China and Japan: New Economic Diplomacy*. Stanford, CA: Hoover Institution Press, 1984. This study describes Sino-Japanese economic relations after 1949 and then analyzes economic negotiations between China and Japan in detail beginning in the mid-1970s. Lee focuses on prominent examples of the collaborative construction of the multibillion-dollar integrated Baoshan steel complex in a suburb of Shanghai, the offshore Bohai Sea petroleum development projects, and Japan's assistance for several of China's main construction programs.

Lee, Chong-sik. *Japan and Korea: The Political Dimension*. Stanford, CA: Hoover Institution Press, 1985. Lee assesses relations between Japan and the Republic of Korea after World War II, focusing on describing political, psychological, and economic differences. Following a brief discussion of the legacies of the Japanese colonial occupation of Korea, he examines the normalization of relations in 1965, negotiations over Japanese loans to Korea after 1981, and the controversy about Japanese textbook descriptions of World War II that began in 1982.

McMillan, Charles J. *The Japanese Industrial System*. Berlin, NY: DeGruyter, 1985. This book comprehensively covers Japan's complex industrial system in the 1980s; topics include business-government relations, industrial planning, technology and knowledge acquisition, education and management recruitment, management strategy and organization, human resource strategies and work, production and operations management, marketing, Japanese management abroad, and money and banking. McMillan minimizes the nation's unique social values and institutions, instead attributing its economic success primarily to the ability to "apply textbook management principles in everyday work life."

Morita, Akio, with Edwin M. Reingoid and Mitsuko Shimomura. *Made in Japan: Akio Morita and Sony*. New York: Dutton, 1986. In this autobiography of the cofounder and chairman of the Sony Corporation, Morita relates his experiences and those of his family but also addresses various topics related to Japanese business. These include differences between the Japanese and Western styles of management, lifetime employment, market research and quality control, competition and technology, and trade relations between Japan and the United States,

Nakamura, Takafusa. Translated by Jacqueline Kaminski. *The Postwar Japanese Economy: Its Development and Structure*. Tokyo: University of Tokyo Press, 1981. This book describes the evolution and inner workings of the Japanese economy since World War II. The author, a respected economist, provides a historical account of Japan's rapid growth after World War II and examines the "dual structure" of the economy, changes in agriculture, government economic policies, the banking and monetary systems, and foreign trade relations.

Okimoto, Daniel I. *Between MITI and the Market: Japanese Industrial Policy for High Technology*. Stanford, CA: Stanford University Press, 1989. This comprehensive study challenges conventional views about MITI's place in "Japan, Incorporated" and attributes the nation's economic development to many interrelated factors. Okimoto explains Japan's economic growth as the result of the totality of influences in Japanese society and policy flexibility in adjusting to changing conditions. The author's focus is on showing how MITI's influence is complex and varies within the industrial structure, but he does cover the impact of politics.

Olsen, Laurence. *Japan in Postwar Asia*. New York: Praeger, 1970. Olsen traces Japan's postwar attitudes, actions, and policies throughout Asia. After regaining independence in 1952, Tokyo pursued a low-key policy to overcome the wartime legacy of hatred and distrust among its Asian neighbors until 1964; thereafter its activism was increased to create a new network of economic relationships in East Asia.

Orr, Robert M., Jr. *The Emergence of Japan's Foreign Aid Power*. New York: Columbia University Press, 1990. This study explains how Japan overtook the United States as the world's largest foreign aid donor; factors include (1) the government making foreign aid the highest budget priority, (2) the appreciation of the yen after 1985, and (3) U.S. reductions of foreign aid budget deficits. In terms of who receives Japan's aid, Orr's answer is more complex; bureaucratic politics play an important role. One-third of the book is a region-by-region, country-by-country examination of Japanese foreign aid distributions.

Packard, George R. *Protest in Tokyo: The Security Treaty Crisis of 1960*. Westport, CT: Greenwood Press, 1978. This study explores the workings of Japan's political process in describing and analyzing the background of the actions for revision of the U.S.-Japan Security Treaty. Packard discusses support for treaty negotiations among the conservatives and vigorous opposition from the political left, asserting that the crisis did not derive from one single cause but rather "from the convergence of international and domestic forces."

Rix, Alan. *Japan's Economic Aid: Policy-Making and Politics*. New York: St. Martin's Press, 1980. This book examines Japan's postwar foreign aid decision-making process, showing that "bureaucratic interests were the main determinants of the articulation of Japan's aid and economic cooperation policies." Describing four major types of development aid and analyzing the politics of the budgetary process for foreign aid, Rix also discusses the interaction of the agencies implementing foreign aid programs and the activities of private firms and recipient nations.

Sanders, Sol. *Honda: The Man and His Machines*. Boston: Little, Brown, 1975. This is a well-written biography of the founder of the Honda Motors empire that began with the building of motorcycles and then became one of the world's dominant automakers. Sanders describes Honda's innovations, concluding with a discussion of "Hondaism," an assessment of the company's future prospects, and comments about Honda's business philosophy.

Schaller, Michael. *Altered States: The United States and Japan since the Occupation*. New York: Oxford University Press, 1997. In this account of U.S. relations with Japan from the end of the U.S. occupation in 1952 to the Nixon Shocks in 1972, Schaller portrays the partnership as tortured because of the asymmetry in power and the rising friction over economic affairs. Japan exploited the U.S. obsession with stopping communism, but its refusal to view the partnership in a geopolitical framework led to mutual misunderstanding, clashes of interest, and mistrust. The last pages briefly trace relations into the 1990s.

———. *The American Occupation of Japan: The Origins of the Cold War in Asia*. New York: Oxford University Press, 1985. Placing the U.S. Occupation within the context of overall U.S. security strategy in Asia from 1945 to 1950, Schaller focuses on the evolution of U.S. policy toward Japan through an examination of the bureaucratic politics of the Truman administration. Schaller argues that the critical moment came in 1947 and 1948 with implementation of the "reverse course" when the U.S. government decided to promote Japan's economic recovery to contain the expansion of communism.

Stephen, John J. *The Kuril Islands: Russo-Japanese Frontier in the Pacific*. Oxford, England: Clarendon Press, 1974. This is a comprehensive study of the chain of islands stretching between Hokkaido and the Kamchatka Peninsula. It describes the entire history of the Kuriles, exploring early Russo-Japanese disputes over them, their strategic and military importance during World War II, and Japan's postwar efforts to regain these "Northern Territories" from the Soviet Union.

Stockwin, James A. A. *Japan: Divided Politics in a Growth Economy*. 2nd ed. New York: Norton, 1982. First published in 1975, this book provides a substantially revised and enlarged second edition of Stockwin's introductory text describing contemporary Japanese politics. Presenting balanced institutional descriptions, the author emphasizes the close interrelationship between government and business in Japan's political system. He also shows how Japan's political process has experienced discord over the same issues during an extended period of stable conservative rule.

———. *The Japanese Socialist Party and Neutralism: A Study of a Political Party and Foreign Policy*. London: Cambridge University Press, 1968. Though dated, this is the authoritative work on the Japan Socialist Party, the main opposition to the Liberal Democratic Party. Stockwin relies on thorough documentation and balanced analysis to explain "what Japanese socialists mean when they talk of neutralism, and what kind of party it is that puts forward this . . . set of policies"

Swearingen, Rodger. *The Soviet Union and Postwar Japan: Escalating Challenge and Response*. Stanford, CA: Hoover Institution Press, 1978. Swearingen provides a detailed description of Soviet policy and practice in occupied Japan, covering Moscow's indoctrination of repatriated Japanese prisoners of war, ties with the Japan Communist Party, and handling of negotiations to normalize diplomatic relations. The author also discusses the joint economic ventures in Siberia, bilateral trade, haggling over Japanese fishing rights off the Siberian coasts, and the dispute over the "Northern Territories."

Toyoda, Eiji. *Toyota: Fifty Years in Motion*. New York: Kodansha International, 1987. This autobiography of the president and then chairman of the Toyota Motor Corporation interweaves his personal life history with the emergence of his company as a world leader among automakers. Although entertaining, it is more descriptive than analytical.

Viner, Aron. *Inside Japanese Financial Markets*. Homewood, IL: Dow Jones-Irwin, 1988. In this nontechnical overview, Viner provides an explanation for the postwar evolution of the Japanese financial system that focuses on the securities market rather than money markets or the market in foreign exchange. The author discusses the government's role in shaping the structure and function of securities companies and banks, as well as in regulating the stock exchange, and he also describes the Japanese socioeconomic structure and value system to reveal how they influenced Japan's investors.

Watts, William. *The United States and Japan: A Troubled Partnership*. Cambridge, MA: Ballinger, 1984. Watts relies on public opinion surveys in this study of differing views, attitudes, and perceptions that Japanese and Americans have toward each another. His particular concern is to explain contention and misunderstanding in economic relations and the security partnership, describing the relationship as "both remarkably strong and yet weak."

Weinstein, Martin E. *Japan's Postwar Defense, 1947–1968*. New York: Columbia University Press, 1971. Weinstein describes the origins of Japanese defense policy during the U.S. occupation and its evolution from the Korean War to the tumultuous debate over security treaty revision in 1960. He also traces the history of the Self-Defense Forces, concluding that the Japanese consistently defined defense policy in accordance with national strategic needs, rather than in "response to American initiatives and to pacifist, anti-rearmament opinion."

Welfield, John. *An Empire in Eclipse: Japan in the Postwar Alliance System*. Atlantic Highlands, NJ: Athione Press, 1988. This book examines the close relationship between the United States and Japan from 1945 to the breakdown of Soviet-American détente in the late 1970s. Organized chronologically and covering major events, Welfield's book succeeds in "exploring the roots of the Japanese diplomatic tradition, examining the background and objectives of Japan's postwar leaders, tracing the movement of public opinion, and carefully analyzing the interaction between domestic political and foreign policy."

Yasutomo, Dennis T. *The Manner of Giving: Strategic Aid and Japanese Foreign Policy*. Lexington, MA; Lexington Books, 1986. Yasutomo analyzes the emergence of strategic aid as a political tool in Japanese foreign policy toward Third World countries. He argues that Japan's foreign aid became "a foreign policy tool for achieving political and security objectives as well as economic benefits." During the 1980s it became a central pillar of Japan's overall diplomacy, especially its broadly conceived national security policy.

Yoshihara, Kunio. *Japanese Economic Development: An Introduction*. New York: Oxford University Press, 1979. This survey of economic growth in modern Japan places major issues within a general framework of postwar global economic development, instead of concentrating on uniquely Japanese problems.

———. *Soga Shosha: The Vanguard of the Japanese Economy*. New York: Oxford University Press, 1982. This study traces the evolution, role, and organization of the large and diversified Japanese trading companies that handle the movement of imports and exports on a worldwide basis. Yoshihara first summarizes the history since the nineteenth century of major firms such as Mitsui Bussan, Mitsubishi Shoji, Marubeni, Toyo Menka, Nichimen, Gosho, Iwai, Ataka, Nissho, and Sumitomo Shoji, explaining their success. He then analyzes the background for the growth of *soga shosha* and their role as marketing and financial intermediaries in Japan's industrialization.

Yoshino, Michael Y., and Thomas B. Lifson *The Invisible Link: Japan's Sogo Shosha and the Organization of Trade*. Cambridge, MA: MIT Press, 1986. This study examines Japan's six largest trading companies that coordinate the purchase of raw materials, the production of finished goods, and sale both at home and abroad. Exploring the historical evolution of the *soga shosha*, the book covers their dynamics and strategy, culture and organization, administrative structures and processes, personnel practices, and sectional and network organization, as well as the challenges of continuing transformation of the Japanese economy.

This annotated bibliography benefited from reference to Richard Perren, ed., *Japanese Studies from Pre-History to 1990: A Bibliographic Guide* (New York: Manchester University Press, 1991). Readers also may wish to consult Peter Duus, ed.,

Index

About the Author

JAMES I. MATRAY is Professor of History at New Mexico State University. He has written or edited three books, published fourteen journal articles, and contributed seven book chapters.